'THE WOLF AND THE BOAR'
THE LLOYDS OF BRONWYDD CARDIGANSHIRE:
LORDS MARCHER OF CEMAIS

By

Leslie Baker-Jones

Quatrefoil
Books

Published by Quatrefoil Books,
Danygribin House, Felindre, Llandysul, Ceredigion, Wales. SA44 5HR

2005

Printed in Wales by
PROPRINT, Carmarthen

Rock of Cashel, Ireland

Architects Perspective of Bronwydd

by R.K. Penson 1816-86

Contents

i

Acknowledgments

I wish to express my gratitude to many people and institutions who have been of assistance to me in bringing about the publication of this book – a history of the Lloyd family of Bronwydd, Henllan, Cardiganshire, Lords Marcher of Cemais, in North Pembrokeshire.

Professor David W. Howell, University of Wales, Swansea, kindly read the transcript, advised on various aspects of the work and wrote the Foreword. Mr Thomas Lloyd, lent family photographs and was a constant source of encouragement and support. The Rev. J. Towyn Jones provided an attractive cover design to remind one of the grandeur attached to the name of Bronwydd.

Others deserve to be mentioned with thanks, for information, photographs, recollections and source material – the late Mrs. Joan Gregson-Ellis, Mr S. J. Havard Evans, Carmarthen, Mr. John Evans (John Y Gwas) Felindre, Mr B. Howell Jones, Penrhiwllan, Major Francis Jones, Carmarthen, Mr John Jenkins, Llangeler, Mr. J. Rees Jones, Felindre, Mr. T. Lewis, Penrhiwpal, the Misses Lewis, Pwllgwair, Mr. B. Phillips, Drefach, and Mr. J. Williams, Capel Newydd.

In addition, I am indebted to Messrs. Ronwy Davies, Trebedw, Roy Davies, Penbre, R. Evans, Penrhiwllan, Dillwyn Miles, Haverfordwest, G. Nash, St.Fagans, Gwylon Phillips, St. Dogmaels, Basil L.V. Richards, Carmarthen, Andrew Williams, Llandysul, the Misses M. and D. Jones, Coedybryn, C. McCann, Llansaint, and the Rev. and Mrs. J. Edward Lewis, Carmarthen.

Dr. Huw Walters of the National Library of Wales, along with other members of staff, past and present, gave advice and guidance; likewise the staff of the Royal Commission on Ancient and Historic Monuments, Aberystwyth; the Cardigan Library; Mr. Dewi Thomas and Mrs. J. Gammon and others of the Carmarthen Library; the Haverfordwest Library; the Carmarthen and Haverfordwest Record Offices; the former Public Record Office, Chancery Lane and the Library of the Society of Antiquaries, Burlington House, London.

Lastly I wish to thank my nieces Hilda and Sarah for putting the whole work on 'Disk' and to Pro-Print, Carmarthen for their skilful workmanship. Blemishes and faults are entirely my own.

L.B-J.

Abbreviations

Arch. Camb.	Archaeologia Cambrensis
Cd. Ad	Cardigan and Tivyside Advertiser
Cards. Antiq. Socy. Trans.	Cardiganshire Antiquarian Society Transactions
Char. Comm. Reports	Charity Commissioners' Report
Cm. Jnl.	Carmarthen Journal
Carms. Antiq.	Carmarthenshire Antiquary
Carms. Hist.	Carmarthenshire Historian
CRO.	Carmarthenshire Record Office
" /EG/...	Evans George/Deeds. Etc.
DNB.	Dictionary of National Biography
DWB	Dictionary of Welsh Biography
FG	The Francis Green Papers at NLW and HRO
Gent. Mag.	Gentleman's Magazine
HRO	Haverfordwest Record Office
NLW.	National Library of Wales
NLW. Jnl.	National Library of Wales Journal
Pembs. Hist.	Pembrokeshire Historian
PRO.	Public Record Office
RCAHM	Royal Commission of Ancient and Historical Monuments
RCSEW	Royal Commission into the State of Education in Wales
RCMCEW	Reports of the Royal Commission on Municipal Corporations in England and Wales
RCLWM	Report of the Royal Commission on Land in Wales and Monmouthshire
ROL	Return of Owners of Land
THSC	Transactions of the Honourable Society of Cymmrodorion
WWHR	West Wales Historical Records

Note - The original spelling of gentry houses, farms etc. has been retained as in the original manuscripts at the time of writing.

Conversion Table

12 pennies (d)	=	1 shilling (s)
20 shillings	=	1 pound (£1)
21 shillings	=	1 guinea (£1 – 1s)

List of Illustrations

Foreword

Dr. Leslie Baker-Jones's fine book on the Tivyside gentry, published in 1999 under the title *Princelings, Privilege and Power*, furnishes one of the most scholarly treatments we possess of the Welsh gentry. Readers of that volume will have high expectations of this follow-up study by Dr. Baker-Jones of the Lloyd family of Bronwydd in Tivyside, whose 'fairy castle' so caught his imagination as a small child. They will not be disappointed. Grounded in meticulous research, *'The Wolf and the Boar'* - *The Lloyds of Bronwydd Cardiganshire: Lords Marcher of Cemais* affords us a fascinating, vivid insight into a world that is lost, a world in which possession of broad acres and, in this instance, the proud title of Lord Marcher, bestowed immense privilege amounting to no less than the right to rule local communities.

Dr. Baker-Jones writes authoritatively on every aspect of the family's history. His richly embroidered narrative thus takes in the family's ancestry and acquisition of lands; the management of the estate, which explores the family's involvement in farming and its treatment of tenants and dependants; the acquiring of the barony in the late eighteenth century and the family's struggle to assert the rights and privileges of the lord marcher; the huge generosity of the Lloyds towards worthy causes within the local community; and the highly 'public' family celebrations which emphasised its consequence in the neighbourhood and further afield and which sought to buttress deference. But changing, more radical and democratic times inevitably undermined such traditional public acceptance and esteem. For Dr. Baker-Jones, it was the loss of this, together with the heavy encumbrances on the estate, which had been mounting alarmingly from the mid-nineteenth century, that led to the break-up of the estate from the 1920s and to the waning of a sometime proud and esteemed family.

The history of the old, privileged landed families with all their ostentatious display has never ceased to interest, indeed fascinate, later generations. I know that this absorbing book will be enjoyed and appreciated by all its readers.

David W. Howell.

'The Wolf and the Boar'
The Lloyds of Bronwydd Cardiganshire: Lords Marcher of Cemais

Introduction

i

The late Major Francis Jones, Wales Herald Extraordinary, doyen of Welsh family historians and genealogists, used to comment that the writing of a family history could be a formidable and daunting task. Indeed, in the case of an old, noble and landed family, there are often massive archives consisting of lengthy pedigrees (albeit, at times of questionable veracity),rentals and details of family income, the geographical distribution of the estate, marriage settlements and other family arrangements, mortgages, debts and encumbrances. Moreover, diaries, journals, letters, domestic bills and accounts, and (in the last two centuries) newspaper reports tell a great deal about the social life enjoyed in the grand houses.

In such cases, the raw materials are available for the author to write a family history. The recollections of elderly descendants and loyal retainers of a famous family are, by now, coming into their own as one of the accredited sources of history. On the other hand, through neglect, loss by fire, flood, war, calamity or wilful destruction, vital evidence has disappeared for ever. The elderly are amongst those who pass this way only once – consequently, the historian is faced with a 'formidable and daunting task'.

A shift has taken place in historical interest over recent years in relation to the old mansions that once presided over the countryside. The impact of television programmes and the crusading work of the heritage industry have witnessed a growth in the popularity of visits to country houses open to the public. The tourist or the casual visitor has become absorbed in the lifestyle of the occupants of these places, their 'oddities and quiddities', their amusements, level of culture and their pastimes. The lesser manor house or palatial ducal residence attracts droves of people agog with curiosity about its architecture, landscaped park, laid out gardens, parterres, kitchen garden, farmyard, dog kennels and game larder. They are transported back in time to view a lifestyle which has almost totally disappeared – the trappings of gracious living, the splendour of fine works of art, the grand salon, dining room and library, not forgetting the kitchen, the 'offices' and the lavatorial and sanitary arrangements of long ago. All the social gradations – the scullery maid, cook, footman, butler, coachman and groom are represented in the rooms (beyond the green baize door) as well as the individual tasks they had to perform.

Game books, laundry lists, old cookbooks and utensils and much more – have become 'respectable' and are no longer dubbed as items of 'mere

1

antiquarianism'. Here, the subjective element is strong and individual taste and curiosity differ so much. If the family has sprung from royal and noble stock, prominent in the service of the king or foreign potentates, having trod the stage of sinister plots, international alliances and intrigue – to emerge unscathed so as to participate in the domestic politics of modern times, then (with luck) state papers and related material will have survived for the historian to work on a large canvas.

Other sources like the Gentleman's Magazine, the European Magazine, the London Review and later on, Cobbett's Parliamentary Review and Hansard, along with less known political 'gazettes', highlight the contribution of the powerful in the annals of their day and age – their political allegiances, the campaigns they fought for King or Parliament, for the Jacobite or Hanoverian side, and as more sober supporters of the emerging political parties of Whigs and Tories.

ii

The Bronwydd collection of family deeds and documents (consisting of some thousands of items) deposited at the National Library of Wales by the late Sir Marteine O. M. Lloyd and Lady Katherine H. Lloyd in 1933, and by their grand-daughter, Miss Morfa Audeley Withington in 1952, is unique in many ways. A massive archive, it records in great detail the administration of a vast tract of land in North Pembrokeshire, known as the 'Barony of Cemais' along with its constituent manors. It includes the literary, genealogical, historical manuscripts and the copious interesting ephemera of that remarkable Welsh Elizabethan and Renaissance man – George Owen of Henllys, in the parish of Nevern. The transactions of the Court Leet and the Court Baron, the 'presentments' or complaints of rural folk (often trivial and petty in a virtually closed community) were nevertheless real problems which were dealt with summarily by these local courts. Legal actions between quarrelsome gentry neighbours, amongst whom George Owen was a prime example, were heard at the Council of Wales and the Marches and in the Courts of Great Sessions - and these matters are well recorded in the Bronwydd collection.

Because the little town and port of Newport in Pembrokeshire was the place where the Lord Marcher had his castle, documents relating to the 'governance' of the town: the authority of its burgesses and mayor and the relationship of the 'town' vis-a-vis the rule of the Lord Marcher are prominent.

The deeds of the Bronwydd estate proper, date from 1562 to the 1930's, and are largely concerned with land transactions, marriages and inheritance which contributed to the rise of a large estate (in terms of landownership in the lower Teifi valley). We see its development from a 'tyddyn' [small holding] of a few acres in 1560's to an estate of about eight thousand acres by the end of the nineteenth century. Moreover, various land purchases and sales were made from

2

time to time to improve and enhance the estate and to get rid of profitless areas. Commons were enclosed through private initiative and public acts of parliament in order to bring about more efficient cultivation, the acquisition of 'ye mines and minerals' and not least, to extend the broad acres and consequent rule and influence of the lord.

Every aspect of estate development is well preserved in the Bronwydd records.

Remarkably, and perhaps unusually so in the annals of many country houses, detailed accounts have survived of the rebuilding of Bronwydd during the years 1853-1856.[1] Unfortunately, for those with an inquisitive interest and curiosity in the gossip and tittle-tattle of country house life, intimate letters and diaries relating to extra-marital liaisons, the mis-adventures and losses at the gaming table, the drunken revelries, brawls and fisticuffs of Squire Weston and his ilk, are totally absent.

With regard to the contents of the mansion house of Bronwydd, its furniture, ceramics, pictures, objets d'art and the like, very little is known (save for a few odds and ends taken to Gernos by Anne Davies Lloyd after leaving Bronwydd in 1849). However a detailed inventory of the contents of Newport Castle in 1875 still exists, but no sale catalogue of Bronwydd has survived, even if there was one in the first place.

Fortunately, there are abundant and detailed reports (dating from the nineteenth century to the early decades of the twentieth) in local newspapers, describing important family events at Bronwydd: marriages, births, coming of age and the rites and solemnities after the death of the Lord Marcher and members of his family. During these occasions the 'display' including hospitality, jollification, merrymaking, dining and wining (all private functions) are openly reported to an admiring and perhaps, envious populace.

Obituary notices of the gentry, like those of eminent and public figures, have always contained a strong element of hagiography,and the personalities described are transformed into glowing figures as in a stained glass window. And this is true of the reports of the decease of Sir Thomas and Sir Marteine Lloyd, and other members of the family. Nevertheless, local folk memory, some three generations later,still confirms what was printed many years ago. Here and there in this study, a chance remark or an anecdote by an elderly person, often adds to the significance and validity of some odd reference in the manuscripts. Ideally, one should have all the evidence relevant to the topic researched in all its aspects: a counsel of perfection, indeed, having regard to the nature of the Bronwydd muniments as outlined above. Consequently, an attempt has been made to examine the major features in the long history of a Welsh estate, the place of the family in the community, and the worth and merit which were the buttresses supporting the dominance of the house of Bronwydd, its popularity and esteem for many generations.

The author's interest in Bronwydd goes back to early childhood; to the garden parties and fêtes held to raise funds for local charities, such as the Henllan and District Nursing Association. Then, crowds of people from 'Tivyside' came together to support the good cause of the day and to enjoy the 'prospect' – the terraced gardens (their walls garlanded with fragrant and exotic roses, bearing grand recherché names like the Duchess of Mecklenburg, Commandant Beaurepaire, Felicité, Madam Stoltz and the like). The terraced gardens led to the shrubbery, with choice azaleas and rhododendrons, and beyond to the American garden.

Above the terrace aged members of the Bronwydd Band entertained the visitors from a stand built at the time of the 'new' Bronwydd of the 1850's. Some of the music makers had been trainee bandsmen in the days of Sir Thomas, the first baronet.

Here and there, stalls had been arranged with various types of produce: cakes, bread, butter, cheese, provided by the generous wives of the tenants and their neighbours. Small children darted between the 'standings' or crowded around that 'mystery of mysteries', the bran-tub, dipping their short arms in the hope of getting a surprise toy or gew-gaw to take home in triumph. Others discovered, for the first time perhaps, the shiny steel drum with a lady in a spotless white overall, dispensing something very new indeed in the locality – ice cream!

The tall figure of Sir Marteine was seen greeting new and old friends: farmers, clerics, doctors, ministers, school masters and those many volunteers who loyally supported Lady Lloyd's various charities. The flag of the Barony flew from the square tower, bunting fluttered from pinnacle and turret, and there seemed to be an air of jollity all around.[2.]

But there was an undercurrent of gloom. Sir Marteine, like other landlords and their tenants, was only too aware of the 'slump' of the 1920's, the depressing state of the economy and (to himself) pondered upon the shaky financial base on which the Bronwydd estate itself was creaking.

The fête of 1929, like many previous ones, was a success, but was the last to be held. Less than ten years later the proud owners of Bronwydd had died; the house and the estate were sold. The mansion house of Bronwydd was dismantled and plundered to become one of the 'lost houses of Wales'- a mere memory of a bygone age.

In the following pages an attempt will be made to recall something of the forgotten past of Bronwydd, its owners, their way of life and place in society as 'Lords Marcher of Cemais'.

Ancestry and 'Estate'

i

In his account of a walk through Wales during August, 1797, the Reverend Richard Warner described how he met a '...Mr. David Pugh, a thickset little Cambrian...a character [whose] pompous manner and affected dignity were truly diverting...and the triumph with which he dwelt on the antiquity of his family afforded a whimsical example of that harmless pride with which the Welsh...possess'.

Although a caricature of a Welsh country squire, it has to be remembered that for centuries the Welsh, like other nations, have been proud of their ancestry. And at a time when rather vain and exaggerated notions of ancient blood were discounted, Lady Lloyd of Bronwydd published her book – 'The Lords Marchers of Kemes' in 1930, in memory of her only son Martin Kemes Arundel Lloyd (who was killed in France in 1916) and '...his great ancestors the Lords of Kemes...'. Indeed, it was a statement of that 'harmless pride' which the Reverend Warner had observed and Lady Lloyd was only expressing a natural sentiment to extol an honourable tradition cherished for centuries by the Lloyd family – their noble descent, the martial prowess of knights in armour, the valour and worth of courtly chivalry and their benevolence to the poor and to the deprived[1].

While it has been possible for scholars to discount some of the glamourous claims, the inevitable errors, and at times the deliberate concoctions in some genealogies, these pedigrees have a special significance. The 'mystique' of the longevity of the clan and the pride in the heroes of a dim and distant (albeit mythical) past, provided an impetus to many a modest but far-sighted squireen to aim for 'estate': status, a special position in society and the dignity and wealth attached to the ownership of land. After all, land was at one time held of the crown; every acre was the property of the king; all honours were derived from the sovereign. Those who held land had duties in the military field against the king's enemies and in the preservation of law and order in the towns and in the countryside.

Since the days of the Tudors land had been acquired by inheritance, marriage to a wealthy heiress, purchase or royal favour. The rise of a large estate, especially that of Bronwydd which survived from the Tudor period to the 1930s, amply demonstrates this process. As a result, the wealth which the squire derived from it enabled him to educate his children and to travel to far-off places. Centres of fashion like London and Bath, and the capital cities of Europe attracted him more and more. The backwoods 'booby' squire was gradually becoming sophisticated in 'conversation', taste, manners and in his social relationships. As time went on, he married someone outside the immediate circle of parish and county, and even sought a bride from beyond the borders of the principality. He became cosmopolitan in outlook and served in the army or navy of the sovereign. He spoke of lands beyond the seas, of strange folk who prattled their own peculiar gibberish. He had adopted the English tongue of 'His Britanic Majesty' and that of polite society. Welsh, his native tongue was regarded as only becoming to country bumpkins and clodhoppers. His farmhouse-style 'plas' was abandoned for a mansion house furnished with elegance and style – a symbol of power and privilege and the wherewithal to provide patronage and protection.

ii

For the purposes of this study of the Lloyd family, the place name Bronwydd, occurs for the first time in a deed of July 1562, when Thomas John ap David of Llandysul, Cardiganshire, gent., sold part of his estate to Philip Brwyne gent. of Ffoshelyg, in the same parish, namely a tenement called 'Tyddyn y Bronwydd' [the homestead on the wooded hill-side] together with a piece of land described as 'Llain y Bronwydd' [llain-a strip of land]. The transaction also included 'Tir Dyffryn Llech' in the neighbouring parish of Llanfair Trelygen [Trefhelygen]. 'Tyddyn y Bronwydd' and other holdings formed the nucleus of an estate which, during the next four centuries, was to become one of the largest and most noteworthy of the estates in the lower Teifi valley, popularly known as the 'Tivy Side'[2.]

Philip Brwyne belonged to a gentry clan who were already well established in Cardiganshire, Carmarthenshire and further afield. Described as 'gent', like many of his kinsfolk and not yet of the 'esquire' class, he was one of many who through their 'wit and acumen', could take advantage of the new opportunities which the Tudor settlement: the union of Wales with England, the introduction of English land law - 'primogeniture' [inheritance by the eldest son]- and the uniformity through the use of the English language, were to bring about. One of Philip Brwyne's 'cousins'(a term used by country gentry to denote all sorts of near and indefinable distant relations) Thomas Bruyne was a squire of Penbuarth, a farm on the slopes of the Moelfre, a hill contiguous to the parishes of Cenarth, Cilrhedyn and Penboyr, not far from Newcastle-Emlyn. Tradition dies hard and the nineteenth century cleric and antiquary, the Rev.Benjamin Williams [Gwynionydd],claimed that the name Dôl Bryn, a short distance from Penbuarth, was at one time one of the homesteads of the Bryn?, Brwyn, Bryne family. Through diplomatic negotiation, Thomas Bruyne had brought about the marriage of his daughter Jenett to Rees Lloyd, of the family of Lloyd of Forest in the parish of Llanfihangel-Rhosycorn in Carmarthenshire. Lloyd claimed that he was descended from Rhodri Mawr (the Great) king of Gwynedd,Powys and Deheubarth, who died in 877. Moreover, his brother Jenkin Llwyd ap David ap Rhys Lloyd, 'esquire', had attained a position of power in the county as the first

6

High Sheriff of Carmarthenshire in 1539, and was 'esquire of the body' to King Henry viii. In Wales, the office of sheriff was an innovation through the Union and the laws affecting Wales enacted in the years 1536-1541. Whereas, the sheriff had, by this time, lost much of his power in England, the office attracted many of the most ambitious squirearchy in Wales by its novelty, pomp and pageantry. Other offices: that of justice of the peace, deputy and lord-lieutenant along with the shrievalty helped to consolidate the power of the king, and enabled those who held them to realise their social and political ambitions. Maud, the daughter of another kinsman, Thomas Brine (and by now, the reader will have realised that the surname was spelt in many different ways) of Llanllawddog, Carmarthenshire, married Reynald Jenkins of Carrog, Llanddeiniol, in north Cardiganshire, and in this instance too, ancestry and a substantial dowry were the essential constituents of a marriage alliance between the two gentry families. Jenkins was able to boast that one of his ancestors was none other than Blegwyryd ap Dinawal whose coat of arms 'azure, a wolf salient argent' [on a blue field, a leaping silver-coloured wolf] depicted valour and tenacity in battle. That the Bryne family were well connected and influential has now become clear, and they made further family alliances with that of Owen of Hafodwen, St. Peter's parish Carmarthen, one of whom Morgan ab Owen (1585-1644) was bishop of Llandaff.

Like many families with non-Welsh sounding names, namely, Barrat, Blome, Byrt, Colby, Havard, Higgon, Mortimer, Revell, Ryd or Read (to name but a few) the Brwyn clan may well have belonged to the 'advenae' or the 'adventurers' – to use Sir Anthony Wagner's designation – who since the Norman Conquest, had arrived in Wales as court or government officials or as urban tradesmen. Indeed, they may have been the offspring of Norman knights or English barons. The Bryne family were concentrated in south west Wales but had their roots going back to Thomas Brine ap Hugh Brine, esquire, of Llanffynnon-wen, i. e. Chirbury in Shropshire. It is tempting to speculate that all those with the names of Brein, Brine, Brwyn, Bruyne and the like, were in some way connected to the distinguished Sir Guy de Bryan (c. 1309-90) son and heir of Sir Guy de Brian of Walwyn's Castle, Pembrokeshire, and of Tor Brian, Devon. Futhermore, because of the proliferation of names like Burian, ap Urien, and others in the Welsh Marches it is not inconceivable that Bruyne of Pantdafydd, Llangunllo, might claim descent from the north British hero of sixth century romance – Urien Rheged, as might the Hugh Brine of Chirbury, mentioned above. But setting aside genealogical fantasy, the Brine clan seem to have been important in their day, but by the sixteenth and early seventeenth centuries were gradually disappearing from the scene: absorbed by other families, the failure of male heirs or because they were unable to face the economic and social changes which more resilient families were able to overcome.

Philip Brwyne, mentioned at the beginning of this account, moved to the parish of Llangunllo and settled at Pant-Dafydd, a small homestead in the picturesque dell known as Cwm Pant-Dafydd or Cwm Cunllo (named after a nearby stream). According to Lewys Dwnn, he boasted a coat of arms, - 'or a double headed eagle, sable' [gold, a black doubl-headed eagle]. In June 1589, he leased for thirteen years and for the sum of £33 his tenements of Tir Noyadd Holl [Hywel] Decka and Pantyfelin-Boeth to Ievan ap Lewis of Llangunllo parish and, as part of the rent, the following dues and services –

'...eight capons at Christmas and Easter, a day of ploughing in Winter, a day of harrowing in every harrowing time, a bushel of oats yearly, a day of reaping with one man every harvest and for carrying dung to the field yearly, 2d years [dues] for kilch march [the stallion's round] one day to dig turves and a heriot [the best beast surrendered to the lord of the manor on the decease of the tenant] when it falls due...'[3].

Bryne must have fallen on hard times, because in December of the same year he sold some neighbouring property to the Rev. Thomas Lloyd of Llangunllo, and in July, 1591, mortgaged to Lloyd for £53:6:8d, the 'capital messuage and lands called Plas y Bronwydd where the said Thomas Lloyd inhabits...' Apparently, the rector of Llangunllo had rented the 'tyddyn' of Bronwydd and had converted the rustic homestead into a 'plas', a gentleman's residence befitting a 'squarson' – a squire cleric. And the annals of the Lloyds of Bronwydd commence here at a 'tyddyn' which was to become in time a 'country house' of social distinction and pre-eminence.

iii

By the autumn of 1593, the Rev. Sir (as clergy of the day were addressed) Thomas Lloyd, MA.rector of Llangunllo and vicar of Penbryn, a parish on the Cardiganshire coast, was the virtual owner of Bronwydd and adjoining land. A few years later, Philip Bryne died, leaving a widow 'Ellen verch Rees of Henllan...late wife of Philip Bryne deceased...' who sold her remaining interest in Plas Bronwydd, in July 1611 '...where the said Thomas Lloyd dwells...' for the sum of £16[4]. Thomas was the younger son of David ap Rhys and Margaret, daughter of Thomas ab Owen ap Jenkin of Crynfryn in the parish of Nantgwnlle, Cardiganshire. The Lloyds of Crynfryn were wealthy gentry.

Thomas claimed that he was the twelfth in descent from Cadifor ap Selyf, lord of Cilycwm, in north Carmarthenshire, and from Tudwal Gloff one of the sons of Rhodri Mawr. The family were prominent in public affairs – David Lloyd, attorney-at-law, was under-sheriff from 1550-1560. Other members of the family also held important positions in the county and enjoyed the sovereign's favour and patronage, for example, John Lloyd, esq. was High Sheriff in 1638, and was a fervent Royalist. However, like many of his contemporaries, he trimmed his sails to the prevailing wind by submitting to the

8

Parliamentary forces at Cardigan in October, 1645. After the Restoration two of the Crynfryn Lloyds were High Sheriffs in 1662 and 1694. Like other gentry families they intermarried with those of similar rank, such as those of Trawsgoed in Cardiganshire and Aberglasney and Berllan Dywyll in Carmarthenshire. By the end of the eighteenth century they had died out in the main male line.

Thomas Lloyd of Bronwydd, the youngest of several children had ambition; he was a pluralist cleric; he was proud of his ancestry and armorial bearings which his family had borne from time immemorial. This was not merely an antiquarian pastime but, as Professor J. Gwynfor Jones has shown, there were very cogent reasons for preserving heraldic emblems and genealogies: to resolve disputes, settle inheritance and legal matters, as well as to consolidate kindred affinities and to confirm merit for public office. Although the Brwyne (Brine, Bruyne, etc) family was in decline – selling their property and unable to cope with the social and economic changes of the day, Thomas Lloyd was disposed to marry Sage daughter of George Brwyne of Pant-Dafydd ap Philip ap Thomas Brine of Llan-Ffynnonwen, a surgeon and a person of standing by now, especially as the Royal College of Surgeons had been founded in 1518, to aim at professional expertise and status.

In every way, Sage Brwyne was a suitable match for the squire cleric in terms of social rank – possibly, on account of her dowry, although there is no exant information about how much it was. Thomas Lloyd, was the owner of property in the parishes of Betws Bledrws, Caron, Llanddewi-Brefi, Llangeitho, Llangybi and Nantgwnlle in mid-Cardiganshire, as well as Bronwydd. Here he lived from the 1580s until about 1629. He improved the 'plas' and its surroundings, farmed his demesne, and asserted his domanial rights, for example, in February, 1619/20 he went to law against one Howell Morgan who had enclosed land near 'Rhydyvoydw' which impeded Lloyd's right of way from Bronwydd to a '...common regial [the king's] highway leading from the parish of Llanvair [tref] helygen to the market town of Llanpeder Pont Stephen...' and the matter had to be resolved before the Council of Wales and the Marches at Ludlow[5].

Thomas Lloyd's will was proved in 1629, by which he left his real estate, namely, land, farms, dwellings, etc., to his two sons: David and Rhys Lloyd. According to one source, David Llwyd or Lloyd, the eldest son, '...for his profuse way of living had but a small proportion of his father's estate...'. He had committed a grievous offence by marrying without his father's consent, and although he was the elder son, had forfeited the major part of his patrimony. Consequently, Thomas Lloyd was succeeded at Bronwydd by his second son Rhys Lloyd. A perusal of Thomas Lloyd's will gives some indication of his wealth in terms of landed property (albeit in the absence of precise details of acreages and rents). To David Lloyd he left some ten holdings of lesser value, described as 'tyddynod' which were entailed to his sons and future generations. Rhys Lloyd was far more fortunate and was left some twenty major properties in the parishes of Betws Bledrws, Caron, Llanbadarn Odyn, Llangeitho and Llangybi, subject to an '...annuity of £40 payable to my third son John Lloyd, until he is worth 300 marks yearly...' charged on them.

The major prize was the messuage and lands of 'Dery Worman', later to be known as Derry Ormond in the parish of Betws Bledrws and 'Ffynnhon-wen' and 'Tyr Pwll Cornor' in Llangunllo parish – the latter forming part of his expanding estate near Bronwydd. To his unmarried daughters Mary and Ann he left £160 each, to be used ultimately as marriage portions. To his daughter Jane, wife of Lewis ap Ievan, gent. (Lewis Bevan of Pencoed, High Sheriff of Carmarthenshire in 1634) and her children £20, and to his niece Lettice and nephew Thomas, children of his brother David Lloyd of Crynfryn the sums of £50 and £20 respectively, and the residue to his son and executor Rhys Lloyd[6].

Rice or Rhys Lloyd of Bronwydd, was High Sheriff of Cardiganshire in 1632, the first of eight members of the family to hold the office as a royal appointee, a duty which George Owen of Henllys described as fit for '...the chief man of substance in the shire...the chief officer of trust and credit...'. Rhys Lloyd married as his first wife, Mary daughter of John Parry of Blaenpant in Llandugwydd parish, and by her had a son Thomas and a daughter Sage (named after his mother). She married Colonel John Robinson of Gwersyllt Park, Denbighshire, and of Mynachty, Anglesey, High Sheriff of Denbighshire in 1630. He was a distinguished Royalist who defended Holt Castle in 1643, against the Roundheads. After the death of his first wife, Rhys Lloyd married Elizabeth, daughter of Thomas Byrtt of Llwynduris, near Llechryd. These marriage alliances consolidated the influence and prestige of Lloyd of Bronwydd as a rising family of standing in the locality and in the county. Astute and prudent, Rhys Lloyd extended his demesne and rule in the neighbourhood of Bronwydd by purchasing, in May 1632, the corn mill known as 'Melin Pwll y Corner'. This provided him with an additional source of income through 'suit of mill' by which he secured for his own farm and household, a proportion of the corn ground there, as well as the personal ascendancy of the lord over his tenants and dependants.

Rhys Lloyd died in 1642 and in his will of 28 September, 1634, bequeathed 12d to St. Davids Cathedral, 6/8d to Llangunllo church, to footmen and servants – Morgan Jones 40s, Edward Goddard 20s, Joanne Evans 'my maid servant' 20s, to five male servants and two female servants 6/8d each – a total of ten domestic servants, evidence that he was a country squire in comfortable circumstances. He remembered in his will John Bruyne, his uncle, to whom he left £5 and to his son Thomas Lloyd the sum of £100 '...when he shall be of discretion and yeares to keep house...' and the rest of his 'goods, chattels and cattle...' to his daughter Sage Lloyd who was appointed the executrix of his will. He left precise instructions that he was to be buried in the parish church of Llangunllo '...interred not in a coffin but in a linen shroud...'

Rhys Lloyd was succeeded at Bronwydd, by his only son and heir, Thomas, who married in July 1642, Magdalen, daughter of William Robinson of Gwersyllt Park in the county of Denbigh, and a sister of Colonel John Robinson, the Royalist mentioned above. There were two sons and three daughters from this marriage: Thomas, his heir, John of Lodge Park (also known as Bodvage park or 'Bodfrigan', in Welsh) a mansion house in the parish of Llangynfelin in north Cardiganshire. Very little is known of the three sisters: Sage was supposed to be alive in 1730, Magdalene in 1701 and married to David Lewes of Llysnewydd and Dôl-haidd, High Sheriff of Carmarthenshire in 1706. Jane the eldest, was married in September, 1674, to John Blome of Abergwili. Her dowry or portion amounted to a comparatively large sum of £500, and, according to the marriage settlement, the following properties in Abergwili parish were settled on her: the messuage and lands of Tyddyn Nant y Mab, Llwyn Picka, Tyddyn Penpont yr Annell, Melin Rees Lewis and other lands. Usually, a marriage settlement contained conditions which would safeguard the rights and benefits of the wife during widowhood, and to ensure that her family retained a legal interest in the property settled upon her. Moreover, the amount of her dowry, often showed her status in society, and that of her family.

An inventory of the goods and chattels of Thomas Lloyd of Bronwydd, deceased, were 'apprised' on 4th May 1663 by Thomas Parry of the parish of Llangunllo, gent, and John David of Llangeler,gent.

The total valuation came to £851-2-4d, including the sum of £600 in 'ready money'(kept in the house before the days when banks were set up throughout the land) and loan bonds worth £80. His farm stock included 26 head of cattle, 3 oxen,52 young beasts[cattle], 5 mares, 6 horses, 10 colts, and also 200 sheep, ploughs, harrows and various implements of husbandry. Lloyd's household effects display the comfortable life-style of a practising farmer-squire who could boast of items of plate [silver], brass, pewter, linen, coverlets, cushions, chairs, tables and bed-steads, as well as, barrels, hogsheads, spits, racks, tongs, and stylish wearing apparel.

Because Thomas Lloyd had died without making a will, letters of administration were granted to his widow Magdalen Lloyd, on 20 June, 1663. Perhaps the 'paper-value' recorded of the farm and house do not reflect the true financial position of the Bronwydd Estate. Indeed, in August 1649, Thomas Lloyd had made a grant by way of mortgage of property in Llandysul, Llanfair- Orllwyn and Llangunllo parishes to Sir John Price, Bart. Sir Evan Lloyd, Kt. Sir John Corbett and others to raise the sum of '...£1,000 payable at Michaelmas 1652...' It is conceivable that the crisis of the Civil War, fluctuating rents, unsettled tenantry, debts or other causes may have put the Bronwydd estate in jeopardy, like those of many other lesser gentry and yeomen. On the other hand, raising a mortgage was becoming an easy and cheap means of acquiring cash temporarily for estate purposes: farm improvements, refurbishing the mansion house, raising portions for unmarried daughters and the like. It had the advantage of making it possible to recover the ownership of the mortgaged land and to retain it in the family[7]. Be that as it may, Magdalen Lloyd took the stewardship of the estate seriously. Between the years 1670-1675 she purchased some neighbouring properties, so as to complete a ring fence about the mansion house: Pant-Dafydd, the ancient home of the Brwyne family, 'parcels of land in Cwm Cunllo...abutting a brook called Lleach...Blaengwenllaeth (Blaengwenllan)...Tir y Bedw called Llain Keven Llanfair in the parish of Llanvairdreflygen...'

When Magdalen Lloyd died in 1680 at Bodvage Park, the home of her sister, Dame Dorothy Price, the 'plas' of Bronwydd was one of the largest and most commodious of 'Tivyside' houses. The 'chimneymen', as the Hearth Assessors were called, came round in 1670 and Bronwydd was recorded as having eight hearths. She had made her will in April 1680, and devised all lands purchased in Cardiganshire and Carmarthenshire to her son John Lloyd. To her eldest son, Thomas Lloyd, she left the derisory sum of five shillings and a similar sum to her daughter Magdalen Lewis[es] of Llysnewydd. All her personal property - cash, jewels, plate furniture, pictures and the like she bequeathed to her son John Lloyd named above. She appointed Sage, her eldest daughter, as executrix and her brother John Robinson of Gwersyllt and her brother-in-law, Sir Thomas Price of Bodvage park, Bart, as 'overseers' of her property[8].

Thomas Lloyd, the eldest son of Thomas and Magdalen Lloyd, was married to Bridget Johnes of Dolaucothi. He was High Sheriff of Cardiganshire in 1680, and little else is known about him. But, in a deed, dated 22 May 1684, he entered into an agreement with John Jones of Abermayd, esq. John Lewis of Coedmore,esq. Thomas Lloyd of Castell Howell, Cardiganshire, and William Pugh of Mathafarn, esq, in Mongomeryshire to sell or mortgage 'Dery Worman' andmost of the properties (named in the will of his ancestor, the Reverend Thomas Lloyd, who first settled at Bronwydd) in parishes in mid and north Cardiganshire, in addition to parts of the Bronwydd estate in 'Tivyside' including the mansion house of Bronwydd. As only the 'lease' has survived (without the 'release')[9] it is not certain what happened, save that he conveyed the Bronwydd estate to his uncle John Lloyd of Bodvage park. It is possible that he had mortgaged his estate to his uncle. Outright sale of what would have been entailed property is not likely, without complicated legal process. One may ask,- Did he lead a dissolute life? Had he dissipated his fortune? Most certainly he was out of favour with his mother who, as has been mentioned, cut him off with only five shillings in her will.

At any rate, he died in 1692 having signed his will on 10 October of that year and had sufficient means to bequeath £300 to his brother John Lloyd, to John Lewes, grandson of David Lewis (his brother-in-law) £6 yearly '...towards his schooling or to such a time as he may be capable to be settled in some trade or as his father thinks it best to dispose of him and then to pay him £100 the said £6 shall be void .....to his sister Sage Lloyd £40 mortgage on lands called Llwynbedw in the parish of Brongwyn.....'

In passing, two interesting features of gentry will-making are seen here: the provision of an annuity or lump sum to younger sons of the family to enable them to acquire a modicum of education or to be apprenticed in a craft, trade or other calling, such as that of a 'peruke maker', 'saddler', 'corvisor'amongst others. Although on the lowest rung of the inheritance ladder they could become self supporting, whereas an unmarried daughter(especially one of several sisters) could be an encumbrance on an estate for life. In his will Thomas Lloyd made other bequests in kind to honour his memory and as a part of the protocol of the obsequies of the deceased – to twelve of his 'best and loving friends' (well known county gentry) he left 'a dozen rings to the value of fifteen shillings'. Again bequests were made to the deferential and deserving poor – lengths of cloth for 'mourning scarves' and other wearing apparel. Lloyd's estate was modest indeed, assessed at £190 – 7s of which John Lloyd of Newcastle-Emlyn received a '....shute [suit] of cloathes and 20 shillings, and James Bruyne of Pant-Dafydd (his kinsman) £4.....'

v

Thomas and Bridget Lloyd's elder son, Thomas , born in 1679, was a Land Commissioner for Cardiganshire in 1702. About that time he married Ann Wogan the sole heiress of Lewis Wogan's estates of Wiston and Cilrhiwe. The latter had become the owner, through his wife Ann (daughter of James Lloyd) of the Cilrhiwe estate. In many ways this was a most propitious match in terms of 'estate' and family importance. According to Lewys Dwnn, the Wogans claimed descent from Gwrgan, son of Bleddyn ap Maenarch of Brecon. Throughout the centuries the clan of Wogan had distinguished themselves as influential magnates in Wales, England and in Ireland, as justiciars, escheators, bailiffs and governors of towns and large tracts of territory. In 1281, Sir John Wogan had the king's 'protection while going beyond the seas' with authority over important Irish castles. Col.Thomas Wogan was one of the judges at the trial of King Charles I and signed his death warrant, but was pardoned later at the Restoration. In Pembrokeshire, the Wogans were in turn High Sheriffs and Members of Parliament. Ann Wogan, who married Thomas Lloyd of Bronwydd was, also, descended from the Phillips or Philipps family of Tregibby and Cardigan Priory – some of them 'parliament men' in the Civil War, army colonels, 'Commissioners of Sequestration' and Judges. Katherine Philipps, the well-known poet, writing under the pseudonym Orinda, who died in 1664 was one of the family.

The Lloyd family of Cilrhiwe were descended from the Reverend Henry Lloyd, rector of Cilrhedyn, whose forebears had come from Montgomeryshire in the

13

early seventeenth century and claimed Bleddyn ap Cynfyn, king of Powys, as their ancestor. The Lloyds had in 1644, joined the 'Association' in Pembrokeshire in support of the Parliamentarians. They held the important offices of the day, but saw how the wind had changed and came to favour the Restoration in 1660. Indeed, James Lloyd was granted a pardon and became High Sheriff of Pembrokeshire in 1661. Towards the end of his life he lived at Penallt Cadwgan near Cilgerran. He made his will on 8 November, 1703, 'infirm in body...but otherwise completely competent'. His bequests were:-

'...10s to the poor of the parishes of Cilgerran and Llanfihangel Penbedw, 10s to the poor of the parish of Cilrhedyn, sums of 10s and 20s to [various servants], to a man servant Hugh Mary 'two lambs or the equivalent', to William Wogan son of Lewis Wogan one piece of gold known as a guinea, to my great grandchild James Lloyd son of Thomas Lloyd of Bronwydd, gent. One gold 'signett' which belonged to my father Henry Lloyd...to my grand daughter wife of the said Thomas Lloyd one third of my books, one suite of 'arras [rich tapestry] hangings', half of the china dishes...along with all real estates to my eldest grand-child Ann Lloyd,... in the parishes of Llanfihangel Penbedw, Llanfyrnach and Penrith, and to two other grand children, Bridget and Catherine Wogan land in the parishes of Abernant, Cilrhedyn, Clydai, Llangeler and Trelech ar Betws....'[10].

Thomas Lloyd left Bronwydd and took up residence at Cilrhiwe and Vaynor,Maenordeifi, where he lived until his death about 1737. of the union of Thomas Lloyd and Ann Wogan there were four sons – James, Thomas, John and Robinson. James inherited Cilrhiwe in 1727, and married Elizabeth, the daughter of James Ladd, MD. of London. Her brother was Steward of the Barony of Cemais in 1744. Thomas Lloyd, the second son, succeeded to the Bronwydd Estate on the death of his great-uncle John Lloyd of Bodvage who had died without issue.

No doubt, John Lloyd had inherited the lion's share on the death of his aunt Dame Dorothy Price of Bodvage. In her will of 12 January, 1700/01, (apart from minor bequests to her Robinson blood relations of Gwersyll Park in Denbighshire) she devised and bequeathed '...to my nephew John Lloyd, all the messuages and tenements and land which I hold from any person or persons by way of mortgage and all sums of money due to me by mortgages, bills, bonds, 'spetialties' [specialties, i.e. chattels] and all rents, arrears of rents and all real and personal estate whatsoever...'.

In his will of 21 July, 1730, John Lloyd left 'all lands and tenements with the appertunances thereof' to Thomas Lloyd, the second son of Thomas Lloyd of Cilrhiwe, as sole heir and executor and to his heirs and assigns for ever. He gave instructions to be buried 'within the church of Llangunllo' left £10 each to his nephew John Lewis of Vaynor ' for a suit of mourning' £10 each to his nephew John Lewis of Carmarthen, and his niece Ann Lloyd of Dolgelynen, to James Lloyd, his nephew ' a ring value 21 shillings' and likewise to John Robinson of

Gwersyllt, to his sister Sage Lloyd an annuity of £20 chargeable on estates, £100 to 'my faithful servant Simon Humphreys', to a servant maid Susanna Jones,£20 and £5 for a 'suit of mourning'.

Robinson Lloyd, who died in December, 1742, was a squire farmer (albeit of modest fortune). From a damaged inventory of his worldly goods, assessed on 6 January 1742/3, he owned –

"a horse and saddle, £5, 11 horses and a colt, £5-10s; 3 yoke of oxen and two steers, £1; 11 cows and a heifer, £8;5 calves,£1-5s;corn and hay in haggard, £11-11-5d; pigs and poultry, 10/6d; all implements of husbandry, £2-2-6d;corn, butter and cheese in the storehouse, £5-1-6d; brass, pewter and furniture in house £12-12s; all other things…2/6d…apprised total £63-00-6d".

vi

Thomas Lloyd (1703-1775) succeeded to the Bronwydd estate in 1730, and on 5 October, 1739, he married Anne Lloyd, daughter and heiress of William Lloyd of Henllys, Penpedwast and Monken Hadley in Middlesex. Of all the matrimonial alliances engaged in by the Lloyds of Bronwydd, this was very significant because Anne's mother was Joan [Ford], daughter of Owen Ford of Bury [later, Berry Hill], who owned, according to the marriage settlement 'half part of the manor Kemes'. William Lloyd , the bride's father, had since January 1717/18, held the office of 'deputy to the deputy vice-admiral of South Wales, Thomas Ferrers of Bageston, with special responsibility for the coast between St. David's Head and Cardigan'. This appointment was a particularly important and, even, profitable one. It entailed the examination of goods and wrecks cast upon the shores, collaboration (if not collusion) with excise men and other officers of the law. It also carried local influence and prestige, notably, as the coast line co-incided with the western limits of the Barony of Cemais.

The title 'Lord Marcher' (and its territories) was by now partly owned by Thomas Lloyd of Bronwydd in virtue of inheritance by his wife. Due to various family settlements there were by now, virtually two separate estates – Cilrhiwe and Bronwydd – owned by the brothers, James and Thomas Lloyd[11].

The deeds relating to the marriage between Thomas Lloyd and Ann Lloyd of Penpedwast were drawn up on the 28/29 September, 1737, after long negotiation. As was usually the case, several important considerations had to be taken into account: control over the estate to guarantee that its revenues were not wasted by the extravagance of a rash speculator, inveterate gambler, unrestrained builder of new mansions or drunkard. Encumbrances too, such as portions for unmarried daughters and younger sons, unpaid debts or mortgages inherited from the past could prove to be a heavy burden on estates generally. For her part, Ann Lloyd had inherited vastly scattered properties apart from the closely spread lands in parishes around Henllys and Penpedwast. Some farms were in the distant parishes (and one must not forget the difficulties of travel in

15

the eighteenth century) of north west Carmarthenshire. These lands were to be held by trustees 'for the use and behoof [advantage, benefit] of Thomas Lloyd and Ann his wife as her jointure estimated to be worth £200 of yearly value'.

Compared to sums recorded in other marriage settlements for the area, it could be said that it was adequate and only so. There was also, provision for the sum of £1000 to be raised 'for the benefit of any younger children'. Unfortunately, there were difficulties arising from previous transactions, for example, an agreement had been made by William Lloyd (the bride's father) of Penpedwast, and Adam Ottley, bishop of St. Davids on 30 May, 1723, for the lease of the 'Forests of Trymints, otherwise Bishop's Forests in the lordship, of Llanddewi Brefy at the yearly sum of Four Marks, [mark=13/4d] payable to the said bishop and his successors...' But this was a small matter compared to the yearly charges of £50 to Ann Lloyd's stepmother Susan Lloyd of Monken Hadley, £30 apiece to her sisters Beatrice and Bridget, on settled land yielding only £160 only per annum. Furthermore, the trustees were able (in the event of a fall in rent) to sell Ann's property in Pembrokeshire in order to raise £600 to pay off her two sisters and a debt of £1000 on the estate of her father William Lloyd.

The legal documents laying down the terms of the marriage settlement had not been completed by May, 1740, because when it came to the point, Ann Lloyd flatly refused to add her signature. Much to the chagrin of her husband and '...notwithstanding such a tender request made by her said husband ...she...absolutely refused to execute the same...!' And she also, refused to give reasons!

Thomas Lloyd thought now that he had to annul and revoke the original settlement as far as his own real estate was concerned.

It occurred to him to sell the distant parts of the Carmarthenshire property in order to clear his own debts and incumbrances, especially, as '...those lands lay remote from those of the said Thomas Lloyd and Ann his wife...' It was expected that these would fetch a good price and negotiations commenced with '...diverse persons...[who]...actually contracted for the sale of some parts thereof...' But, unfortunately for Thomas Lloyd, the proposed buyers had second thoughts: their lawyers advised them that Thomas Lloyd's power to revoke the settlement was suspect, and any future purchasers might be afraid they would be bound by encumbrances, such as the annuities to be paid out and maybe more.

In order to extricate himself from this impasse, Thomas Lloyd had to resort to costly legal processes; he had to consult 'learned counsel' (a phrase frequently occurring in the Bronwydd deeds) and all were baffled by Ann Owen's refusal to sign in the first place, and more so, that she had refused to give a reason! Eventually, Thomas Lloyd had to secure a disentailing deed (which allowed him to sell parts of the estate irrespective of any claim by an eldest son). By July, 1740 an 'Act of parliament for vesting the estates of Thomas Lloyd, esq. and Ann his wife in Trustees for discharging incumbrances affecting the same and for settling other estates to the Uses [trusts] in their marriage settlement' was obtained, with a proviso to discharge all debts and liabilities on the Bronwydd and Penpedwast estates in the counties of Cardigan, Carmarthen and Pembroke and to pay the sum of £170 a year settled on Thomas and Ann Lloyd for life; £500 for [any] younger children; £1,000 (after her death) for the benefit of younger children, and, in the event of her death without children, the sum of £1,000 each to be raised for Beatrice and Bridget Lloyd her sisters. Any surplus money arising from the sale of Thomas Lloyd's Cardiganshire estate was to be invested in the purchase of lands in Pembrokeshire[12].

Thomas and Ann Lloyd had a large family of ten children, many of whom died young. Thomas the eldest was born in 1740; Owen Lloyd became an army colonel and in 1765 married Dorothy Elizabeth, heiress of Thomas Lloyd, esq. of Abertrinant in the parish of Llanfihangel-y-Creuddyn, by his wife Elizabeth Vaughan, the sister of the earl of Lisburne. Their son, the Revd. William Lloyd became the rector of Maenordeifi, and was the maternal grandfather of Henry Williams Lloyd Howell (1871 – 1916) of Glaspant, Newcastle Emlyn.

Thomas Lloyd was ambitious; he had acquired a 'moiety' [a half share] of the barony of Cemais and had served as High Sheriff of Cardiganshire in 1733. In 1750, the opportunity came to buy the other half of the barony. It was owned by John Laugharne of Llanrheithan, a 'cousin' of Lloyd. Having lived a prodigal life and squandered his fortune, Laugharne was hounded by bailiffs and creditors and, finally, ended up as a prisoner in '...the common gaol or prison for the county of Pembroke and chose rather to continue in prison than surrender his estate and affects to his creditors...' But, mulish stubbornness could not save him and at last, he was compelled to sell everything he had. Now, it was Thomas Lloyd's chance and for the sum of £2,000 Laugharne sold his share of 'the lands and profits' and not least, the prestige attached to the 'Barony of Kemes' – once again in its long history, the barony (estimated to cover some 60,000 acres) was held by one Lord Marcher – Thomas Lloyd of Bronwydd[13].

The new lord of the barony had to face the serious task of making his enlarged estate economically viable by clearing it of the encumbrances which had accumulated over many generations. Amongst those the heaviest, perhaps, was a charge of £800 on his Penpedwast estate, and, a mortgage of £6,000 raised in 1734 which had not been repaid.

Thomas Lloyd was eager to revive the power and pageantry which was traditionally associated with the Lord Marcher. He would wish to set himself up as a fashionable country squire, to refurbish the mansion house of Bronwydd, to acquire costly artistic objects, carriages and equipage. The more land he possessed the greater was his responsibility to see that it was cultivated efficiently and that rents were paid on time. More and more land was being enclosed and there was the challenge from new and more efficient methods of farming. The names of Jethro Tull and Lord (Turnip) Townsend were becoming well known throughout the country.

Lloyd's aim was to buy land here and there, and much of it was acquired from the estate of his brother James Lloyd of Cilrhiwe. The latter seems to have been in financial difficulties, and there is evidence that he was borrowing sums of money amounting to, at least, a thousand pounds from his brother Thomas Lloyd of Bronwydd in order to pay his attorneys in Pembrokeshire and in London, not to mention the day-to-day running costs of his house and estate at Cilrhiwe. Thomas Lloyd saw clearly that Cilrhiwe was in jeopardy and in order to save what was, after all, the family patrimony and to expand his own Bronwydd estate, he bought up many of the properties which his brother would have to sell.

From 1755-1760 some dozen farms and tenements in the parishes near Bronwydd (forming part of the Cilrhiwe estate) as well as a few houses and warehouses in the town of Cardigan in 'High Street, St. Mary Street...in the north of Quay Street with Mwldan or Mill Dam Brook on the west thereof, two stables...two gardens near the west of Bridge Street...' which cost him about £2000. The ownership of these houses and business premises appealed to Thomas Lloyd as a profitable commercial venture and the initial outlay could be justified. Cardigan was a flourishing market town and port. To be freeholder in the town brought its civic and political privileges – 'faggot' voters could be bought to support a candidate favoured by Bronwydd as member of parliament for the Cardigan Boroughs [Cardigan, Atpar, Lampeter, Tregaron and Aberystwyth]. Burgesses too, had the right to trade without paying market tolls, and much else besides[14].

Mounting debts (and, reading between the lines, ill health) made it impossible for James Lloyd to continue at Cilrhiwe and in April, 1758 he signed a deed authorising his brother Thomas Lloyd of Bronwydd to dispose all or any part of his estate and 'take to himself for my use such sums of money as shall arise or become due to the sale thereof...' He ended the document with a cryptic note '...James Lloyd of Cilrhiwe in the parish of Llanfihangel Penbedw for divers causes and considerations me hereunto moving......'[???]. He left Cilrhiwe and went to live in various places in England such as Buscot Hall in Walsall, Staffordshire and Gittisham in Devon. He died about the years 1780/81. His will was proved in the Probate Court of Canterbury on 4 September, 1781.

James Lloyd devised to his brother Thomas Lloyd of Bronwydd farms and other holdings in the parishes of Eglwys Fair a Churig and Llanfyrnach, with remainder in trust for the sons of Thomas Lloyd in tail male and a sum of £2,000 for various relations. He left instructions that he was to be buried in St. Augustine's church Bristol, in the same vault as his wife Ann (Owen, daughter of Wyrriot Owen of Great Nash in Pembrokeshire). According to Francis Green, the burial register of that church records her burial on 4 August, 1779 from Shirehampton, and the memorial states that she was fifty two years of age.

18

There is no mention of the burial of James Lloyd and in her will of 16 October, 1769, Ann Lloyd left some land (held by lease from Sir Richard Philipps of Picton Castle) to her husband and add '...Would that I had more to give..'a sad comment on the sorry plight of this impoverished gentlewoman[15].

While the Cilrhiwe estate and the fortunes of James Lloyd were in decline, Thomas Lloyd continued to expand his Bronwydd estate. Perhaps family pride and ambition rather than prudence motivated these transactions. In buying back what had been Bronwydd property a few generations previously – Pantbach, Pwll Cornor and Pwll Cornor Mill, in the neighbourhood of Bronwydd , Lloyd wanted to consolidate his Bronwydd demesne. But he had further ambitions. He bought Aberarthen Fawr near Penbryn Beach and lands in the parishes of Eglwyswrw and Llanycefn, in north Pembrokeshire, and elsewhere. According to the marriage agreement between Thomas Lloyd and Ann Lloyd of Henllys and Penpedwast, lands in mid and north Cardiganshire were to be sold to provide for the purchase of lands nearer home. Consequently, Olmarch-isaf, Glandiwlas and Gellygarnedde in the parishes of Llangybi and Bettws Bledrws were bought by David Jones of 'Derry Ormond' and it will be recalled that 'Dery Worman' was part of the inheritance of Rees Lloyd from his father the Revd.Thomas Lloyd,MA., rector of Llangunllo, the first Lloyd to live at Bronwydd, but had been sold about the year 1740.   Because the Bronwydd estate (comprising parts of Cilrhiwe, Henllys and Penpedwast) was widely spread and subject to very tangled legal arrangements, resort had been made to the provisions of an act of parliament in 1748 to partition and sell the estate in mid Cardiganshire. Fortunately, by the 1760's there were willing buyers – Herbert Lloyd of Peterwell, John Johnes of Dolaucothi, Thomas Johnes of Croft Castle, Herefordshire and John Pugh Pryse of Gogerthan. The cash derived from these sales became available to acquire, once more, former Bronwydd lands and some new ones as well. But, as it turned out, Thomas Lloyd overstretched himself and caused serious pressures on the Bronwydd estate which his son Colonel Thomas Lloyd (1740-1807) had to face some years later[16].

vii

Col.Thomas Lloyd, the eldest son of Thomas Lloyd and Ann Lloyd of Henllys and Penpedwast, succeeded to the Bronwydd estate after the death of his father in May 1775. He served as a Captain in the 10th Foot Regiment, and in 1798, was appointed Colonel in command of the Fishguard and Newport Fencibles. He was a magistrate and a Deputy Lieutenant of Cardiganshire, and held the office of High Sheriff of the county in 1793. On 31 July, 1784, in his forty fourth year, Thomas Lloyd married Mary Jones of Haverfordwest, spinster, and further described as of '..the manor or lordship of Llanfyrnach...' She was the daughter of Dr.John Jones, MB, and Sarah Williams of

19

Haverfordwest, who was descended from the well-to-do Williams family and Owen Howell of Llanddewi-Velfrey, whose money was derived from commerce as well as from land. The marriage took place at St. Ishmael's church, Camrose, with the Rev. Owen Perrott Edwardes, rector of St. Bartholomew the Great, London, officiating.

In the annals of family alliances, diplomatic matchmaking, economic and social advantage which greatly affected fortunes of the Lloyds of Bronwydd and their estate, this marriage provided to be most desirable. Taking into account ancestry, inherited wealth and social position, Dr. Jones could hold his own in the polite and elegant gentry circles of Pembrokeshire. A graduate in medicine from Trinity College, Oxford, he had proceeded to the degree of Doctor of Medicine of the University, and styled himself as 'John Jones, doctor in physic'. His services were much in demand in the mansion-houses of the county; he was a 'confidant' of the squirearchy, a 'persona grata' whose professional advice and discretion could be trusted. Like many of those with whom he was friendly, he could boast of his distinguished ancestry, namely, descent from Cadifor ap Dinawal of Castell Hywel in Cardiganshire, through the line of Ffoshelyg and Llanllyr. He had, in 1745, claimed the right to a scholarship, and if possible, to a Fellowship at Jesus College, Oxford, on the grounds of 'Founders Kin', namely, family links with Dr. Griffith Lloyd (the younger son of Hugh Llywelyn Lloyd of Castell Hywel and Joan, daughter of Griffith ap Henry of Llanllyr) the second principal of the college. Dr. Jones was sworn in as a burgess of Haverforwest in 1750. In 1757, he married Sarah Williams, daughter of a prosperous 'mercer' in Haverfordwest, and whose mother was the daughter of the Owen Howell, mentioned above.

The doctor was the owner of considerable landed property which was spread over a wide area – in the parishes of Llanboidy, Clynderwen, Henllan Amgoed, Eglwys Fair Churig and in the 'townred' of Keeston, in Carmarthenshire and Pembrokeshire, as well as in distant parts of Cardiganshire, such as, Silian, Mwnt and Verwig.

Not lacking in enterprise, he leased, in May, 1784,

'... for the lives of the three youngest sons of George iii, the buildings called the Old Chapel of the town of Tenby (the whole foundation avenue from the pier head on the south side of the chapel and the ring fence of the chapel... for mooring ships and the profit of the same, also the causey [causeway] leading along the slip on the south side... below high water mark with the drang or path and parapet wall on its north side, together with the emoluments belonging thereto, in consideration of emoluments which may accrue to the town from a company which the construction of baths may induce to resort thither. Rent.1/ - annually...'

This move on the part of Dr. Jones shows him as a far sighted developer and benefactor who realised the need for leisure facilities in the increasingly popular resort and town of Tenby[17].

According to the marriage settlement between Thomas Lloyd and Mary Jones, the income from about thirty farms and holdings, was settled to provide for her during widowhood. But in the early years of the marriage, the Bronwydd estate was still managed by Ann Lloyd, Thomas Lloyd's mother. As executrix, she had the responsibility along with trustees, of administering the property. She had to secure her own rights and pecuniary benefits as a widow, raise portions for younger children; exercise prudence and good management in choosing industrious tenants and take quick measures to acquire money for any contingency. For this purpose, Ann Lloyd had in 1777, to raise a mortgage of £3,600 on Bury[Berry].Nant-yr-Helygen Fawr and Eithinduon, in Nevern and Eglwyswrw, to provide annuities for Owen Lloyd and four unmarried sisters. She insisted on including feudal dues and services in rent agreements, for example, the provision of eggs, poultry and other farm produce, as well as the carrying out of farming tasks during the year.

On inheriting a large estate, the life-tenant had to take stock of the financial state of his properties, and it was not long before Thomas Lloyd realised that serious trouble lay ahead. Firstly, with two large mansions, Bronwydd and Cilrhiwe, he decided that he had no need for the old and unimproved house of Penpedwast. Consequently, in June 1779, it was let 'for three lives' to one Joseph David of the parish of Eglwyswrw, yeoman, at at annual rent of £70. Leases and rents were reviewed; the estate was surveyed and accurate maps were drawn up. Some of these contiguous properties were bought, although an exchange of such lands was the course often chosen[18].

Shortly after his father's death in May 1775, Thomas Lloyd commissioned Richard Jones of Pantygarn, Eglwyswrw (later of Pantirion, near Cardigan) to survey and map parts of the Bronwydd estate. Further examination during the next few years showed that the situation was serious: there were unpaid loans, rent arrears, servants' wages, family portions, mortgages and a host of debts of all sorts which amounted to, at least, £9,000. The lord's rights over the 'waste' throughout the barony were being flouted: 'cotts' and 'tai un-nos' were erected without permission, the cutting of 'matts' [peat turves] for fuel ruined pasture land, with scant regard for the lord of the barony. While any possible baronial rents were only minimal in the economy of the estate, the utter disregard of the ordinary people was an affront to the dignity and rule of the lord (as will be shown later in this account).

Thomas Lloyd bemoaned the profligacy, in land purchase and reckless borrowing, which his father had indulged in, particularly, parts of Cilrhiwe and those of John Laugharne of Llanrheithan. The acquisition of the title 'Lord Marcher of Kemes': its pageantry, prestige and chivalric fantasy, altogether, proved to be costly and extravagant in the long run. Indeed, Thomas Lloyd had to confess that '...It was the ambition of the day to covet many acres not to cultivate the few...' With regard to sorting out his financial problems, he added '...this promise I hold most sacred and, indeed, it concurs with the soundest

21

policy to unhamper myself from debts.'[19]

Thomas Lloyd's marriage to Mary Jones, the daughter of Dr. John Jones, was to provide a lifeline, partly, at least, in saving the solvency of the Bronwydd estate. The character and temperament of Dr.Jones were, by no means, the least important factor; he was a determined and unremitting speculator in property; he probably acted, too, out of affection for his only daughter and heiress, and wished to save his son-in-law from financial ruin.

He bought Henllys, which, by this time, comprised Henllys Fawr and Henllys Fach, along with Cwmeog, from his son-in-law, Thomas Lloyd, for £3,700 in 1787. Shortly afterwards, in 1778, he cast his eye on the Pendine estate of Gwynne Vaughan of Jordanston Hall (Trewrdan) in Dewsland, which had come on the market. For this he paid the sum of £3,000, and this property comprised, not only good farming land, but also '...collieries,lime kilns and limestone quarries...'

By 1805-1806 Dr. Jones had bought the manor of Llandilo-Abercywyn, Carmarthenshire, and lands in neighbouring parishes, from Sir Henry Protheroe of Bristol, for the very large sum of £23,000. One prime consideration for the acquisition of '...these valuable properties was their contiguity to the water carriage and good markets...the prospects of peace have greatly advanced the value of this property and the terms are such as can be seldom obtained'. Dr. Jones insisted that '...all deeds, writings, Court Books, Court Rolls and Muniments' had to be handed over to the purchaser. He knew well the ways of shifty characters who might claim manorial and mineral rights, the long forgotten customs and dues, and the fraudulent demands made by opportunist landowners. At the time, he was deeply involved in Chancery Court proceedings, as a trustee of the Orielton estate, to safeguard the 'infant' [i.e someone who had not attained the age of twenty one] Sir Hugh Owen's interests, against the trickery of his uncle and guardian, John Colby of Ffynone.

Advowsons were another popular investment, and in May 1805, within two years of his death at Bronwydd, the doctor repurchased the advowson of Newport for the benefit of his son-in-law, Thomas Lloyd, for the very large sum (for such transactions) of £2,250. He knew that they could be traded, from time to time, as profitable sources of income to the estate. In his will of 10 August 1806 he devised all his real estate, namely, land, and two '...perpetual advowsons to his daughter Mary Lloyd; the lordship and manor of Abercowin and Pentrewyn to his grandson James Lloyd after the decease of Mary Lloyd, Clyngwynne and Pante in the parish of Newchurch and real estate in the parishes of Llanboidy and Eglwys fair a Churig, to his grand-daughter Sarah Mary Lloyd when she reached the age of twenty-five; all personal estate to his daughter Mary Lloyd...' Dr.Jones died at Bronwydd in 1807, and was buried at Llangunllo. His memorial inside the church records that he '...was an eminent physician and a highly literary character...' One might add, that through his foresight his sound business sense and enterprise, he saved the Bronwydd estate at the time, and added considerably to its broad acres, in some twenty parishes in the counties of Cardigan, Carmarthen and Pembroke.

A few months after Dr. Jones death, Thomas Lloyd (Colonel Lloyd) died on 13 July, 1807 and was succeeded by his eldest son Thomas Lloyd (1788-1845), James Lloyd (1795-1827) and a daughter Sarah Mary. In his will made during June and July, 1795, Thomas Lloyd left all his real estate, except some small properties in Llandyfriog, to his eldest son Thomas Lloyd. The sum of £4,000 was to be raised and use and benefit of his younger children James and Sarah Mary Lloyd, £200 towards their maintenance and education, £400 each to his sisters Anna Louisa, Bridget and Beatrice Lloyd, to his brother and 'sister Lewes' of Llysnewydd 10 guineas for a 'mourning ring' and £600 to trustees in support of a 'chapel built by me in the parish of Henllan Divy and commonly called Capel Drindod...'[20].

viii

Colonel Lloyd's son, Thomas Lloyd served in the East Kent Regiment (the Buffs), was a Justice of the Peace, Deputy Lieutenant, and High Sheriff of Cardiganshire in 1814. In July 1819, he married Anne Davies Thomas, the only surviving child and heiress (after 1823), of John Thomas of Llwydcoed and Llety Mawr in the parish of Llannon, Carmarthenshire. John Thomas of Llety Mawr had died in 1812, and his heir, John Davies Thomas, esq., (who had matriculated at Christ Church in 1815), died in 1823, at Jesus College, Oxford. John Thomas' wife Anne, was the daughter of Arthur Davies, esq. of Llandovery, son of Rees Davies of that town who was - an 'ironmonger' a term used in the eighteenth century of 'ironmasters' who smelted iron and manufactured swords, guns, 'militaria' of all kinds, the metal accoutrements and trappings of horse-drawn vehicles, 'fowling pieces', farming implements, household utensils and the like, at his 'manufactories' in Swansea and other places.

John Thomas, esq. of Llety Mawr, boasted a long and distinguished ancestry: he was the fifth generation from Thomas Rees Treharne, the son of Rees Treharne (who died in 1660) a descendant of Sir Hugh Treharne, Knight, of Llety Mawr in the time of Edward iii, and one who fought with Lord Audeley under Edward the Black Prince at the battle of Poitiers in 1356.

The Davies family claimed that one of their forebears was a Captain Davies, who had fought on the continent under the command of John Churchill, Duke of Marlborough, at the battles of Blenheim, Oudenarde and Malplaquet, in the early 1700's.

The historical and social background of the Davies family is important   because much of the wealth from industry and land was, partly, to devolve by succession to Anne Davies Thomas, the heiress who became the wife of Thomas Lloyd of Bronwydd.

The will of Rees Davies 'ironmonger', of 11 December, 1773, gives some indication of his status – he had lands in the parishes of Caio and Llandingat, Carmarthenshire, and in Ystradfellte, Breconshire; he made several bequests of £200 each to relatives; he possessed a 'gold watch'; he had a great deal of 'plate, enough to fill a large trunk'- all the 'indicia' of a well-to-do man of business. By the time that his grand-daughter, Anne Davies Thomas, married Thomas Lloyd in 1819, the family were prominent landowners in the new industrial areas of east Carmarthenshire, in the parishes of St. Mary's, Swansea, Oystermouth, Llandeilo-Talybont, Llanrhidian, Llansamlet, Llangyfelach, Llanguicke and Llandewy (with Reynoldston) in Glamorgan as well as properties in Middlesex and Essex.

The Davies family had taken advantage of prosperous times (with England engaged in a war against France) from the 1790's to the early 1800's, to purchase land from old but impecunious gentry families such as, the Dawkins and Mansels. A grandson of Rees Davies, the 'ironmonger', by now styled as 'esquire' had moved to Swansea about 1809, and after him, Anne Davies Thomas inherited the sum of £5,000 and estates in Llandeilo-Tal-y-Bont and elsewhere. In this connection, it is interesting to note that her 'kinsman' Dr. David Davies, Doctor of Physic, married into the family of Saunders of Clynfelin and Pentre, Pembrokeshire, - later to be known as the Saunders Davies family.

Thomas and Anne Lloyd lived for some years at Cilrhiwe, while his mother, Mary Lloyd, stayed on at Bronwydd and managed affairs there, where she had a life interest. Thomas and Anne Lloyd had five sons: Thomas Davies Lloyd, who succeeded his father, James John, Rhys Jones, Owen Treharne and George Martin, who died while he was a young lad. James John, who served in the 13th Hussars, married Susan Maria Anne, daughter of David Arthur Saunders Davies, MP. of Pentre, Boncath, from whom are descended the Lloyd family of Court Henry, in the Tywi valley. Rhys Jones Lloyd, was educated at Exeter College,Oxford; was ordained and served for many years as rector of Troed-yr-Aur. He was described as a 'man of wit and learning' and 'the most noticeable figure in the society of the Tivyside'.

One of the picturesque 'squarsons' of the countryside, Rhys Jones Lloyd kept horses and hounds;followed the 'Tivyside' hunt several days during the week; was chairman of public bodies, such as, the School Board, the Board of Guardians and the Lower Troedyraur Bench of Magistrates. In court, his linguistic skill in translating English legal terms into Welsh was often appreciated by monoglot Welsh speakers. His theatrical mannerisms, idiosyncratic intonation of the Liturgy (relics of a bygone age) and fluent and powerful preaching in the Welsh language drew large crowds[21].

Up to his death in 1845, Thomas Lloyd of Bronwydd, was, in his rôle of Lord Marcher, troubled by the most vocal radical elements in the population within the barony of Cemais and the constantly warring factions who were jockeying, unashamedly, for the office of mayor of Newport, as will be shown later in this account.

Like the other squires of Bronwydd, Thomas Lloyd was bedevilled by financial problems; he had to resort to temporary and long term loans, estimated to amount to a total of over £10,000, not to mention the payment of portions and other encumbrances according to previous family arrangements – one of which was the redemption of Henllys and Cwmeog and lands (about 1271 acres) in the parish of Nevern, from John Beynon, to whom the properties had been mortgaged by Mary Lloyd (Thomas Lloyd's mother) for £5,000.

While Thomas Lloyd was engrossed in trying to solve the problems of the barony from his home at Cilrhiwe, a convenient and strategic base, his mother continued to live at Bronwydd until her death at 1830. From the rents of the lands left to her by her father, Dr. John Jones, it would appear that she could have lived very comfortably. But the perennial problems which beset the gentry – shortage of immediate cash, overspending, generous gifts to charitable causes, the blandishments of spendthrift blood relations, the repayment of inherited debts – also faced Mary Lloyd and seriously diminished her income.

She generously but unwisely, agreed to a grant of '…the mansion house of Bronwydd, with rights of common…at a peppercorn rent…' in exchange for the [surrender] of rents and emoluments of some twenty properties to her son Thomas Lloyd. Whereas, by this arrangement, Mary Lloyd was freed from encumbrances, such as, raising the sum of £3,000 to provide portions of £500 each for her and her late husband, Colonel Thomas Lloyd's younger children, she was however habitually forced to borrow on a large scale, estimated to be about £24,000 from 1809 onwards, a sum which had not been repaid by the time of her death[22].

James Lloyd, her younger and, apparently, prodigal son, was a constant drain on her finances, and there is some evidence that his brother, Thomas Lloyd, had frequently to come to his aid. James, died young in 1827 – of some tragic illness or a dissolute way of life, one cannot tell. For the last ten years of his life he had amassed debts of several thousand pounds, a large sum for a younger son. Creditors were ready to pounce at any time – small tradesmen, cobblers, saddlers, blacksmiths, farriers, keepers of hostelries and taverns – all clamouring for payment of bills and loans ranging from a few pounds to thousands. James Lloyd had been foolish enough to entrust his affairs to the notoriously crooked attorney-at-law in Newcastle-Emlyn, John Beynon of Atpar Hill. On one occasion, Mary Lloyd had to challenge a bill of £1,000 from Beynon '… for want of proof of the sum due..' Some money borrowed was from neighbouring gentry, one of whom, John Lloyd Williams of Gwernant, scribbled a hurried note to Thomas Lloyd, asking him to repay a loan to James which was 'long overdue'.

As a footnote he added – '...excuse haste as dinner is on the table and the company is waiting...!!'

Many of James Lloyd's money problems were no doubt, due to his convivial and generous nature and his friendship with and concern for the unfortunate poor in the locality. One of his creditors was Samuel Jones, shoe-maker of Aber[banc] who sent a bill (in respect of some one hundred items from January, 1821 to March, 1827) amounting to a total of £34-16-6d, '...for work and labour done for the said James Lloyd in his lifetime and also for goods sold and delivered at his special instance and request...'

One item was '...12/6d for half-boots supplied at Mr Lloyd's request, to Twm Cawl Llath...' Unfortunately, nothing is known about this character, save that he seems to have survived on a diet of gruel!

James Lloyd made his will on the 27 January, 1822, and appointed Mary Lloyd, his mother as his executrix and sole legatee of '...any goods, ready money, horses and all lands to which he had claim' In an inventory of 17 December, 1827, his personal possessions were listed as follows:- ' Horses, harness, etc. £182-5-6; Wearing apparel £92-11-6; Household goods, furniture. £82-0-6; Books. £28-6-0; Plate. £17-14-0; Wearing ornaments. £43-10-0. [Total - £423-7-6] His interest in land was limited to his lifetime. When Mary Lloyd died in 1830, her personal estate was calculated as follows – Cash in house, £692-2-6;-do- at Bankers, £129-2-1. Total: £821-4-7. Debts on simple contracts: £84-0-0; Insurance policy on life of testatrix per Rock Insurance Co. £3000; -do-per Pelican Insurance Co. £300; return of probate because of debts: £132-0-0; Total - £7461-4-7.

Cash expenses - £ 7816 - 16 - 1
Cash received - £ 7461 - 04 - 7
Deficit - £ 355 - 11 - 6

The residue of Mary Lloyd's other personal estate amounted to – Household goods, furniture, etc. £157-11-6; Plate, linen and china. £133-1-0; Books, prints and pictures. £5-0-0; Wearing apparel. £10-0-0;Jewels, trinkets and ornaments of the person...£51-10-0; Horses and carriages. £110-0-0; Other effects not converted into money... wine, and other liquors. £20-0-0. Total £487-11-6.

Deductions: Balance of cash due   - £ 355 - 11 - 6
Retained in part of debts paid by
Executor out of his own money   - £ 132 - 0 - 0
                                        £ 487 - 11 - 6 [23]

The next (and most well known) squire of Bronwydd to succeed was their eldest son, Thomas Davies Lloyd, who was born at Bronwydd on 21 May 1820. Educated firstly, at Harrow School, he matriculated from Christ Church, Oxford, in December, 1838. On leaving Oxford, Thomas Davies Lloyd joined the 13th Light Dragoons when he was twenty-one years of age. He later served with the 82nd Foot in Canada, but returned from Ottawa on the death of his father. In December, 1846, Thomas Davies Lloyd married Henrietta Mary, the fourth daughter of George Reid of Bunker's Hill and Friendship estates in Jamaica, and of Watlington Hall, Norfolk. Her mother was Louisa, daughter of Sir Charles Oakeley, Bart. Of the famous Oakeley clan who had connections with the University of Oxford and the East India Company. There was a previous Welsh connection too, namely – a William Oakeley had married the daughter of Ifan Gruffydd of Plas Tanybwlch, Merioneth. Moreover, the Oakeleys were connected by marriage to the nobility – the Russells (Dukes of Bedford) of Woburn Abbey.

Thomas Davies Lloyd was breaking with tradition by seeking a bride outside his peer group and also outside the Principality – a process which was to be seen more and more amongst the Welsh gentry – through the contacts made in the Universities, the Inns of Court, the Army and Navy, and with wealthier gentry and nobility.

There is no evidence to show that Henrietta Mary contributed in any way to the broad acres and coffers of the Bronwydd estate. She was however, the grand-daughter of a baronet who had lived at the Chateau of Meysenbrock '...a beautiful old family residence owned by her mother née the Comtesse de Lormet...' (according to Lady K.M. Lloyd's description). Henrietta's husband, Thomas Davies Lloyd, was a mere Welsh squire, albeit, with a large estate in south west Wales. The match seemed well arranged from Lloyd's point of view and that of his relations. Moreover, to the Oakeley family the title of 'Lord Marcher of Kemes' and the possibility of a peerage could adequately compensate for inferior rank.

Like his predecessors (and other landowning gentry), Thomas Davies Lloyd was appointed a Justice of the Peace and in 1851, was High Sheriff of Cardiganshire. In his campaign to revive an ancient peerage he failed, but had to console himself with a baronetcy in 1863. He served as a Liberal Member of Parliament for Cardiganshire from 1865 – 1868 and for the Cardigan Boroughs from 1868-1871. He was greatly influenced by the 'Gothic' revival and undertook the restoration of Bronwydd, Newport Castle and churches, especially, Llangunllo, amongst other projects. He was an inveterate spender, and along with his grand schemes as 'Lord Marcher', the many encumbrances on his estate and his conspicuous display, he sank deeper and deeper into a quagmire of debt, often, to those who had trust in the 'good name of Lloyd of Bronwydd'. One example is typical: one 'Evan Thomas, late coachman at Bronwydd' lent his former master the sum of £350 – probably his life savings – a telling act of devotion![24].

From the time he inherited the Bronwydd estate (as the following examples show) Thomas Davies Lloyd was in constant financial trouble: in 1849, he owed his mother, Anne Davies Lloyd, the sum of £1,870. Between 1852 and 1858 he was in debt to London and country lawyers for about £12,000. He bought the estate of Penybeili adjoining Bronwydd, in the parish of Llangunllo, for £3,000 and in order to discharge many other immediate payments, he borrowed from a firm of money lenders? – the Swinney Trustees – the sum of £13,000. There were, also, inherited debts (outstanding from his father's time) of £10,000 together with other encumbrances amounting to about £35,000. An annual charge of £600 a year, for the benefit of his mother, Anne Davies Lloyd, during her widowhood (and she survived her husband by forty three years) in all, came to £35,000, while the Cilrhiwe estate had been mortgaged for over £20,000 to provide annuities to Sir Thomas' brothers – Rhys Jones, James John and William Owen Lloyd.

Sir Thomas Davies Lloyd died in July, 1877, his estate heavily in debt, his political and social ambitions unfulfilled. His wife Henrietta Mary had predeceased him in 1871[25].

x

Sir Marteine Owen Mowbray Lloyd, the 2nd baronet, was born on 8 February 1851, the only child of Sir Thomas Davies Lloyd and his wife Henrietta Mary. He was educated at Eton, and afterwards by a private tutor at Bronwydd, Charles Robert Hutchings, BA (Oxon). When he was twenty six years of age he inherited the Bronwydd estate which, as has been mentioned, was heavily encumbered with debt. The entire property comprised some 8,000 acres in the counties of Cardigan, Carmarthen, Glamorgan and Pembroke. At the time its annual rent was about £7,000, together with royalties from the Llanfyrnach lead mines and other industrial enterprises, mainly, in Glamorgan.

Sir Marteine was faced with a Herculean task – his father had left very heavy mortgage debts of £94,000 and a bank loan of £10,000 – in all some £100,000, a colossal sum which, in modern terms, could be calculated in millions. In order to reduce these debts Sir Marteine sold off parts of the estate from time to time, so that the debt was gradually paid off, but not entirely. The once large Bronwydd estate was, by the 1930's, only a fraction of what it was a century earlier.

On 8 November, 1878, Sir Marteine married at Helensburgh in Scotland,

Katherine Helena (his 'cousin' through the Oakeley line) daughter of Alexander Dennistoun of Golfhill, Glasgow, by his wife Georgina, daughter of Sir Charles Oakeley, 2nd baronet and Charlotte-Francoise-Augusta-Gisberte Ramadier, Baroness de Lormet, and niece of the Marquis de la Tour Mauburg, the French ambassador in this country. Lady Lloyd was passionately proud of her royal Scottish descent from King Robert 1, in the early fourteenth century. She was enamoured with Bronwydd – its towers and turrets – which reminded her of the old Scottish castles which she knew in her childhood. She recorded the warm welcome she had received from 'the kindly Welsh people' and during her life time at Bronwydd she was the mainstay of many charitable and worthy causes. A very colourful personality (according to Dillwyn Miles), she is still remembered by elderly folk in the Teifi valley. Lady Lloyd published an epitome of the history of the 'Lords Marcher of Kemes' – a miscellany of personal recollections and comments which reflect 'her pride in, and devotion to the lordship and to her husband'.

Sir Marteine served as a Justice of the Peace, Deputy Lieutenant of Cardiganshire and High Sheriff of the county in 1882. His patronage of agriculture, country pursuits and local cultural events will be dealt with later, and like Lady Lloyd he had the welfare of the community at heart. Sir Marteine and Lady Lloyd had a son and three daughters: - Marteine Kemes Arundel, Nesta Constance Muriel, Peverel de Lormet and Joan Henlys. Sadly, Sir Marteine and Lady Lloyd's lives were deeply scarred by the loss of their only son and heir Kemes, who was killed in action on the Somme in 1916. Sir Marteine died in April, 1933, and Lady Lloyd in March, 1937. Thus came to an end centuries of growth and development, continuity and change, caused by irreversible, uncontrollable, economic, political and social forces – and above all, the demise of an ancient, benevolent and patriarchal family[26].

Squire Lloyd – Farmer and Landowner

i

The Bronwydd estate had developed over three and a half centuries, from a dozen or so acres in the Teifi valley, to one which extended into the four counties of Cardigan, Carmarthen, Pembroke and Glamorgan. During its long history, marriage, inheritance and purchase had added to its broad acres and to the influence and sway of the Lloyd family.

Through the legal processes of entail and primogeniture, whereby the eldest son inherited, an estate could continue undiminished and intact for generations, provided the life-tenant was industrious, provident and followed the advice of wise trustees. The obvious dangers to the well-being of an estate, which had been built up over many years, were the whims and extravagances of a spendthrift who wasted his resources on reckless 'display': houses, the race course, foolhardy elections, or the wild pastimes of drink, loose women and the gaming table. Sometimes, excessive ambition to acquire vast acreages, unwise land purchases, a lavish life-style, political ambition, wastefulness and pursuit of the glamour and prestige of titles of honour cost dearly. Examples of this occurred in the history of the Lloyds of Bronwydd: the many land purchases of Thomas Lloyd in the mid-eighteenth century, the happy-go-lucky prodigality of James Lloyd in the early 1800's and the 'grand design' of Thomas Davies Lloyd to become 'le seigneur par excellence' as Lord of the Barony of Cemais.

Notably, amongst the gentry landowners of 'Tivy-side', there was a very close bond between the Lloyd family and their tenants and dependants within the community. They ruled over their demesne with paternalistic benevolence which meant that they showed care and concern for those who had to rely on a social welfare system which was, perhaps, a remote relic of a feudal view of the natural order. Central to the legal relationship of landlord and tenant was the lease, namely, a contract whereby the landlord, as lessor of agricultural land and tenements (large and small) conveyed land to a tenant, for a specified period of time, in consideration for the payment of rent, which was the gentry landowner's chief source of wealth[1]. As will be seen, there were sometimes sources of income other than rent: the sale of produce and livestock from the home farm and of timber growing on the estate; mining and mineral enterprises, such as the lead mines on the manor of Llanfyrnach, Pembrokeshire, and coal mines in east Carmarthenshire and Glamorgan. The coming of the railways resulted in the sale and lease of land and wayleave payments arising from industrial activity. The Lloyds of Bronwydd, as Lords Marcher, derived chief rents and other 'dues' from the barony. To a lesser extent, some of them invested in the small craft which traded along the coast of west Wales and, as lords of the barony, had limited right to items cast up along the shores. As patrons of many clerical livings they held the advowson, namely, the right to appoint rectors and vicars to several parishes; or if they chose, they could sell or lease out these rights. But these non-agricultural enterprises played a relatively minor role in the economy of the estate.

ii

For centuries the Welsh squire (like many of his English peers) was a working farmer, and the 'plas' where he lived was surrounded by barns and beast houses, the muck and the mire inevitable in such circumstances. Farm and household inventories show clearly that live stock and farm implements were considered to be more value than the furniture and other items in the house. In the history of the Lloyds of Bronwydd, one can take into account the goods and chattels of Thomas Lloyd 'apprised' in May, 1663 – his '…26 head of cattle, 3 oxen, 12 young beasts, 5 mares, 6 horses, 10 colts, 200 sheep, ploughs, harrows…' and various other implements of husbandry. The home farm was a vital element in the life of the squire and his family. It provided food and other necessities for the household and the servants; for the sick and poor of the locality and any surplus could be sold in local market places and fairs. The home farm was the centre of a self supporting establishment. Its management and cultivation reflect the changes in the theories of good husbandry and stock rearing[2].

Colonel Thomas Lloyd who inherited the Bronwydd estate in 1775, along with Thomas Johnes of Hafod, was one of the pioneers of the 'new agriculture' in Cardiganshire. Determined to make the estate pay its way, Lloyd compiled two volumes of detailed information and advice on farming which he applied himself, and which was also intended for the enlightenment of his tenants. This 'manifesto' deserves close scrutiny. In it he maintained that meadows should be mowed and 'fed' [fertilised] year by year and that one and a half acre of green clover would keep a cow for six months and upwards. A 'milch' cow needed an acre and a half of 'good meadow pasture' to keep her well from May to November. At Bronwydd, during one season he had a stock of eighty-three loads of lime which he applied to the land at the rate of four loads per acre. This had been brought from Aberporth, and he recorded – '…I carried myself thirty cart loads, in amount seventy eight teals [a dry measure of five Winchester bushels]…'.

Thomas Lloyd was not oblivious to the needs of his carters and workmen, allowing them '…a pint of ale each at Aberporth and Bread, Cheese and Butter with Quart of Good Beer on their return…[he adds that]…when they went at night owing to the heat of the weather, I allowed my carters 2 pence apiece for another pint of ale…' He advised that horses were to be kept in their stables as much as possible to produce manure which with straw bought from neighbours would produce about 28 loads yearly. It was advisable to cut and stack up

31

stubble for manure. At every field gate there should be a compost heap or dung hill made up of 'headland pairings', and what was dug out after cleaning ditches was to be placed in a shady corner with each layer intermixed with lime. According to his advice '…Happy is ye farmer who has marl on his ground…' to be applied at the rate of twenty to thirty tons per acre. With regard to '…lands that had become Foul from tillage…' he recommended cleaning them by summer fallow, and '…the dung heap must ever be regarded as the foundation of future wealth, but no manure on wet lands until they had been drained…' The scouring of old ditches and drains and the sediment waters with lime would sweeten and improve grassland. A convert to the 'Norfolk Husbandry' he believed in the following crop rotation: barley, clover, wheat, oats, turnips, and 'lay' [land temporarily under grass][3].

He was familiar with the novel methods practised on the estates of Coke of Holkham, Lord Adam Gordon of Preston Hall, the Duke of Buccleuch and others. Colonel Lloyd was, by all accounts, a keen reader of authoritative books on agriculture : – '*Museum Rusticum*', '*Principles of Vegetation*', '*Annals of Agriculture*', 'Rural *Economy of Norfolk*' and the popular journal '*The Gentleman's Magazine*' which contained useful information on a variety of farming topics – how to destroy rats, get rid of moles, make 'Bath Cream Cheese', fatten geese, cure the ailments of horses and how to dose cattle with '…strong brine…' against suffocation after gorging themselves with clover and so on.

The Bronwydd home farm in the 1780s and 90s amounted to some one hundred and eighty three acres and Lloyd's policy of crop rotation was applied to about thirty fields on which seasonal improvement could be closely monitored by the squire, or in his absence, by his bailiff. Colonel Lloyd was very particular with regard to the essential qualifications of such a person – he was to be unmarried, so as to have no domestic ties to detract him from looking after his master's interests. He was to be 'active, austere, communicative and acquainted with the customs of the county' and such a one was preferable to a stranger unfamiliar with the locality and its ways. A book of accounts was to be kept and balanced every Saturday night; all monies were paid to the squire so that no temptation to dishonesty should arise. Regular stock taking was to be at regular intervals and the 'Baily' awarded with gratuities to 'quicken his diligence'. Labourers were to work as a team under the eye of an overseer and '…to be rung out and home by a bell,' and this was the routine followed at Bronwydd up to the last decades of the nineteenth century.

In May, 1796, the labour force consisted of 'fifteen adult males, one lad and two women'. Thomas Lloyd paid his workers at a rate of 7d a day throughout the year except during December, January and February when the rate was 6d. However during busy periods such as harvest time, the rate was '…1/- shilling a day…and 3d a day in lieu of beer…and the glite[lees] of whey and buttermilk they fetching it…' Other labouring tasks and the wages paid are of interest: labourers doing heavy manual work such as '…raising [digging out] roofing tiles on Gigfran [Penrallt-y-Gigfran received]… 4 shillings per thousand…' Women too, had their own special tasks: weeding rows of turnips and carrots, and during wet weather they were occupied in cleaning and lime-washing dairies, saddle rooms and the like.

Thomas Lloyd was conscious of the need to provide proper homes for his estate workers, the emphasis being on their health and welfare and, not least, to keep up the good name of the squire. Influenced by contemporary ideas of the aesthetic and 'picturesque' he argued that 'a pastoral farm needs a degree of polish or ornament' and this was true considering the tumble-down and dirty shacks which (as some topographical writers had observed) often marred the face of the countryside. Again, farm buildings should blend with trees, erected near a brook or rill to provide clean water for livestock and '…the refreshment which attends the appearance of water must not be denied to the scene…'[4].

All in all, Colonel Lloyd could be considered, like Thomas Johnes of Hafod, one of the most distinguished circle of pioneers of the 'improved agriculture' praised so much by Walter Davies (Gwallter Mechain) in his 'General View of the State of Agriculture and Domestic Economy of South Wales' in 1815. He was imbued with a rare idealism to be a model landlord of many a 'ferme ornée' on his estate. After Colonel Thomas Lloyd's death in 1807, the management of the Bronwydd estate was carried on for many years by his widow Mary Lloyd, with the assistance of her younger son James Lloyd who died in 1827. The farm and garden employees during these years included, gardeners, hedgers, threshers, hay makers, potato lifters, furze pounders, timber sawyers, quarrymen, wheat rickers, a shepherd and craftsmen, such as, a smith, carpenter, saddler and stone mason. A few months later a farm sale was held at Bronwydd, in February 1828, and the Auction Account Book has interesting information on the live and dead stock of the home farm: 4 horses, 1 horse 'pie ball', 2 horses (cream colour accustomed to run together in double or single harness), 1 grey Galloway mare, 3 poneys, 1 heifer, 1 steer, 1 boar, 3 pigs' – a sufficient number of animals to provide for the cultivation of the land, the carting of lime and manure, corn and hay, for riding and hunting, and to supply the household with milk, butter, cheese and bacon. There was an interesting collection of 'implements of husbandry' – '1 waggon body, 1 broad wheel wagon for a team of four horses, 1 cart, 4 ploughs, 1 hay machine (London made), 1 turnip machine, smith's tools and bellows, for the trade complete, a gig and harness, a handsome double bodied phaeton with shafts and pole for one or two horses…' The leisure activities of the gentry are reflected in the following items: 4 capital guns, 2 large fishing punts with oars, poles, sails, nets 'with a caravan for the same', and, for the elderly genteel, 1 bath [chair] and 1 sedan chair.

33

H. M. Vaughan observed that very often, on the small south west Wales estates, sales of farm stock, household goods and effects were made on the death of the life tenant. And a number of reasons are possible – as an immediate source of cash to pay off the debts of the deceased, an interim measure until the next life-tenant could decide whether to continue farming or not and also, to allow time to make a survey of the estate and to assess its profitability. In any case, it appears that Thomas Lloyd (1788-1845), for the time being, however, decided to restock the home farm with new breeds of animals and the most up-to-date 'engines' of husbandry.

He held several collective sales from time to time to avoid the inconvenience and vexation to drovers and to the animals by driving them to distant fairs and to display them at their best in the environment of a well equipped and well managed farm. Moreover the culling of some stock, both live and dead, was the policy of an enterprising farmer. One of these sales, held in 1834, included the following: 6 milch cows, 6 four year old oxen, 1 fat ox, 6 three year old steers, 20 two year old steers and heifers, 13 calves, 4 horses, 20 pigs, and 'a capital car with a Head and Harness built in Dublin'.

Eight years later in 1842, Thomas Lloyd had made up his mind to give up farming. The whole farm stock sale was advertised in '*The Carmarthen Journal*' and took place in April of that year: 1 bull, 10 excellent milch cows of the 'real Roos and Castlemartin breeds' 1 Guernsey bull and cow 'thorough bred and very large', 2 four year old oxen, 1 five year old spayed heifer, a number of two year old heifers, steers and yearlings, 6 excellent draught horses, 2 promising bay fillies, 'a good match for a phaeton and likely to make good hunters or hacks', a capital large brood mare, several ponies of the true Breconshire breed, 20 ewes and lambs, 30 wethers, a considerable number of store pigs, timber and firewood...[5]

Why Thomas Lloyd gave up farming the home farm is not clear: the appendage of the home farm, the experimentation, the cost, and the trouble involved, in all, meant that it had become an expensive luxury. Direct farming, a useful supplement to other financial resources, was seldom sufficient in itself to lever families far up the social scale. The times and conditions, and the current economic climate did not favour the gentleman farmer. And, perhaps, home farms in the occupancy of the landlord were seldom profitable concerns, often the reverse. Moreover, Thomas Lloyd's interest and attention lay elsewhere. There was constant unrest brewing within the barony: squatters were building 'cotts' on Newport common without the lord's permission; burgesses in the town were up to their necks in intrigue concerning the choice of mayor and the claims of the lord himself were challenged by upstart radicals. He was embroiled in the legal morass relating to the Priory Estate reversion claim. But, perhaps, more then anything, the social and cultural horizons of a remote country squire had widened so much by the early decades of the nineteenth century that the glitter and sparkle of the metropolis and foreign capitals were more alluring than the farm. The daily round of pigstye and cow byre, turnip field and stockyard, had become a very dull pastime indeed!

The 'golden age' of farming at Bronwydd had passed with the death of old Colonel Lloyd. The home farm had become of less importance in the life of many squire landowners. Its main function from now on was to provide food for the household, fodder for the farm stock, stables and kennels. Cows, pigs and hens roamed about in paddocks and in the vicinity of the cow house and barn. But, it was *de rigeur* for the squire to retain his horses and hounds; such expenditure was not a part of the estate's economic equation. But, it must be remembered that the Lloyds like other landowners, did not cease to sponsor agricultural shows, ploughing matches, public lectures by agriculturalists to educate tenant farmers and all sorts of farming enterprises. It was part of the squire's public rôle in the community.

The squire's support of agriculture was one aspect of the general patronage of good causes in which he was the mainspring. In 1786 the Cardiganshire Society for the Encouragement of Agriculture, was formed and Colonel Lloyd was one of its chief supporters. Because of their considerable land holding in Pembrokeshire, the Lloyds were keen to revive a similar society in the county 1805. As a prominent public figure Sir Thomas Davies Lloyd was a patron of many movements where the welfare of the farming community was paramount. The young squire, Sir Marteine Lloyd, was the president, along with Sir G. E. G. Philipps of Picton Castle, of the Llanboidy 'Poultry, Root and Provision Show' in December 1879. The event was followed by a dinner for the landlords and tenants at the Maesgwynne Arms, and a debate on 'The Various Modes or Ways of Farming in this District, best suited to Present Times'. Such events continued from time to time during the lifetime of Sir Marteine and in 1925 the Annual Cardigan County Agricultural Show took place at Bronwydd. He, himself, had tried to farm the Bronwydd demesne farm, but gave up the idea in the 1885, because it was more cost than profit; and, only retained a field or two for the keep of a cow to provide milk and cream for the house hold[6].

iii

With the extension of the Bronwydd estate, comprising lands in four counties, necessity demanded that it had to be administered by a properly qualified agent or steward. According to Walter Davies, such a person had to be '…well versed in the several departments of the rural economy… - sometimes, a local practising farmer-squire who possessed wide knowledge of crop husbandry and the necessary skills of surveying and land valuation. The Lloyds of Bronwydd made use of persons well known within the county (sometimes local people and near relations) with intimate knowledge of the soil and climate, the customs and traditions of the locality and its inhabitants, indeed, the whole spectrum of society from squire to peasant. The names of J. Rees Stokes, 'Mr. Wogan',

Richard Jones, Pantirion and Owen Lloyd of Cardigan, come to mind. In view of land enclosure, improved agriculture and the possibility of the discovery of minerals for industrial purposes, it was essential to have properly delineated plans of estates and farms. And, there was always the constant threat to valuable assets by greedy neighbours. Moreover, as the estate was an economic unit, the keeping of orderly systematic accounts certainly marked an improvement in estate administration by persons possessing a high profile of professionalism.

Colonel Lloyd appointed his kinsman Mr. Wogan to survey Bronwydd lands in north Pembrokeshire, who '...rode over it at 20/- per acre if sett in parcels which is the best way of setting it.' With regard to Bury [Berry] he commented that '...the superior fertility of enclosed ground points to the advantage of further enclosure and the tenant should by his lease be bound to raise yearly two hundred perch of hedge which would amount to Ten Pounds for a few years till the open bank should be hedged in...' Mr. Wogan added, that the tenant of Berry '...should give due attention to the Rabbits that no shooting is suffered in the warren or any other means of destroying them, that he encourage their breeding and keep a warrener to inspect it...' To safeguard his fishing and shooting rights, Thomas Lloyd commissioned, in 1775, Richard Jones to survey Newport Marsh, an area of 80 acres or more. One, Owen Thomas, showed where the boundaries were and was paid £2:12:6d for vellum.

The rest of the Bronwydd estate, amounting to about 3,800 acres, was also surveyed and mapped. But this did not take into account the much disputed commons, 'waste', sheep walks and 'cotts'. Jones of Pantygarn, Eglwyswrw (later of Pantirion near Cardigan) was paid at the rate of 2½-4d per acre. His total bill came to £38-17s which also included '...15/- for two and a half reams of vellum for mapping and 2/6d for 5 sheets of Imperial Paper...'

As land owners, the Lloyds preferred local men, to act as stewards and agents, rather than those, perhaps more professional agents from England and Scotland, like John Butcher, Samuel Bartley and John Plumbly of Bath. William Smith (1769-1839) who settled in Cardigan, styled himself as '...geologist, irrigator, engineer, builder of sea defences...' and much else besides. He could produce evidence of his competence from Lord Cawdor, Lord Dynevor and other worthies. But, Thomas Davies Lloyd, strange to relate, thought it best to employ his talents, mainly, in compiling the Lloyd family tree in 1846! The employment of an agent set a precedent for this estate and many others; the squire could not be tied down to visiting his farms and tenants; he might be away on other business or travelling abroad or spending his leisure time in London and Bath. This was particularly important when Mary Lloyd was left a widow in 1807, although she was actively interested in the administration of the estate and the welfare of those living on it, while practical matters were left to her son, James Lloyd[7].

From many scattered references the agent of the Bronwydd estate had to act as steward for the barony of Cemais, especially to see that chief rents and tolls in addition to farm rents were fully paid when due. In 1817, John Beynon of Newcastle-Emlyn, attorney-at-law, was appointed to act as agent for Thomas Lloyd. He was not incapable of indulging in shady practices. To make matters worse, he was paid from 'profits arising out of the Chief Rents, Estrays, Mortuaries and Alienations derivable from the barony…' He was considered a rapacious character, who wielded power as Clerk of the Peace in the county of Cardigan and his infamy became known within the barony and elsewhere. It was a wise move on the part of Thomas Lloyd to appoint Thomas George of Cardigan, in 1837 to administer the Bronwydd estates, the barony and to oversee the mining enterprises in the three south-west Wales counties. To avoid peculation and malpractices with consequent ill-feeling between landlord and tenant, Mr. George was paid an annual retainer 'free from tax and deductions' and other cash burdens on tenants and dependants within the barony. In this way harmony and goodwill existed, and it is noteworthy that descendants of Thomas George have been stewards of the barony of Cemais up to the present time, although their duties have by now, become largely ceremonial.

Later on qualified professional valuers and estate surveyors were appointed, such as John Morgan Davies of Froodvale (known to country folk as Ffrwdfâl Dafis) and John Evans, Cardigan. He was the last agent of the Bronwydd estate. The very nature of their work made the agents unpopular with tenants (as appears in evidence before the land Commission in the 1890s) and some might suggest that one reason for their appointment on some estates was to take the blame from the landlord. But, John M. Davies and John Evans were Welsh speaking, were natives of the Welsh country-side and fully aware of the innate problems in landlord/tenant relationships. Even so, they were not beyond reproach, as these examples show – in 1871, Mr. Davies, Ffrwdfâl, valued the Bronwydd estate and from the allegations of a Mr. Evan Rees, no allowance was made for improvements made by his father on his holding. The higher valuation was considered harsh and unconscionable. But, it has to be remembered that the agent's function was to value property in relation to prices current at the time and he was obliged to report what was commercially honest vis-à-vis his employer, namely the landlord. In the case of Bronwydd, tenants often appealed directly to Sir Thomas Davies Lloyd and later, to Sir Marteine when generosity and leniency prevailed more often than not. John Evans was not popular with the Bronwydd tenants and when a tenant (in great distress) asked for the matter to be discussed with Sir Marteine he met with a sharp rebuff 'Fi yw y Syr…' [I am the Sir]. So presumptuous was he of his power over the tenantry of Bronwydd, that sometimes it was the agent himself who should be held to account for the allegations of harsh and unfair treatment laid at the door of some country squires[8].

Landlords were of necessity, as Professor David Howell has argued, involved in the business of agriculture, and landownership meant that they had to invest capital into their properties in the form of buildings, fences, roads and drainage schemes. They had to oversee, personally, or though their agents, the quality and efficiency of what their tenants were doing, otherwise, an estate could soon fall into rack and ruin. It was discovered that many farms on the Bronwydd estate in the parish of Camrose, in south Pembrokeshire, were 'extremely out of repair' in 1840. Consequently, Thomas Lloyd ordered a full survey and valuation for new gates, door frames, thatch for rooves and the rebuilding of walls. Thomas Davies Lloyd, on inheriting the estate in 1845, seems to have carried out essential repairs which continued on his very scattered lands (as far as records survive) until 1876, a year before his death. According to one Bronwydd Buildings Book, the sum of about £5,000 was spent on the Bronwydd demesne farms and the out buildings of the mansion house. This sum included £800+ on repairs on the farm of Ffynnon-Fair. But, it has to be admitted that the amount he spent on his farms was small in relation to other expenditure. Sir Marteine Lloyd, with the enthusiasm of a young squire who had, only a few years earlier, inherited the Bronwydd estate, in 1883, commissioned George Morgan, the Carmarthen architect, to design what might be called a 'model' farm at Penpedwast in the parish of Bayvil. It was the ancient home-stead of his ancestors the Lloyds, and here the improvements comprised: a new dairy, kitchen, new cow and yearling houses, a straw and chaff room, stables, loose boxes, cart-houses, troughs for slurry with drainage to pits, a spindle connected to a water wheel to provide power for chaff and turnip cutters, threshing and sawing machines. Sir Marteine requested especially, that the farm buildings were to be erected with eliptical arches, Carnarvon slates and Chester crests. The 'poverty' of many of the smaller estates, often because of the excessively grand lifestyle, (amongst other reasons) of their owners, prevented any adequate long-term investment. The tenants were impoverished more often than not, in arrear with their rents, and unable to pay any increase to compensate any cash investment by the landlord. And this was the situation on the heavily encumbered Bronwydd estate. Towards the last decades of the nineteenth century, some measure of relief came about from the government and private companies (incorporated by Acts of Parliament) in order to improve farm buildings and to provide essential facilities for good husbandry. Sir Marteine Lloyd took advantage of such provisions to a certain extent and some improvements were carried out on farms, such as Penpedwast, mentioned above. From a few scanty and isolated accounts which have survived, one can only estimate, (in very broad terms) that Sir Marteine availed himself of the financial services of companies like the Land Loan and Enfranchisement Co. from the years 1877 to 1927. Various sums of money were borrowed, a thousand pounds or so at a time, and by 1927 about £1027 still remained unpaid[9]. Perhaps, Sir Marteine, was often moved by sentiment rather than by the harsh realities of economics.

38

For instance, in November, 1932, a few months before his death, he authorised repairs and additions to the 'Sergeants Inn' and the 'Sessions House', at Eglwyswrw. These were not farms which produced rent, but places where Courts Leet and Courts Baron had been held whence the Lord Marcher had led his Perambulation with pomp and ceremony throughout the centuries.

As in other parts of the country, the landowners of the lower Teifi valley had long realised the importance of tree planting to enhance the value of their estates for aesthetic and commercial reasons. In particular, from the end of the eighteenth century there was a growing demand for timber: for ship building, mining and other industrial purposes, the rebuilding of farms and mansion houses and was thus a valuable part of an estate's economy. Colonel Lloyd was unremitting in planting trees, in the 1780's, like his neighbours Brigstocke of Blaenpant, Colby of Ffynone and Lewes of Llysnewydd, amongst others. Lloyd's 'master plan' for the administration of his estate, mentioned already, included the mass planting of trees. The ideal farmstead needed trees for shelter, and leases included conditions with regard to hedgerows and groves on the less fertile parts of each farm. Near the squire's own home, tree planting had to be carried out according to strict rules: acacia, beach, birch and larch in combination '…arranged beautifully in clumps, altogether having pendent boughs…'. They would be best appreciated in autumn '…during the fall of leaf …the time to notice the tints of leaves…' Drives, paths and walks were to be constructed to provide a 'sudden vista' or 'prospect', to be seen occasionally, that '…they do not destroy themselves by Familiarity…' The work of John Nash in the locality, for example, at Ffynone and Llysnewydd, was well known to Lloyd, as were the ideas of Payne Knight and Humphrey Repton concerning the 'antique' and the 'picturesque'. In addition grottoes, shell houses, statuary, follies, rustic lodges and dovecotes could be placed to add surprise and dramatic visual impact amongst the plantations. It is uncertain whether Colonel Lloyd's theories were ever carried out in his day. Certainly, his grandson, Thomas Davies Lloyd, when Bronwydd was rebuilt, some sixty years later, redesigned the drive and the 'pleasure gardens', in keeping with his own particular 'grand design'.

Taking advantage of the timber which had reached maturity on land (part of the Bronwydd estate) through the marriage of Thomas Lloyd to Mary, daughter of Dr. John Jones, a sale of timber was held in 1796. Two hundred oak trees, together with sycamores, hazels and willows were felled in the vicinity of Pendine. The oaks were not more than 12" in girth, and were considered useful for house building. Four hundred feet of deal and ash could be sold @ 14d per foot, with 68ft of beech and sycamore which were expected to fetch 10d. In these sales, much of the timber was '…very crooked and only fit for colery or cord wood…' – according to the agent's report. In 1813, Mary Lloyd sold to James Miles of Pengwern, in Cenarth, and David Davies, Towyn, Ferwig '…two groves of wood…' at Henllys, Nevern, for the sum of £500. One can reasonably assume (in the absence of detailed timber accounts) that a consistent policy of tree planting and felling was carried out on the Bronwydd (and other estates) during the century. According to information from old estate workers, for every free felled, at least two or three trees had to be planted in its place, as a cash crop for the future[10].

The sale of timber for the industrial areas of south Wales was becoming an important item in the economy of many estates from the 1850's. But, unfortunately, the timber accounts for the Bronwydd estate are too sporadic to determine the exact contribution to its coffers. Some figures may be quoted – a sale of timber from the Pontardulais area in 1873 yielded £1,525, and timber was sold from other parts of the estate as occasion demanded. During the years 1918 to 1925, surveys and a valuation of timber to be felled were made. One area of woodland was singled out and a quantity of over 3,500 cubic feet of timber was for sale @ about 3/9d per cubic foot. It was estimated that the benefit to the estate would be about £4,000 at least.

At a time when the survival of the Bronwydd estate seemed to be very doubtful, Sir Marteine Lloyd in his old age continued to plant trees. Other landowners like Fitzwilliams of Cilgwyn, had long realised that afforestation was a poor investment on account of cheap imported foreign timber. The demand for home produced wood had declined after the end of the war in 1918. Even so, Sir Marteine, in March 1925, employed George Bough 'of the Bronwydd Stables' to supervise the re-planting of the woodland. The outlay was £39-15s and was carried out by Evan Evans of Penlôn, Cwrrws, who was paid £2-0-0 for eight days work, and Arthur Davies of Gwernllwyn chapel house £1-10s for six days. In addition, Owen Jones, of Cross Roads, spent sixteen days ' cleaning, torri claw (hedge cutting), railo (fencing), ceibo lle i'r netting (digging a place for the wire netting), plant 100oaks....' . By April, 1925, 500 trees had been planted 'in the Voel', namely, the east-ward slope bordering the south drive. Not many years afterwards, the plantations of many generations, the noble oaks, beech, chestnut trees, Scottish pines and ornamental varieties like the 'sequoia gigantea' and many others were felled in the wanton devastation between the years 1939-1945, not only to support the war effort but also to satisfy the greed of crafty speculators. The despoliation of the house inevitably followed[11].

iv

The existence of good roads, safe bridges and, in time the coming of the railway to hitherto remote parts of the countryside was a matter of primary concern to the squire-farmer and his tenants. Railways were vital in opening up rural areas to the growing centres of urban demand. The coming of the railway to the Teifi valley in the 1860's and as far as Newcastle-Emlyn in 1895, provided access to scattered properties, comfortable modes of travel, and easier transport of produce and livestock to distant markets. In addition, lime, coal, culm, and other supplies could be brought to farm and mansion.

The gentry of 'Tivyside' had been active promoters of 'Turnpike Trusts' at the end of the eighteenth century, which linked up the towns of Carmarthen, Cardigan, Lampeter and Newcastle-Emlyn and beyond. The Lloyds of Bronwydd, like other gentry landowners in the area invested money in support of these trusts. But, from the 1840's onwards the impact of railway development and its possible extension to south west Wales, met with a cool response from many a landowner. In spite of the general demand, resulting in a series of parliamentary acts for railway development, some 'Tivyside' gentry (like their counterparts in the rest of the United Kingdom) dismissed railways as new-fangled and eccentric. At worst, they posed a threat to 'rural quietude', causing disturbance to game preserves, and were an invasion of domestic privacy by the 'riff and raff' from outside. One suspects that there was an undercurrent of social opposition to the railway. It was promoted by new gentry: Lloyd Hall of Cilgwyn, a London barrister, J. Lloyd Davies of Blaendyffryn, born in an Aberystwyth tavern and Gwinnett Tyler (although, one of the Tylers of Cottrell in Glamorgan) had been a 'railway manager', but had the good fortune to marry the heiress of Gernos. Initially, Thomas Davies Lloyd of Bronwydd was not over enthusiastic in his support nor had he the cash to invest in the new railway companies. Socially, too (as Professor David Cannadine has observed) railway development demoted the aristocracy and the gentry. No longer did they travel in their own carriages, displaying their heraldic shields on the doors, to be greeted by obsequious landladies, waiters and liveried flunkies – '...on the trains they were indistinguishable from other wealthy travellers and at large railway stations they often went almost un-noticed...'.

The project was the brainchild of 'arrivistes' with money from the professions and trade. Fitzwilliams of Cilgwyn, J.Lloyd Davies of Blaendyffryn, and Lloyd Williams of Gwernant were prepared to 'dig-deep into their pockets', in order to acquire a 'facility' which could give the Welsh farmer the means to dispose of his goods, the lack of which was one of the causes of distress and poverty of the agricultural community. In the first stages of proposed railway development Fitzwilliams lost a great deal of money, and the original plans had to be abandoned. It was in the second phase of activity that Thomas Davies Lloyd became involved in the enterprise. At heart, he was living in a world of mediaeval romance (as is described elsewhere in this study). He regarded the railway as the product of a mechanistic age. Eventually, he took a pragmatic view, and differences of class and culture did not prevent him from showing support for railway extension by addressing gatherings in towns like Cardigan, when the benefits to the farming community of landlord and tenant were put before the general public and, especially, to those who were likely to invest in it[12]. Moreover, land could be leased at a premium to railway companies; its development value had increased and prosperous times ahead would lead to higher rents as well. In the years 1852 to 1859 land on the Bronwydd estate in the parishes of Newchurch, Carmarthen, in Llandeilo Talybont, Glamorgan, and later, in Sir Marteine Lloyd's time, in the Pembrokeshire parishes of Clydai, Llanfyrnach, Penrith and Stainton was sold for railway development.

At a meeting held in Carmarthen in 1871 the case for the railway was revived. The line had been constructed as far as Llandysul in 1864, but did not reach Henllan and Newcastle Emlyn until September 1895. Shortage of capital investment and lack of enthusiasm and, especially of cash, on the part of the gentry, the main landowners in the area, were some of the reasons for the delay Sir Thomas Davies Lloyd had become a supporter of the extension of the railway line to Newcastle Emlyn. Using his influence as member of parliament, he had to face opposition from press comments – that landowners were charging an exorbitant price for land, that drovers would be deprived of their livelihood, and that some landlords were reluctant to sell land because their tenants argued for reduced rents to compensate for the diminution in the latter's acreage.

The Lloyd family of Bronwydd gained from the expansion of the railway in some ways: in 1867 land in east Carmarthenshire was sold to the 'Llanelly Railway Company' for £886, which was to be invested in Stock Consols, the income there from to be enjoyed by Anne Davies Lloyd during her lifetime and, afterwards, by Sir Thomas Davies Lloyd. He died many years before his mother and it was Sir Marteine Lloyd who was to profit from the transaction. In the early 1900's the Great Western Railway rented 376 acres of land, namely, the Bronwydd farms of Priskedwyn, Morfeydd, Pentre, Coedsaeson Fawr and Bolgoed-uchaf, in the parish of Llandeilo-Talybont. But it has to be borne in mind that, these rentals were one of the lesser sources of income to benefit the Bronwydd estate. They were often fraught with problems: the pollution of land and water supplies, loss of amenity, aggravation to tenant farmers, and sometimes, the costly legal actions which followed. One such instance was a case for £1,174 compensation involving Sir Marteine Lloyd, through his agent J. Davies, Ffrwdfal, and the G.W.R. at the Swansea County Court in 1910. The financial gain was small in view of the problems inherent in such assets. The permanent benefit of railway extension to the Bronwydd estate and its tenants was the easy transport of farm livestock and produce to distant markets and, to be able to receive fertilisers, lime, coal, farm machinery and consumer goods almost on their door-step. However, the opening of the station at Henllan, about a mile from Bronwydd, was a 'great facility' which the family, their guests and staff, as well as the local community was to enjoy for many years[13.].

One commercial activity, in which the gentry were to invest any spare cash available, was the maritime trade from Cardigan and the small fishing villages along the Cardigan Bay. But, what had been once a thriving trade declined after the coming of the railway. 'Shipping Shares' were regarded as valuable forms of personal wealth and squires like Oliver Lloyd of Coedmore, Thomas

Howell of Glaspant, and Captain James Lloyd of Bronwydd, were participants in such investments, as were many other gentry and a few wealthy farmers during the years 1820-1850. Thomas Lloyd of Bronwydd, and his kinsman G.Saunders Davies of Pentre, with fourteen landowners, gentleman farmers and merchants formed a company to promote trade, by sea and rail, along the coast of Cardiganshire following the passing of the New Quay Harbour and Railway Act in 1835. For over the next sixty years an ambitious plan was put forward which included the construction of a light railway along the coast, with collecting points at Newcastle Emlyn, Llandysul and Llanybydder, but nothing came of the scheme[14].

v

Landowners had been keenly aware of the potential financial advantages of mineral resources on their estates, and restrictive clauses in deeds relating to land testify to the importance of retaining those rights for the owner. In the early decades of the eighteenth century, William Lloyd of Monken Hadley, wrote to his son-in-law, Thomas Lloyd of Bronwydd of the importance of enclosing land and the protection of '..ye mines and minerals..' within the barony.

Unlike the estates of Gogerddan and Nanteos, Cawdor and Dynevor in Cardiganshire and Carmarthenshire, with lands over rich deposits of lead and coal, Bronwydd had only very limited mineral resources of coal, lead and slate on the estate.

Because actual involvement in trade and commercial enterprise was largely frowned upon in gentry circles, and because there was only limited cash available for capital investment, it was the custom to lease land to entrepreneurs. But not totally, as the following examples show,-

James Lloyd of Cilrhiwe, owner of part of the manor of Llanfyrnach, (bought from the executrix of Maurice Morgan, Blaenbylan) made an agreement for three months with Samuel, Benjamin and Jenkin Jones, miners, '...to work mines on land called Llandre, in the parish of Llanfyrnach...50/- per fathom to sink, dig and cut...45/- for every ton of Oar, other than and except Candles, Gunpowder to be found by workers themselves'. The ore was to be '..cleaned, washed, merchantable and fitt for market..' and after '...this said term, to yield up and quitt the said work and implements of Jas.Lloyd in good and workmanlike order..' From subsequent operations, this seems to have been in a trial exercise.

In March 1755, James Lloyd entered into a partnership with his brother Thomas Lloyd of Bronwydd, in the hope of a profitable yield, to work land '... in the tenure of Philip Owen Dafydd at a peppercorn rent...for working the mine at Llandre..' Nothing is known of the outcome. In 1764 a full scale survey was made of the Llanfyrnach mines '...shewing where each vein produceth Ore, their meeting and intersection as far as hath been hitherto discovered the condition of each bottom, and the method to produce ore'. From this survey, it was revealed that a certain level contained 'bunches of ore' about 23 wide in 'very kind soil' and other shafts with 'layers of lead from 4"-30" wide pretty solid'. As in many similar undertakings, water was a problem, and it was observed '...that the river Tave may with small expense be so directed as to forse an Ingine or Ingines to sink...a perpendicular shaft...there is no doubt of success....and [in a certain part] the adventurers cannot lose...if well managed...'

After James Lloyd had moved from Pembrokeshire to Boscott Hall, in the parish of Walsall, Staffordshire, he leased in May 1759, the lead mines in '..the parishes, townships, vills or hamlets of Llanfihangel, Penbedw, Capel Colman, Manor Divy, Llanvernach, Penrith, Kilrheding, Clydey and Killgarran, with licence to work the same..' to George Blackden of Loxley, gent. and Roger Holmes of Walsall, gent. for thirty one years. The rent was computed as '..two thirteenths of merchantable ore, and partnership in the venture..' From the deed of agreement one is informed that '...the lead mines till lately unworked and not of any profit to the said James Lloyd,[and] that the working of such mines will be of such expense and risk...'The terms of the agreement suggest that the operation of the mine was to be carried out in a professional and business-like way by the Walsall partners: they were '..to erect and build engines, smithies, smelting houses (except those for habitation, cleansing, dressing ores and the like)...'They were not to allow water to over-run other lands; they were'...to drain properly, not to cause injury to fences, loss of herbage..' And, if the mining activities were to stop for six months '...except for lack of wind [for power] and annoyance by water,' then the lease was void, and buildings and engine houses were to be dismantled. According to the agreement the 'proprietors and co-adventurers' were to appoint an 'overseer' to manage the 'works', and he was 'removable' by the proprietors. His name was to be entered in a book; he was entitled to make contracts, buy materials, attend meetings and keep a book of accounts of '...candles, powder, ropes and other items in use..' Lastly, every eight months a meeting of all the parties was to be held to review the level of profit and loss.

How far this mining company was prosperous is difficult to measure. Some fifty years later, Richard Fenton in his 'Historical Tour of Pembrokeshire' (published in 1810) stated that the mines of Llanfyrnach had been '...a great work...carried on with great success and held out so flattering a prospect from the quality and quantity of ore raised, as to become a fair object of speculation...[for]...persons of the first rank and fortune..'. Fenton further cast doubts on any profit gained lately, by those who had invested in the mines '...who had not even lead for their gold..' The operation had been bedevilled by problems and Walter Davies, in 1815, refers to a rich vein of ore worked in the parish of Llanfyrnach '...which is now under water, for want of hydraulic powers...to drain the mine...'[15.]

Further attempts were made to revive the mines: John Beynon, Thomas Lloyd's agent, put an advertisement in the '*Carmarthen Journal*' in November, 1816, drawing attention to the lead mines and minerals in the parishes of Llanfyrnach and Clydai, which had the great advantage of being situated '...within about ten miles from the sea-ports of Cardigan and Newport...' Possibly, as a result of this publicity, in April, 1817, Mary Lloyd of Bronwydd and her eldest son, Thomas Lloyd of Cilrhiwe, negotiated with Thomas Foster, of Theobalds, Cheshunt, Hertfordshire, esq., George Bouser of Keccross, and Thomas Gaunt of New Lodge, Pembrey, Carmarthenshire, for a twenty-one year lease of lead mines under Llandre, Llanfyrnach. The annual rent was £25 and every ninth dish [a gallon of ore fit for the smelter] The lessees were responsible for providing and setting up '....engines and furnaces, a weighing machine..' and various implements and tools for their trade; to make '..waggon roads for the delivery of stone and gravel...and to make a railway...' an interesting innovation in the mechanisation of industrial enterprises. By March 1824, the mines were extended over a property known as Llwyncelyn, let by Mary Lloyd to Samuel Parker of Treleigh House, Redruth, Cornwall, at a rent of every '...tenth dish of ore except Halvan ores [i.e. ore given as part of produce of labour instead of wages]....' Such was the enthusiasm created by this and similar ventures, that the '*Carmarthen Journal*', in April 1825, reported that the Llanfyrnach mine was being worked in a 'very spirited manner. [and]..engines of great magnitude..' had been installed; workshops had been built and most encouragingly, specimens of ore were discovered which contained a mixture of lead and silver. The possibility of laying a 'railway road' from there to the nearest seaport, to link up with the extensive quarries in the vicinity of Maenclochog, would be of 'incalculable benefit to the agricultural interest and slates could be exported to different parts of the world'

As far as can be ascertained, Lloyd of Bronwydd neither gained much from this mining enterprise, nor was he able to risk capital in any extensive and far-reaching ventures.

By 1845, other gentry speculators, including E.C.Lloyd Hall (who later used the surname Fitzwilliams) of Emlyn Cottage, the principal shareholder, along with R.Goring Thomas and R.J.Nevill, mine owners and industrialists from the Llanelli area, and Thomas Davies, shipowner and tradesman of Cardigan, lost a great deal of money. Flooding was a major problem below a depth of fourteen fathoms, the maximum depth that could be worked using hand pumps, so Lloyd Hall (Fitzwilliams) explained to Thomas Davies Lloyd in a letter of 11 January, 1853. As an antiquarian footnote, he added that the mine had been worked by the Romans and that Egyptian and Greek coins had been found there!

It took some years for the mines to show any profit. It is estimated, that during the period 1861-1871, the total value of ore produced, amounted to approximately £18,000, of which Sir Thomas Davies Lloyd received royalties of one twentieth. During the last quarter of the nineteenth century, mining activity gradually came to a halt, in spite of the optimism of a few speculators. In May 1891, the engines, machinery and equipment were advertised for sale. Eventually, buildings were demolished and thus, a chapter in the industrial history of Pembrokeshire came to an end and an enterprise which only in a small way added to the estates' revenue.

The mining of coal and and industrial development on Bronwydd land in the parishes of Llan-non, Carmarthenshire and Llandeilo Talybont, Glamorgan, is only partly recorded in the Bronwydd archives for the years 1873-1880 and 1909. From these sporadic and crude sources, one gathers that during the 1870's the following farms with mineral rights, were let to various companies and sub-let to tenants.-

Pentre Priskewyn	79	acres ....Rent p.a. £160
Bolgoed	315	.... £500
Coedsaeson (pt.of)	19	.... £100
Coedsaeson	32	.... £100
		£860

plus royalties of 10d for every ton of coal produced, together with 50 tons of coal to be delivered to Sir Thomas Davies Lloyd. Allowing for any gain to the estate from this rented land, it also had its problems: the maintenance of river banks and weirs. Much of the land sublet for agricultural purposes was poor, wet and marshy, its 'humus' sour and, owing to industrial contamination, became depasturised. The sinking of new shafts often resulted in the water supply to farm stock becoming 'short in summer'; caused serious problems to tenants and was a constant source of worry to the landlord. Consequently, when Sir Marteine was selling parts of the estate to pay off his debts, he was prepared to include mineral rights as well, for example, in December, 1890, he made such an offer to the tenant of Coedsaeson, Llandilo Talybont, for £1,875. [16.]

vi

As has been mentioned already, one of the incidental sources of estate income was the advowson – a curious form of real property which granted to its owner the right of patronage and presentation to an ecclesiastical living, i.e. the choice of the incumbent of a parish. Advowsons were assets which could be bought, sold, leased or left by will. Moreover, they were the means whereby the social and political patronage of the landlord could be strengthened, apart from their economic value. (see chapter 6)

The Lloyd family of Bronwydd were particularly fortunate to hold the right of presentation to many clerical livings within the barony of Cemais – Dinas,

Llanllawer, Llanychllwydog, Meline and Newport. But the right to an advowson could sometimes be a source of dispute like any other form of property and to take one or two examples – during 1703-1704, a protracted legal suite involved Thomas and Anne Lloyd of Penpedwast, against Thomas Bowen and George Roche which led to a commission of enquiry into the right of presentation which, allegedly, had been wrongly claimed by the Lord Marcher of Cemais. The matter had to be referred to Bishop George Bull of St. Davids and was later heard by the ecclesiastical lawyers of Doctors Commons. To avoid litigation in the church courts Thomas and Anne Lloyd agreed in 1786 to grant the next presentation of the rectory of Meline to William Sanham [Sandham] of Horsham, Sussex, for the sum of £300, making it quite clear that '...they were the true and lawful owners and patrons of the said rectory and are therefore lawfully seized of a good and sure, perfect and indefensible Estate of Inheritance...' In spite of occasional problems of ownership, the advowson was a convenient means to raise cash (without any loss of estate land) which could be redeemed at a future date. Ann Lloyd clung tenaciously to her right of presentation to livings, for example, in February, 1784, she sold the 'next presentation' of the rectories of Dinas, Llanllawer and Llanychllwyddog to John Bateman of Haverfordwest, gent. for the sum of £600. He was one of the prosperous merchants and entrepreneurs who wished to make a profit from the transaction and acquire ascendancy and influence in the power structure of the time. In 1785, James Harris of Cardigan, a wealthy 'mercer', paid the sum of £300 to Ann Lloyd of Bronwydd, in exchange for the next presentation of the rectory of Meline and his '...right to appoint a fit person [to the living] and to receive and take rents...profits...plus all messuages, tenements, glebelands, meadows, pastures...waters, fishings, rights,....whatsoever' In the same year,and again in order to raise a sum of money,namely £200, the right of presentation to the rectory of Whitechurch [Eglwyswen] Cemais,was sold to the Rev.Morgan Jones of Ynyscedwyn in the parish of Ystradgynlais, Breconshire.

The value of these advowsons was usually assessed by a third party, someone well versed in financial matters. A late eighteenth century survey of Bronwydd advowsons assessed their value to be as follows:-

Dinas,Llanllawer,Llanychllwydog (Consolidated worth)	£230 p.a.
Meline	100
Whitechurch	50-60
Newport	120
	£500+

The Bronwydd records show that the right to the next presentation of Dinas c.1770 was sold for £400 and twenty years later fetched £600 'but much undervalued...' The price for the perpetual advowson of Dinas and Newport was £1200 and £800 respectively '...and with other perpetual advowsons,fairs and chief rents should not be dear at £1000...'[17.]

The true value of advowsons was no small matter, and by the early nineteenth century gentry like the Lloyds employed some of the established assurance and financial companies to give their professional advice, for example, Thomas Lloyd in 1804, obtained the services of William Morgan, of the Equitable Assurance office. According to him the next presentation to the rectory of Newport was worth £1088 and a 'perpetual' advowson could be as high as £1577. In arriving at these figures, such considerations as the existence and condition of the parsonage house were very important and whether it had 'ample offices... was it a short distance from a sea port and market town...its glebe lands, their acreage and state of cultivation...' were some of the factors to be taken into account. Not least, was the age of the existing incumbent – the older he was, the greater the value to the new owner! In 1841, another valuation was made of Bronwydd livings, for example, Meline, a parish of five hundred inhabitants, with a commuted tithe worth £160, house and glebe £15, its poor rate of £12 – and subject to the life expectancy of 'the present incumbent of forty years of age' was worth £393, so Thomas Lloyd was informed by the legal and General Life Assurance Company. However, if there were an 'immediate presentation' it could be as much as £1351.

During the nineteenth century, trading in advowsons on the Bronwydd estate seems to have diminished, judging from the sparse evidence which has survived. Furthermore, the Ecclesiastical Commission set up by Sir Robert Peel in 1836 led eventually to a series of laws passed in parliament, especially the Ecclesiastical Benefices Act, 1898. All these attempted to reform the church, redirect its finances, end the abuses of simony (trading in benefices and spiritual things), the sale of advowsons and the exercise of patronage in favour of particular people – a whole body of legislation which diminished the rights of the gentry in no small measure. But the Lloyds exercised their right of patronage until the disestablishment of the Church in Wales in 1920. Apart from the monetary value of the advowson – to be the patron of parish could be of more value perhaps, because the incumbents of such parishes as Dinas and Newport, were the eyes and ears of the Lord Marcher. They could keep an eye on encroachments on the commons and the fate of cargoes washed up on the shore. They were in a position to report any infringement upon the claims of the lord of the barony as in the case of the silver flute found on the beach near Dinas. Moreover, patronage was important in the religious, social and political influence of the squire and an essential element in his role in the community. [18.]

Tithes were closely connected with advowsons on account of their ecclesiastical nature. Questions concerning the ownership of some advowsons which also included the right to tithes were often debateable. In some instances the title did not go with the advowson, and this seems to have been true with regard to the Bronwydd estate. Tithes were paid by parishioners as a tenth part of the produce and profits from land, stock and the like, to maintain the incumbent of the parish. Since the Reformation the right to tithes had been acquired by lay 'impropriators': landed gentry, collegiate bodies amongst others who often had no connection with the parishes so burdened by what was considered as an unfair tax. To quote a few examples – Savile Miles, owner of the Priory Estate, Cardigan, lived in Somerset; Llandysul tithes were paid in part to the Principal of Jesus College, Oxford; Llangeler tithes were shared between Lewes of Llysnewydd and St. David's College, Lampeter.

By the nineteenth century the payment of tithes had become a contentious social and political matter which the Tithe Commutation Act of 1836, (whereby tithes were to be paid in money) did little to assuage ill-feeling between landlord and tenant, churchman and nonconformist. While many landowners profited to a certain extent, from the tithes they claimed, the Lloyd family of Bronwydd do not appear to have gained at all and this, no doubt, was to their advantage in the bitter controversies which took place later. It is true that Lloyd of Cilrhiwe, received £5 from the parish of Llanfihangel-Penbedw in the years 1780-1781.Indeed, Bronwydd accepted liability for the payment of tithes on their property in the parishes of Llandyfriog and Llanfair-Treflygen and Colonel Lloyd of Bronwydd paid the sum of £5-7s to Oliver Lloyd of Coedmore and other 'impropriators' in 1799-1800. In the 1840's the 'great tithes' levied on the Bronwydd home farm amounted to about £40 of which the sum of £11-14s was due on '78 Winchester of Oats'. Later on, Thomas Davies Lloyd had to pay £23-10s in tithe for 260 acres of land in the parishes of Llangyndeyrn, Carmarthenshire and Keeston, Pembrokeshire. So, if anything, Bronwydd was the loser of any profit (albeit, in a very small way) from what was called the 'contentious tithe', but gained considerably as the Lloyds were never a target in the 'Tithe War' of the 1880s and 90s[19].

One cause which contributed to the detriment and impoverishment of many estates was the tendency of landowners to engage in lawsuits. George Owen, the distinguished ancestor of the Lloyds of Bronwydd, was constantly fighting for his rights as Lord Marcher and a constant pattern of litigation appears throughout the history of the family. A large estate and its owners could not easily avoid the problems endemic in its administration, some of which may be quoted as examples.

In 1700-1, before the Court of Great Sessions in Pembrokeshire, the matter of the inheritance and claim to 130 acres in the parish of St. Dogmael's was pleaded by William Lloyd, gent. of Penpedwast against Jane Lloyd, widow, which he claimed as his rightful inheritance, traced back to four generations. But the case went on and on for years when she argued that a much larger share of the land in question was hers: one third of five messuages, cottages and 3,600acres of land in the parishes of Nevern, Monington and St. Dogmael's '..as dower from her late husband Evan Lloyd, gent. Again, in 1734, disputes arose with regard to some twenty tenements, ten cottages, thirty gardens and a corn mill with an annual value of £70, supposed to belong to William Owen of Henllys, and it was some time before he was granted possession on account of irksome and slow legal procedures. Another aggravation was the imprecise and vague bills of costs from certain attorneys, for example, Thomas Lloyd was very puzzled, indeed, when he received an account of £88-14-4d from John Howells of Lincoln's Inn, '.....payment for [unspecified] writings and business'. The future ownership of the Cilrhiwe estate, with a rental of £300 a year in 1748 was the subject of a Chancery Suit, a court to avoid because of its protracted deliberations which could result in the ruin of all the participants.

Wills were often the cource of conflict within families on account of indecisive drafting, complicated provisions and persons making spurious claims. In his will of 17 October, 1742, Robinson Lloyd of Cilrhiwe and Vaynor, left £500 to his daughter Elizabeth, raised on land but subject to a life interest of several other people, one of whom was Ann Ferrier. The legacy involved lengthy proceedings which lasted until the end of the century and it was only after much trouble that Ann Ferrier obtained what was due to her when she married Thomas Howell(s) of Glaspant near Newcastle Emlyn.

The Lloyd of Bronwydd claim to the Priory Estate, Cardigan was particularly foolish and costly. The estate had at one time belonged to the Pryse family of Gogerthan and had been sold in 1776, to Thomas Johnes (the father of Thomas Johnes of Hafod) of Croft Castle, Herefordshire, for the sum of £21,000. Colonel Lloyd of Bronwydd considered that he had a fair chance (although he was only a distant remainder-man) to recover some of the estate for himself. Indeed, the estate in the parishes of St. Mary's Cardigan, Ferwig, Tremain and Llangoedmor produced an annual rent of £1,022-18-6d. In addition, it had its political value: influence over the freeholders and the burgesses and their right to vote in the election of the member of parliament to represent the Cardigan Boroughs. From the mass of correspondence and the labyrinthine complications in the claim, it is clear that Lloyd had very little chance of winning. Leading London counsel refused to fight the case. John Brown, attorney-at-law, Carmarthen, was despondent from the start. The suit lingered from 1787 until 1813 and one single lawyers' bill was for £2,403-3-6d (and probably much more had been spent). Even by 1834, it was still thought that there might be some hope of success. Colonel Lloyd's son, Thomas, remained optimistic[20].

In a letter to Lloyd, enclosing a mass of papers relating to the suit, Michael Clayton of Lincoln's Inn, wrote: 'My opinion remains the same, that the chances are so much against your success that, if I were in your situation, I would gladly confirm the title on receiving any sum of money ....' [by way of indemnity to drop the action]. About the same time as the Priory case occupied

Colonel Lloyd and his son, the colonel's father-in-law, Dr John Jones was involved in the Owen of Orielton chancery suit as a guardian of Sir Hugh Owen, Bart. against the machinations of John Colby of Ffynone and his sister Lady Owen, the young baronet's mother. As took place far too often, recourse to law was adopted with little concern for the cost and consequences. And litigation seems to have played a key role in their lives. The old legal maxim: 'Good fences makes good neighbours' was not always observed rigidly as this example shows – Cwrrws Bank, a tract of high ground bordering on the parishes of Llandyfriog, Llanfair-Trefhelygen and Llangunllo, had been enclosed at the end of the eighteenth century. Portions had been allocated to Lloyd of Bronwydd, Howell of Penybeili and Lewes of Dolhaidd. From 1804 to 1821, it was the source of trouble between Lloyd and Howell, especially when third parties became involved, such as, the Rev. Ebenezer Morris (1769-1825) the Methodistical Divine from Rhydlewis. The latter had built a cottage on Lloyd's land without the landlord's permission. In his own peremptory way, John Beynon, agent for the Bronwydd estate, laid down Morris's obligations in no uncertain manner with regard to the rent he was expected to pay and Mr Lloyd's rights.

Perhaps, this incident marks the beginning of a vocal radical sentiment, as shown by Morris, which led to open protest against enclosures and landlord influence. It shows, too, how bizarre claims were made to establish customary rights: an elderly man swore that as a child of two years of age he had herded cattle and chased trespassers off the land on Cwrrws Bank! Occasionally, the blame for unnecessary litigation lay with the agent. In January, 1825, David Richard, a tradesman from Cardigan, alarmed by a threatening letter, and summoned by Beynon to appear at the Court of Great Sessions in Cardigan, wrote to Mr. Lloyd of Bronwydd to countermand '…your instructions to Mr Beynon to save further expenses of law….'In many ways, the lawyer-agent, could be the source of trouble between the landlord and his neighbours, and the ultimate expense which had to be borne by the estate.

It could be argued that one reason for the insolvency and ruin of the Bronwydd estate was the pursuit of an extinct title of honour: endless and costly legal actions, political jockeying, the investigation of ancient genealogies, charters and the pursuit of spurious claims. The award of a baronetcy to Thomas Davies Lloyd, a seat in Parliament, the pageantry of perambulations in all, the recreation of a myth – the return to Camelot – Lord Marcher as 'knight of the shire' and the 'parfait gentle knight' of mediaeval chivalry and romance, ultimately led to massive debts and financial ruin.[21.]

viii

It has been argued by some modern historians that, until the mid-nineteenth century, a politically unenlightened Welsh rural community had for centuries slumbered under the protection of a dominant family, in return for their deference. When the 'Land Question' (towards the end of the century) brought into sharp focus the relationship – almost of vassalage, according to some commentators – between landlord and tenant, allegations and denials were made of acts of oppression, tyranny and heartless treatment by some of the landed families. The evidence was recorded by the Land Commission in the 1890's.

But an examination of the patrician rule of the Lloyd family of Bronwydd over many generations makes it clear that their tenants (almost without exception) enjoyed a happy and harmonious relationship with their landlords. Indeed, like other 'good' gentry, as Professor David Howell has argued, the Lloyds lived side by side with the rest of the community with kindly feeling and concern.

A survey of the Bronwydd estate, carried out by Colonel Thomas Lloyd in the years 1775 to 1785 demonstrates that equity was to prevail over the letter of the law in dealing with his tenants. He had to make a careful assessment of the profitability of the estate – the level of rents, the practice of good husbandry (or otherwise) on his farms and not least, the circumstances of each farmer. To his dismay, he discovered many arrears of rent. The Pembrokeshire estate of Penpedwast, and that of John Laugharne, had been managed very badly, with rent arrears going back to 1735. Colonel Lloyd confided to his father-law Dr.John Jones, that '...my father, during the early part of his life, had been a very Considerable Purchaser [of land]...it was the ambition of the day to covet many acres not to cultivate the few...and the promise I hold most sacred, indeed, ...is to Unhamper myself from Debts as Interest of Five per cent speedily swallow the Income of a low rented estate...' Part of the Cilrhiwe estate, bought by his father, consisted of '...land ill-sett[let] with Rents worse paid ...he was like a Receiver with one Hand to pay with the Other...a mere agent for the estate...' He had been compelled to sell some tenements and 'resetting' others. As a result '...I again took to the Red Coat, and except for the purchase of the my Company scarcely drew upon the estate...' His army pay was his only source of subsistence. Consequently he had to raise some rents, having regard to the economic climate. On the other hand some tenants were 'forgiven' on account of old age, poverty and ill-health. Where Lloyd and his agent considered that rents were too low individual circumstances, such as, the duration of the lease, the age of the tenant and the like had to be taken into account. The rent of Hyan Isha, Eglwyswrw, £3-11-6d a year, was not raised because '...it is an old lease with one life subsisting viz, the present tenant Mr. Hughes, an Old Man...when he drops it will at least be let for forty pounds per annum as the grounds are exceeding good...' The mutual bond between squire and tenant is further shown in the case of the tenant of a farm near Bronwydd. He did not have his rent increased because the 'lease was promised by my father and the tenant is suffered to hold it at the present rent...' Again, the tenant of College Mill, Nevern, was hopelessly in arrear with his rent, and treated very sympathetically. '...He has suffered great loss as Capital Houses which used to grind plenty of corn are now turned into cottages...'

Acute personal distress arose occasionally, especially, if the rent had not been paid for many years. In 1784, this was the case at Ffynnonfair. The husband had died leaving his widow in dire financial difficulties '....obviously, it [the rent] cannot be recovered any other way than by distraining, it is in the landlord's breast to make further allowances...the widow,' tis to be feared will not be able to continue [farming] unless times mend greatly...' was the agent's comment. But, the equitable decision was left to Colonel Lloyd who, invariably, favoured the tenant in need.

Naturally, the landlord had to safeguard his own interests and the future wellbeing of the estate; rents were expected to be paid at the proper time, his manorial rights had to be safeguarded,and this was a thorny problem in the barony (as will be seen later). The indolence of feckless tenants could not be tolerated when for example in 1781, Cwmeog (a farm of 216 acres) became vacant as the 'tenement' was out of lease', the tenant was given notice to quit, and the rent raised from £30 to £40 a year. The farm was terribly run down: '...the house and buildings in a poor state of repair, the meadow ground had been shamefully neglected and a year's rent would be insufficient allowance for reparation..' It would appear that the tenant was expected to carry out the work of maintaining and repairing farm buildings. The granting of leases for three lives, as was the usual custom, on the Bronwydd estate up to the end of the eighteenth century, probably led to some tenants to take advantage of these conditions, often, to the detriment of the property.[22.]

Feudal dues and services going back to the Middle Ages (as the name suggests) added to the payment of rent in cash, came to be regarded as a real aggravation and was censured in evidence before the Land Commission as a relic of non-monetary economy and antiquated custom. Although these terms were to appear, less and less, in leases towards the end of the nineteenth century on the Bronwydd and other estates, they still survived. H.M. Vaughan comments that the '...fowls and ducks brought to Llangoedmore in my grandmother's time were obviously the skinniest and oldest of their kind...' A few examples may be quoted of the dues and services demanded of Bronwydd tenants over the years. Tenants of Bronwydd and Cilrhiwe, in the parishes of Cynwil Elfed and Llanpumsaint had to grind their corn in 'Velin Dyad' in the hamlet of Cwmduad, in the 1750's. Tirygors,in the parish of Llanfair Orllwyn was let for a rent of '..£3. one hen and two dozen eggs at Shrovetide annually..'

Some of these services were arduous. John Evans of the parish of Troed-yr-aur, a shopkeeper, rented Pantbach, Llangunllo, in the 1756 for '..six pounds a year, six hens at Shrovetide, two horses to carry lime or coal to Cilrhiwe or one man to reap or bind in the corn harvest.' The haulage of coal and lime (probably, imported from east Carmarthenshire to the coastal villages of Aberporth and Llangrannog) to Cilrhiwe meant travelling a distance of twenty to thirty miles along poor country tracks – a burden in terms of time and effort. Occasionally 'services' were undertaken without demur, and were not related to any kind of farm work: Evan Evans, tenant of the large farm of Nanyrhelygen Fawr, Eglwyswrw, agreed with Thomas Lloyd of Bronwydd, to accept the tenancy for an annual rent of £42 per annum and '...six fat hens and sixty eggs at Shrovetide and one man for ten days to collect tolls at Migan [Meigan] fair...' The right to levy tolls at this and other fairs was one which the Lord Marcher of Cemais had a right to, and in this instance, the tenant might well feel privileged to have the trust and confidence of the lord, prestige amongst his peers and, possibly financial gain from such a responsibility. No doubt, many of these terms in leases were a burden – in 1777, David Morris of Eithinduon, Eglwyswrw, rented his farm from Ann Lloyd of Bronwydd, for an annual rent of £24, two hens and twenty eggs at Christmas, with 'suit of mill at Jordan Mill' which belonged to the landowner who could claim a proportion of the meal ground, resulting in loss to the tenant who had to support himself and his family, and was constantly faced with the vagaries of the weather, bad harvests, animal diseases and the like. On the other hand, it was an ancient custom which was accepted by a conservative minded peasantry and less laborious than grinding with a hand mill at home.

Rather unusual terms were included sometimes, for example, in 1792, Thomas Lloyd agreed with John James of 'Colege Mill', in the parish of Bayvil, a joiner, to let the premises for £24 a year on condition he repaired the mill'...in the form of a French Mill..'i.e. with 'French burrstones' of a very high quality imported from France. Broadly speaking the dues and services were in proportion to the acreage of the farm. Thus, John Hughes of Pencnwc Fawr, Eglwyswrw, rented the farm from Thomas Lloyd for £60, eight hens and eighty eggs annually. The feudal custom of paying a heriot (the surrender of the best beast on the death of the tenant) was commuted to a money payment, eggs and poultry. Thomas Lloyd was aware that to claim the best beast could well be a disincentive to good stock breeding.[23.]

From the end of the eighteenth century onwards one can trace a change in farm leases, with conditions which reflected more and more the 'new agriculture': tenants were forbidden to cut 'matts' and blocks of turf for fuel, thereby impoverishing the soil. Straw and manure, were not to be removed from the farm. In time 'good husbandry' clauses became more prominent. In 1817 Mary Lloyd leased a farm to George Page 'for his natural life' for £26 annually, together with '...two couple of fowls at Shrovetide, forty eggs...' but added that he had to apply 'teals of lime, sow 10lbs of clover seed, 1 Winchester of "Ever Grass" per acre with the third and last crop and a proportionate quantity of muck or compost' and after such manuring was not to take more than three crops '...unless one is pease or clover under the penalty of £5 per acre for every such offence...' nor was he allowed to sublet, sell any straw and all manure was to be left on the farm.

In the 1820s Thomas Williams of Castell Gorwen, in the parish of Trelech, a'r Betws, agreed to keep in good repair all buildings, drains, hedges and trenches, as well as to farm the property in the best manner. In 1833, Thomas Lloyd agreed to let the large property of Llandilo-Abercywyn to a partnership comprising Lewis Lloyd of that place, David Lloyd of Woodhouse, and Jacob Thomas of Maesgrove, Laugharne, for an annual rent of £350 (clear of all taxes and abatements). The lease contained all the terms already mentioned with regard to manure, crop rotation, not ploughing meadow land and the like, but stipulating clearly not to cut trees.

The payment of tithes (an aggravation to churchman and non conformist) as noted above, was now being included as part of the rent, for example, this applied to some leases in the parish of Eglwyswrw and Nevern in 1839. But it does not seem to have soured the relationship between landlord and tenant on the Bronwydd estate. The same may be said of leasehold properties, - in 1807, Colonel Lloyd allowed '..Hendry Williams to build a cottage at his own expense on Cross Rode on [the] way to Newcastle-Emlyn.. for an annual ground rent of 6d during the lifetime of Hendry Williams and his wife ...the said Thomas Lloyd, Esq., is to pay full value of the Building at that time when they leave it and [the property] valued by two or more substantial men....' In 1840, Thomas Lloyd made an agreement with David John Allis of Danycapel to allow the latter '...the liberty of building a house on a small plot of ground.. on Park Three Cocks in the parish of Llanfair-Treflygen.. where there is a small plantation with its front facing Bronwydd house, for £2-2s annually'. Thomas Lloyd was to find the timber and stones for building '...but was not to go to any expense other than carting or digging any stone or timber... and was prepared to pay one half of the expense of drawing up a lease..' If David John Allis, at any time, wished to vacate and sell the property, Thomas Lloyd was prepared to buy it at a fair valuation.

The same sense of equity and 'egwyddor' [W. sense of justice] occurred when the tenancy of farms or cottages on the Bronwydd estate had to be terminated, and that for a variety of reasons, such as the sale of the property or amalgamation with adjoining land. There are several instances of an amicable arrangement with tenants by offering a lump sum in compensation or an annuity for life – in 1740, James George, yeoman, and Joseph Llewelin, butcher, (both of the parish of Nevern) surrendered a moiety of Cwmeog Fawr and Cwmeog Fach to Thomas Lloyd for the sum of £500. In the same year, a similar agreement was made with David Evan of Nevern, for the surrender of Coedwinog Fawr and Tyddyn-y-Dderwen.

About a hundred years later, Thomas Lloyd of Bronwydd, granted an annuity of £10 (a sum not to be despised, having regard to wage levels, the means of subsistence and support in food and clothing from the squire and his household) to cottagers in the vicinity of Bronwydd, one of whom was Margaret Drew of Aberbanc.[24.]

On the whole, the harmonious relationship between landlord and tenant on the Bronwydd estate continued during the nineteenth and twentieth centuries. However, Thomas Lloyd, in the 1840's, had little sympathy with squatters and cottages who openly disregarded his rights as landlord. The erection of 'tai-un-nos' built without the squire's permission led to strong action: for example, in 1849, a cottager dwelling on the inhospitable tract of land, known as Waunmorfa in the parish of Newport, was faced with a distress warrant for arrears of rent. His wordly goods amounted to – '…1 Leyn [linen] Press, 15/-, Syve 10/-, 2 tables 11/-, 1 shelf and Dresser 20/-, 4 Chairs 6/-, 2 Cows £6-5s…' And, many years later, Sir Marteine Lloyd, too, caused public dismay, when as a young, inexperienced and ill-advised young landlord, he gave notice to quit, in 1880, to the aged tenant of Henllys, Ebenezer Harries, eighty eight years of age, one of the oldest tenants on the Bronwydd estate, where generations of his family had lived. He still farmed satisfactorily, had paid his rent regularly and had ample security that it would be so always. The old man was desperate and had not the '…slightest idea where he and his family can find the humblest home…'

A public outcry followed in the locality when the community at large-clergy, ministers, farmers, a chemist, an auctioneer and tradesmen signed a petition entreating Sir Marteine to reconsider the matter and allow Mr. Harries to remain at Henllys. It is likely that this incident made a deep impression on Sir Marteine, and in later years, his treatment of tenants was at times unduly lenient. His father, Sir Thomas Davies Lloyd had in the course of his campaign and parliamentary speeches, restated the old and paternalistic values of the country gentleman: one of large territorial possessions '…living with his people and for his people …' All in all, it can be argued that Sir Thomas and Sir Marteine, remained faithful to the much quoted saying of old Colonel Lloyd of Bronwydd: 'Cursed be the first Lloyd to evict a Bronwydd tenant'.

Sir Marteine was generous towards his tenants during hard times. His 'egwyddor' and the reverential regard shown by Marteine Lloyd in particular, was aptly recalled in the 1950's by the aged occupant of the garden cottage at Bronwydd . In the 1880's, his father had suffered heavy losses on the farm, and unable to pay his rent made a personal appeal to Sir Marteine himself. After relating his tale of despair and woe. Sir Marteine told him (in his homely Welsh) 'Ti dim becso, ni talu rhent da'n gili…'[Don't worry we shall pay the rent together] which meant that the farmer did not pay any rent at all for that year.

The mutual regard between landlord and tenant which existed on the Bronwydd estate was not impaired by the pressures of the day and the allegations of radical editors, politicians and preachers. The latter quoted (and rightly so) the eviction of tenants, harassment for political and denominational reasons, extortionate rent increases, insecurity of tenure, the burden of tithes, game and fishery laws, no compensation for improvements and the like – the key issues which gravely affected the tenant farmer and the rural community.[25]

The case for the farmers was put before the Land Commission by such Liberal and Nonconformists leaders as Dr. Enoch Davies, of Bryn Teifi, Bangor Teifi, in the lower Teifi valley. He asserted that because of landlord pressure many tenants were afraid to give evidence of their grievances before the Commission. Whereas tenant farmers who were radical and nonconformist had been evicted from their farms after the 1871 election for voting Liberal against the wishes of Tory landlords in 'Tivyside', not a single Bronwydd tenant had been evicted. Sir Marteine Lloyd had actually encouraged his tenants to come forward to give evidence of any grievance before the Land Commission.

Until the last decades of the nineteenth century, 'statutory' control of the responsibility of landlord and tenant was entirely absent. There were time-honoured customs in different parts of the country, but these were ill-defined and unclear on matters like compensation for any cash outlay on improvements by the tenant on buildings, gates and fences and the like. The Agricultural Holdings Act of 1875 (unlike the Act of 1883) was permissive rather than mandatory. Indeed, leases made by Sir Thomas Lloyd and his mother (for the Cilrhiwe estate) contained clauses which exempted them from paying compensation to their tenants. Even so, the general picture is of a tenantry happy with the old customs, backward looking, indifferent to their legal rights, and too poor to carry out any significant improvements. Above all, they relied on age old bonds between squire and tenant, as was made clear before the Land Commission. The name of Sir Marteine Lloyd was singled out as a landlord who could be trusted.

Certainly, there were grievances, such as the high rents at the end of the nineteenth century caused, perhaps, indirectly by the social and economic trends of the day. Rents had been raised on the Bronwydd estate between 1865 and 1871 due to market forces when ' things were brisk'. One complainant was Evan Rees, who had migrated from his home Wern-Newydd near Bronwydd, to set himself as a butter merchant in Swansea, a prosperous industrial town and port. He argued that the rent of the farm he grew up on had been raised from £14 per annum in 1760 to £106 in 1871. Another tenant complained that, while rents had been raised during prosperous times, they had not been reduced when times were bad. It has to be remembered that farming was a pathetic spectacle during the depression from about 1879 to 1900, caused by bad harvests, higher taxes and the influx of foreign goods. Rents were reduced by some landlords, and in this context, Sir Marteine Lloyd and his uncle the Rev. Rhys Jones Lloyd made allowances of 10-12%. Even so, the landlord was the scapegoat for all the ills of the community, but the Lloyds were held in high regard. Their 'kind and courteous behaviour', 'there was no fear of eviction while Sir Marteine was alive'- were some of the comments made.

During the depression of the 1920s, Lady Lloyd informed the estate agent (John Evans of Cardigan) who had raised the matter of reducing rents '...I expect that we shall have to meet their [tenants'] wishes as these days we must help each other to exist....'[26].

One source of grievance arose from the Game Laws which allowed landlords certain privileges and to impose what conditions they pleased in leases and agreements. Moreover, on the Bronwydd estate the Lord Marcher claimed the sole right to hunt and fish within the barony so that its inhabitants felt that they were being deprived of what was theirs too. This happened from time to time, for example – in the early 1800s Thomas Lloyd prohibited all persons from 'sporting within the barony of Kemes on pain of a fine of £15..' and many landowners were unpopular because of the penalties they meted out to poachers in the courts (and this was one specific cause of the Rebecca Riots some years later). Sentences of heavy fines or hard labour were common, and two examples of harsh treatment can be quoted – in October, 1856, Ebenezer Jones of Drefelin in Llangeler parish was fined £5 or three months hard labour for trespassing in pursuit of game by the magistrates: Thomas Davies Lloyd, Gwinnett Tyler, W. O. Brigstocke and James Bowen. In January, 1862, John Boultbee of Gwernant, Chairman of the Cardiganshire Quarter Sessions demanded stricter laws against persons '...in constant violation of the Game laws...spending their time in idleness and dissipation, illegally trespassing in pursuit of game and rabbits...' The motion was seconded by none other than Davies Lloyd!

But there were some notable exceptions, such as Colonel J. R. Howell of Pantgwyn and Sir Marteine Lloyd of Bronwydd, squires who were aware of the poverty and hardship experienced by many of the poachers and rustic rogues who came before them in their rôle as magistrates. The 'Ground Game Act' of 1880 limited the monopoly of the gentry by granting tenants the right to destroy rabbits and hares on their holdings, notwithstanding any provision to the contrary in their agreements. But some tenants were understandably afraid to exercise their rights if the landlord was known to be hostile to this act. Differences arose on the Bronwydd estate and were made public in evidence before the Land Commission by Evan Rees (mentioned already). He alleged that Sir Thomas Davies Lloyd had given his father permission to shoot rabbits which swarmed over their farm of Wern-newydd, but Sir Marteine had revoked this agreement on condition that this 'heinous sin' [of using a gun] was not repeated – '...we were to ferret the rabbits and not kill with a gun...'

Like other sporting gentry Sir Marteine had a phobia of poachers armed with guns invading game preserves. Such conduct was deemed to be an attack on a gentleman's status and privilege; it savoured of 'revolution' in the thinking of many a squire who regarded game as sacrosanct and a symbol of status in society. The material and pecuniary loss was not so important in their scale of values. But it has to be remembered that, as in other ways, Sir Marteine showed leniency towards miscreants and desperadoes who snatched what they could to provide their families with the next meal. In the Henllan area stories still survive of the stratagems used by the poacher's confederates to give warning where the keeper was lurking – the cornet player (followed by others of the Bronwydd Band) would blow a jolly tune which re-echoed over the countryside! The poacher then took evasive action and made a tactical withdrawal in good time!!![27]

The Lord Marcher

i

When Sir Marteine Owen Mowbray Lloyd, 2nd Baronet, of Bronwydd and Newport Castle, died in April 1933, local and national newspapers expressed public sorrow at the passing of a beloved and revered squire and landowner. The benevolence and patronage of a highly esteemed family, the virtues and 'humanity' of the colourful Lord Marcher of Cemais had come to an end, - an event which was lamented by a wide circle of friends, tenants and the community at large. Sir Marteine, like his forebears at Bronwydd, had represented the best in the values of a social order which was fast disappearing in the face of radical change. Claims to noble ancestry and the possession of broad acres, wealth and status, were being surrendered to the forces of democracy, wider educational opportunities and the challenge from many of those whose ancestors had been 'hewers of wood and drawers of water'.

Burke's '*Peerage, Baronetage and Knightage...*', the '*Annals...*' of T. Nicholas, and other genealogical books and manuscript pedigrees, had recorded the descent of the Lloyd family of Bronwydd, from Cymric and Norman stock: Cadifor, lord of Cilycwm and (through the Owens of Henllys) 'without interruption' from Martin de Tours, the Norman conqueror. Thereby, the lord or baron of Cemais, was entitled to all the rights, privileges and dignities of a 'Lord Marcher'. But contrary to the glamorous and enchanting traditions held by the Lloyd family, modern scholars during the last hundred years have questioned whether this claim was as historically reliable as the Lloyd family sincerely believed. The irate and (according to some) the controversial Oxford scholar J. Horace Round, adviser to the Crown on Peerage Cases, styled by Sir Anthony Wagner, as a 'great genealogist and historian' challenged the Owen claim to descent from the nebulous Martin de Tours and other Norman lords who styled themselves as Fitzmartin[1].

A more recent study by the late Dr. B. G. Charles (based on the massive Bronwydd archives at the National Library of Wales) has indisputably shown that it was William Owen (c. 1488-1574), son of Rhys ap Owen Fychan of Henllys Isaf in the parish of Nevern, a lawyer and member of the Middle Temple, minor landowner and government official in Pembrokeshire, who completed the purchase of the barony of Cemais in 1543, from the impoverished John Touchet, Lord Audeley, a descendant of Henry de Audeley, Lord Audeley of Heleigh, governor of the castles of Cardigan and Carmarthen in 1225.

The barony, lordship or manor of 'Kemeys' comprised the castle of Newport, the manors of 'Newcastle, Kevenllymwyth, Carndeyvo, Bayvil, Moylegrove and Eglwyswrw', 200 messuages, 8 mills, 2850 acres of land,, £30 in rents, along with the advowsons of Newport, Dinas, Llanllawer, Llanychllwydog,

Meline and Whitchurch. William Owen was able to add to his estate through
further land purchases, taking advantage of the prevailing economic and agrarian
conditions when the stronger neighbour was able to oust minor freeholders and
consolidate many scattered holdings into one estate.

The ancient castle of Newport stood partly in ruins and sadly neglected by its
its past owners, and although the baronial demesne of Bury [Berry] was nearby,
Owen had to reside at the humble farmstead of Henllys. Even so, as lord of the
barony, he took no time in swaggering over those who had to render homage,
swear fealty, pay customs and tolls to their new master. The little town of
Newport was within the Lord Marcher's fief, and (in spite of any ancient
traditional rights and privileges of its burgesses and traders) tolls and payments
for 'standings and pitchings' and for the sale of livestock and various commodities
had now to be paid to the lord of the barony, albeit grudgingly. The last traces
of feudalism which had fallen into abeyance because of the absenteeism, shaky
finances, family misfortune and the failure of the Audely dynasty to administer
the barony efficiently could not be re-imposed without some degree of protest
and much latent bad feeling towards the new lord. And an undercurrent of ill-
will can be traced throughout the period of the 'governance' of the barony by
the Lords Marcher later on.

William Owen died in advanced old age in March 1574. He was buried at
Nevern, and the bards Huw Llŷn and Morris Llwyd Wiliam o Fôn came to
bemoan his death. They extolled his patronage of poets, great learning in
languages and 'skill in legal science'. He had shared chambers with Sir Anthony
Fitzherbert, and had published law books which had been printed by none other
than Richard Pynson (d. 1530), printer to King Henry viii. He had married
well, especially, as his second wife, Elizabeth was the daughter of Sir George
Herbert of Swansea. They had a son George Owen (1552-1613) who succeeded
him[2].

George Owen, his life, career and prolific writings are central to any study of
the Lloyds of Bronwydd and the 'saga' of the Lords Marcher of Cemais for
centuries to come. He succeeded his father at Henllys, and became famous as
the 'historian of Pembrokeshire'. Owen was appointed to all the important
public offices in the county, and is considered a 'Welsh Elizabethan' *par
excellence*. He was influenced by the great awakening of interest in the history
and antiquities of Wales as in England at the time. He was on familiar terms
with antiquaries and genealogists like William Camden, Lewys Dwnn, Humphrey
Llwyd, David Powell, Sir John Price and their contemporaries. George Owen
was at the centre of a small group of writers in Pembrokeshire which included
George Owen Harry, Robert Holland and George William Griffith: genealogists,
antiquaries and patrons of bards who enjoyed Owen's hospitality at Henllys.
Moreover, he was a prolific recorder of the geology, topography, ancient
monuments, castles, geneaology, heraldry and government of Pembrokeshire.
Some of his 'writings' have a particular relevance to the annals of Bronwydd,

for example, in 'Proofes that the Lordship of Kemes is a Lord Marcher' and others, Owen 'became inordinately conscious of his status as Lord of Cemais and proud of the somewhat anachronistic title of Lord Marcher', to quote Dr. Charles. With much 'tedious labour' and travel to London and other far-off places, he researched everything relating to the barony of Cemais. He argued that Cemais and other lordships were held of the king of England 'in capite'; that the king's writ did not run within the barony and that the Lords Marcher did not hold their lands by charter but by 'jura regalia'.

While it has to be conceded that some of Owen's conclusions were balanced and cogently argued, his 'historical writings' prolific and wide-ranging, he made exaggerated claims relating to the historical and regal superiority of the lordship of Cemais. He was convinced, on very flimsy grounds, that the right of inheritance had passed for successive generations of blood relations from the heirs of Martin, through the Audeleys to the Owens of Henllys. In 'Proofes that Kemes is an Aunciente Lordship Marcher' George Owen claimed the 'dignites, royall power and jurisdiction of the barony'. He argued that the lord thereof was lord of the Parliament; had the exercise of 'jura regalia' (like Lords Marcher in the past) and even after the Acts of Union, it has to be remembered that many privileges were safeguarded to the lord. These included the right to hold courts baron and courts leet, and to claim treasure trove and wrecks on the sea. Owen claimed he had the right to erect gallows, to execute felons and to take possession of their goods and chattels. In addition he incorporated the town of Newport within his jurisdiction and maintained his right to grant it 'liberties, officers and a common seal'. Owen went as far as to assert that, like other Lords Marcher, the lord of Cemais could be consulted by the king on matters of state, and lead his tenants to 'the warres at his pleasure'. He demanded that the mayor of Newport and all his officers 'accounted' to his lordship... upon oath... as sheriffs and other kings officers doe now at the kinges audit..' And, for good measure, George Owen added that the Lord Marcher of Cemais had built an abbey (St. Dogmaels) '.... which was before the earl of Pembroke...'- a swipe at the claims of the earldom of Pembroke.

This treatise was regarded as an impudent manifesto and bitter feuds resulted between Owen and the leading county gentry such as Warren of Trewern, Gwyn of Trericert, Eynon Phillipps of Tregybi and Sir John Perrot, described as Owen's 'great enemy'. Brawls, abduction and gang warfare followed and allegations of forging deeds and of concocting spurious documents were made against Owen. He clashed with the county magistracy about the appointment of petty constables, the levying of fines and forfeits, and the like.

There was a spirit of revolt against Owen's arbitrary exercise of power in the borough of Newport. Although the old castle had become a ruin it was remembered as the 'caput' of previous lords, and was a cherished symbol of olden times. The town still had its corporate life: its burgesses, claiming the privileges which the Martins had granted them in the thirteenth century. It is true that, as lord of the borough, George Owen was entitled to certain rents, profits of the courts, fairs and markets as well as the customary services laid down by charter. The election of the mayor of Newport had been made (according to tradition) by the lord who chose one name from a list of four nominations. Some of these names were not acceptable to Owen, because they represented a faction who challenged his claims to rents and some other emoluments. On one occasion, he refused to elect a mayor, and, for a time, the government of the town collapsed. The town ceased to function; it was without a mayor; a bailiff and new burgesses had not been appointed. Such was the situation in October, 1606, when Owen coerced the town's burgesses (some of whom were local gentry) to appoint a mayor who could be manipulated to agree with his schemes. Like other Welsh gentry, he resorted to litigation and was constantly in dispute with his peers, neighbours and tenants in the courts of Great Sessions and the Council of Wales and the Marches. He was an ambitious landowner, motivated by the pursuit of power and wealth. In this way, he made himself 'an unpopular reactionary' to quote Dr. Charles, and, with his father William Owen, were regarded as 'pretensious upstarts, who tried to assert their social primacy in Cemais'. Be that as it may, it was George Owen – 'a very versatile man of many parts, and outstanding member of the squirearchy and an important figure in public affairs, a scholarly antiquary...whose writings earned him a high reputation among his contemporaries and enduring esteem to this day..' who recreated the 'myth' of the Lord Marcher of Cemais. In later centuries it was responsible for the prestige (and many of the problems) relating to the Lloyd family of Bronwydd and their estate[3].

After George Owen's death in 1613, he was succeeded by his son Alban Owen (1580-1656) whose mother was Elizabeth, daughter of William Philipps of Picton Castle. Little is known about his education and upbringing. He may have attended the 'College' at Felindre Farchog, where, according to tradition, George Owen had established a school. Alban Owen set out to exact dues and impose the rule of Lord Marcher with no less fervour than his father. He held all the usual 'county' offices of government and was High Sheriff like his father and grandfather, fought cases in the courts of Great Sessions and the Council of Wales and the Marches, for example, in 1614 he appeared against Thomas Lloyd of Cilciffeth in an action touching enclosure of Commons in the lordship of Pontchardson [Puncheston] and Llanycathe, and Lloyd's other misdemeanours as a Justice of the Peace. Owen himself had to answer a charge of dishonesty concerning Henllys tithes, brought by Thomas Birt, gent.

After Alban Owen's death in 1656, the power and influence of the Lord Marcher seems to have diminished, and during the tenure of his son David Owen, there are few extant records of contentious matters in which the Lord Marcher was involved.

David Owen, about the year 1651,married Anne daughter of Robert Corbett of Ynys-y-Maengwyn, Towyn, Meirionethshire, and left a son William Owen, and two daughters, Elizabeth and Anne. As William Owen left no surviving heir, his estate and the lordship of Cemais, passed to his two sisters as co-heirs. For the next thirty years the lordship was in dual ownership.

William Owen does not seem to have been interested nor active in the mediaeval historical role of Lord Marcher envisaged by his great-grand-father, George Owen of Henllys. Neverthless, he insisted on imposing feudal dues on his tenantry, and the following agreement shows how the economy, labour force and farming practices of a squire's holding in the late seventeenth century, depended to a large extent on such terms. In March, 1676/7, William Owen of Henllys, esq. 'leased Hyan Issa in the parish of Eglwyswrw to Hugh David...labourer, and William, son of the said Hugh David, in consideration for 50 shillings and rent of £3 a year with .....1 bushel of marketable oats, 3 persons to reap or bind for one day in corn harvest, 3 hens,3 cords of fire to be cut and led to Henllys, 1 person to make the lessors hay in the said parish as other tenants are wont to do and to load it to Henllys, one man to cut wood before the strippers in barking time, 1 horse to fetch lime,1 horse to fetch coals,2 horses and drivers to load and carry muck, 2 men for one day in summer or autumn to 'stooke' furze and to lead them and make them in a rick, 2 harrows to harrow in sowing time,1 day's ploughing, 2 horses to lead corn,1 person for one day to watch at Meigan's fair and the accustomed duties annually, and 10 shillings in lieu of heriot and the lessees to pay rates and taxes, with an allowance of 5 shillings if a great rate should fail during the term...'

Elizabeth, William Owen's sister and co-heir married Arthur Laugharne of Llanrheithan in 1678, and by him had a son William Laugharne. He married his cousin, Elizabeth, daughter of Francis Laugharne of Llanunwas. John Laugharne, the elder son of this marriage was High Sheriff of the county of Pembroke in 1731. His fortunes declined from now on, and family quarrels, litigation and debts led to the sequestration of his estates: Llanrheithan, half the barony of Cemais and other properties. He died in poverty in 1755. Anne, the other co-heir, married Thomas Lloyd of Penpedwast, who died about 1710. Their son, William married in 1713 Jane or Joan Ford of Berry. The marriage settlement included 'half the manor of Kemmes'. Their daughter Anne Lloyd of Penpedwast, was married (see ch.2.p15) in 1739 to Thomas Lloyd of Bronwydd. By this match, half the barony of Cemais was absorbed into the Bronwydd estate and Thomas Lloyd purchased the remaining half of the barony for £2,000 in 1751, from the (by now) penniless John Laugharne. Through marriage and purchase, the lordship of Cemais became the property of one owner once more[4].

The acquisition of more acres and scattered properties was not without its problems: common land was being increasingly enclosed by rival landlords and boundary disputes followed. The ambitious cottager in his 'tŷ-un-nos' encroached a plot of land to obtain a roof over his head, so as not to be beholden to a landlord for rent, other than a penny or two. Chief rents had not been levied for many generations on the 'cotters' living within the barony of Cemais, partly because Anne Lloyd of Penpedwast, a widow, had along with her son William Lloyd, gent. had come to a formal agreement with William Laugharne of Llanrheithan, gent. for receiving the chief rents of the barony.

Although these rents were an insignificant part of an estate's economy, their prestige and social value rated highly in 'preserving' the interest and influence of the lord, a consideration which could not be ignored. Moreover, other landlords who claimed title to manorial lands kept an eagle eye on their rights: Thomas Lloyd of Coedmore and John Lloyd of Cilgwyn leased, in May 1725, the manor or Lordship of Iscoed Ishirwen and Iscoed Mortimer to freeholders in Llechryd and Llangoedmore, along with the mill and weir and 'fishery' in the Teifi, for an annual rent of 28 shillings. Their neighbours, the Brigstockes of Blaenpant, and Vaughan of Golden Grove, with lands across the Teifi in Cenarth and Penboyr parishes (and one could mention many others) were not slow to make similar claims[5].

A survey of Bronwydd chief rent payments and manorial dues, from about 1760 to the 1920's, reveals that they were in arrear for most of the period. Thomas Lloyd issued instructions to Mr. J. Rees Stokes to warn defaulters of their last chance to pay 'before we proceed to any rough methods'. In the town of Newport, chief rents had not been paid for several years, and, in 1775 even a neighbouring squire, Thomas Lloyd of Cwmglyne, owed £4-5s 'being five years chief rent due last Migantide...' for tenements in Bayvil parish and Ceibwr Mill in Moylegrove. Moreover, storehouses, lime kilns and other buildings had been erected on the quay at Newport. No rent had been paid and, from now on, plans and drawings would have to be shown to Lloyd's steward to safeguard Bronwydd interests against other rival claims. Indeed, many of Mr. Bowen's tenants in Newport had not paid their rent, and Mr. Stokes, in his report, in 1779, stated that '...there was no inclination on the part of tenants, to pay rent to the lord...whether it was Mr Bowen or Mr. Lloyd!'

The rent of properties in the town of Newport were assessed at about a £1 a year, while in the outlying hill parishes, sums like 3d or 6d were usual. The appointment of Mr. Charles Hassall, well known as the author of reports on the state of agriculture in the counties of Pembroke and Carmarthen, for the Board of Agriculture in 1794, as the new steward of the barony of Cemais, failed to bring about any significant improvement in the payment of rent. In the manor of Llanfyrnach-ar-Dav, freeholders, farmers, dairymen and cottagers, all defaulters, openly ignored notices and '...covetously absent themselves from attending...; the manorial court.

By the 1830's matters had reached a critical stage, and Thomas Lloyd aware of the expense of collecting rents, issuing warrants for non-payment, providing dinners, free beer and other forms of hospitality, was compelled to seek counsel's opinion. He was faced with a dilemma: distraint of goods was unpleasant and

65

damaging to the relationship between lord and 'homager' and, whereas, it could be applied to enforce payment, it was all important to establish proof of ownership. But had not George Owen and ancient custom settled that one and for all? In 1835, Thomas Lloyd instructed Thomas George, steward of the barony, to distrain upon the goods and chattels of tenants of Mr Bowen of Llwyngwair. Inevitably, such a course led to strained feelings between the two landlords. Mr. Bowen wished to be fair and equitable and did not dispute Mr Lloyd's right to chief rent, as he himself owned tracts of land over which he too claimed rights. But, when Thomas George distrained to the value of £6, on one of Bowen's tenants, for a debt of 4/6d such unfairness could not be tolerated.

Owing to Bowen influence in the town of Newport, demands by Mr Lloyd of Bronwydd continued to be ignored, and indifference spread to outlaying parishes. A protest movement, urged by the populace, in 1844 urged non-payment of chief rent to landlords, such as George Bowen of Llwyngwair, Lloyd of Trewern and his kinsman Longcroft of Llanina, Cardiganshire. As the chief rent books of the Bronwydd estate show, there was a repeating pattern of arrears and non-payment which had reached its nadir by 1849. Significantly, it coincides with the distress and deprivation of the labouring classes and the disaffection of the Welsh peasantry with the social conditions of the time as had been expressed by the Rebecca riots and similar unrest further afield.

A survey of the level of payment of chief rents and manorial dues, for example, during the years of 1853, 1868, 1890, 1917, shows that in most cases, the demands of the Lord Marcher were largely ignored. In 1868, it is estimated that the occupants of more than four hundred tenements who owed sums ranging from a few pence to a shilling or two, had not paid a single penny. In the manors of Llanfyrnach ar Daf and Llandeilo Abercywyn (part of the Bronwydd estate outside the barony of Cemais) the custom of paying chief rents had long come to an end. The very active agent of the Bronwydd estate, John Daniel Jones of Rhydlewis, gave notice that in 1861 payment of 2/6d per head plus arrears, would have to be paid by, '…every 'cotter' and those living in peasant cottages within the barony, at the Llwyngwair Arms hostelry, Newport, and at the Cwmgloyne Arms in Crosswell, …when the tenants are espectfully to pay up all amounts with all Arrears due and all those neglecting to do so will be placed in legal hands…'

From now on until the 1920's, it gradually became clear that the Lord Marcher had fought a losing battle: the distraint of goods was a procedure which could make the landlord liable for any irregular acts by his bailiff; the uncertain nature of the tenure of holdings added to the complications and, above all, when payments were made, the profit to the lord was very little. In 1917, from some four hundred and fifty five holdings, the chief rents collected amounted to £76-10-8d, while the expenses were £66-4-4d, leaving the Lord Marcher with the paltry sum of £10-6-4d. Clearly, 'the game was not worth the candle'! A few years later, Lady Lloyd added in a letter about Newport Castle and the barony of Cemais to George Eyre Evans, the Carmarthen antiquary, '....feudal rights are dead nowadays....'[6.]

The non-payment of chief rents was only part of wider discontent which had reared its head, especially from the end of the eighteenth century. The administration of the barony had been lax for generations, notably during the days of the Laugharnes of Llanrheithan. By the 1770's Lloyd of Bronwydd realised that more and more plots were being enclosed; 'tai-unos' were sprouting up everywhere; the hedges and fences of legally enclosed land were torn down at such places as Brynberian and Tafarn y Bwlch. One Daniel David had 'the audacity to enclose land on "Commons Vach" and erect a kiln for drying oats...' As a result he was ordered to pull it down in July, 1777. Two years later, gangs committed encroachments on a '...very valuable part of the lordship...where the turfery there is of so much superior quality...' This was a perennial problem on common land where clods of peat were cut during fine weather to be dried for winter fuel. The Lord Marcher was not the only source of dissatisfaction to provoke the 'commonalty'. Acts of physical violence and criminal damage were perpetrated against freeholders who had enclosed land according to what the law allowed. There were many instances of trespass and damage committed by neighbours and disaffected persons, their friends and supporters. Joseph Rees of Llwynybyrian in the parish of Nevern, took to court a gang of farmers, labourers and artisans who 'with force and arms' broke into a close owned by Rees. The indictment dramatically and perhaps with a degree of exaggeration, alleged that '...they had pulled down, prostrated and destroyed trees and underwood to wit: 100 oaks, 100 elms,100 ash trees, 100 other trees and 10 acres of underwood valued at £20, and 100 cartloads of timber and 100 of wood and 100 of bushes worth £20...'But, there was more: 'hedges and fences were pulled down and grassland trampled on, causing damage of £20 and personal injury to Joseph Rees assessed at £40...offences against the peace our lord and king...'

The attitude of neighbouring landlords was not always favourable to the claims of the Lord Marcher. George Bowen of Llwyngwair wrote to Thomas Lloyd at Cilrhiwe, in 1823,enquiring into the legality and authority whereby the burgesses and the lord of the manor (Lloyd) had enclosed commons and had erected buildings on them at Newport 'causing hardship to his tenants and neighbours'. And, ten years later, he threatened going to law 'to prevent any person as may have built houses on the common from doing any act which might have a tendency to establish the lord of the manor's pretensions'[7].

The number of enclosures in and around Newport had increased greatly in the 1830's, and consequently, the little township had become a hot bed of rivalry and intrigue between some of the inhabitants (loyal to Bowen of Llwyngwair or Lloyd of Bronwydd) and certain other disaffected elements bent on causing trouble. A proclamation, supposed to have been sponsored by George Bowen, of Llwyngwair, was made telling the inhabitants that they need not pay rent to the lord of the manor or to the mayor. One Will. Thomas had gone round the town on Pig Fair day, in the midst of a milling crowd of squealing pigs and raucous traders, virtually inciting rebellion against the Lord Marcher and the town's first citizen. A member of the Gap Watch, John David, was sent round with a counter proclamation. Questions were asked as to the authenticity of the original document and various local inhabitants (conscious of the importance of their evidence and of their part as witnesses in the investigation) – a small holder, shoemaker and shipwright, amongst others, swore concerning the wording of the 'cry' but not about the handwriting. The affair was most unsettling when legal advice especially, from leading London lawyers, urged Thomas Lloyd to act with the greatest circumspection in pursuing his claims. Many allegations against Mr Bowen could not be substantiated; the authorship of the proclamation was not proven, and, above all, what was to be avoided in the borough of Newport was the spread of civil unrest. In the spring of 1845, the latent rivalry between Bowen and Lloyd flared upagain by the action of George Goode of Carmarthen, the capable and conscientious agent of the Llwyngwair estate. He, it was alleged, along with a gang of desperadoes had destroyed fences, walls and fences on Newport Common. Goode had '…ridden his horse wildly through standing corn...remarking that he had committed a sufficient trespass for Mr Lloyd to prosecute him a test case…'Adding insult to injury, Goode 'makes great brag that Mr Bowen is determined to pull down every cottage and garden…will do away with the rights of the lord of the manor [Lloyd of Bronwydd], the Mayor and Burgesses altogether.…it is high time this Rebeccaite system should be put a stop to immediately…'according to John Harries of Spring Hill (who was mayor from 1845-50,1861-1863).

The corrosive influence of some outspoken radicals, like Thomas Rees of Brithdir,still prevailed. In 1837, he had refused to pay rent to Thomas Lloyd, on the grounds that the Lord Marcher had no right over his holding. Lloyd brought a court action against Rees and relied on the traditional arguments that his legal title could be traced back to Martin de Tours, and that he had a duty to protect the rights of ordinary people within the barony. Rees was a tenant of the Misses Bowen of Bury and held Brithdir from them; he had enclosed an adjoining piece of land for which he had paid rent to Lloyd at one time but did so no longer. Described as '…that impertinent little cur [who] corrupts the whole them..' Lloyd thought that, by bringing that matter before a court, he could scotch this and any other form of challenge to his authority.

The case opened at Cardigan but was later transferred to Haverfordwest. Such was the public interest and the tense feelings aroused that Lloyd was advised by his London counsel to request a special jury (nine of whom were county gentry) because it was considered that '…the inclination of a common jury will of course be towards their own class…' Thomas Lloyd won the case. The judge had advised the jury to consider whether 'the soil was in the plaintiff or in the burgesses and the homagers…' The latter decided that '…the homagers were only entitled to the herbage…'

The judgement of the court had to be accepted. Nevertheless, old wounds were re-opened and discontent continued. Folk memory could recall how many years since, Bowen of Llwyngwair had claimed that he had in his possession 'records, rolls and other papers' which challenged the claims of the Lord Marcher to chief rents and the privileges alleged by Lloyd of Bronwydd. Indeed, it was in the spring of 1762, that George Bowen had been compelled to appear before the Court of Great Sessions at Haverfordwest, and there produce such documents as he had in his possession. Bowen denied that he had them and his defiance of Bronwydd power was quashed for the time being. But resentment against Bronwydd simmered for generations afterwards. On the other hand, many of the inhabitants of Newport, the mayor and burgesses and those dwelling in the surrounding countryside, were fearful of revolutionary methods which could lead to anarchy. It was openly said that Bowen would wipe out all the courts: courts baron and courts leet and deprive those of them who had been allowed enclosures by Lloyd of Bronwydd. Following the incident when Goode and his men had ridden over growing corn '…poor people who have laboured hard in enclosing gardens and built cottages on the common are greatly afraid of his [Bowen's] proceedings…' remarked one observer.

One persistent troublemaker in the 1850's and 1860's, was a dangerous character by the name of James Thomas, locally known as 'Shemmy'r Halen'. He was responsible for all sorts of criminal acts such as, maiming cattle and livestock, arson, plundering wrecks, destruction of trees and fences, physical assaults against any one who stood in his way or tried to apprehend him. He had had his goods distrained for non-payment of rent, but had been acquitted by the magistrates on criminal charges. He was the scourge of the community. Exasperated by his defiance Thomas Davies Lloyd wrote to Messrs George, solicitors, Cardigan, '…There will be no living with Shemmy on Newport common…put the man's character in the strongest light as to secure punishment by imprisonment…I think Mr Fitzwilliams would manage the affair well for us…Leave no stone unturned to bring this rascal to condign punishment..'[8.]

While the validity of Bronwydd claims and the extent of the 'rule' of the Lord Marcher were issues which brought about unrest and misrule on the part of some radical activists, (especially by some who used the name of Bowen of Llwyngwair as a cloak for their conduct) many were full aware that their own welfare and the future of the town of Newport depended on the acceptance and survival of the lord marchership under Lloyd of Bronwydd. Illiterate and ignorant of their legal rights, and, certainly, without the means to fight any wrong committed against them, the majority of the artisans, peasants, homagers and the 'sans-culotte' of society had always turned to the lord of the barony for redress. The name of 'good Colonel Lloyd' had been spread abroad; his sympathy and 'egwyddor' had become a byword. Like the 'good Sir John [Philipps] of

Picton Castle, he was ready to give ear to those in straightened circumstances: in March 1790, the Reverend Enoch Thomas, curate of Whitchurch (Eglwyswen) and Evan Parry, his church-warden 'invoked the compassion' of Colonel Lloyd, on behalf of one Joseph William, a parishioner '…of sobriety and industry who was in narrow circumstances'. The latter had with 'the assistance of neighbours, and without any place to go, put up one night a small cottage on the common…[and they requested]..that he may retain it unmolested of rent…' And to quote another example, amongst many over the generations: some of the inhabitants of Newport in the 1830's and 1840's had to resort to 'the support and clemency of Thomas Lloyd, the lord of the manor'. Maria Phillips, a poor widow, was greatly concerned to know who her lord of the manor was. Her neighbour, James Thomas, was in a similar plight and unable to pay his rent 'because the times were bad', and the mayor of the town and 'his flunkies' had, in the spring of 1844, compelled one John Jenkins to demolish his garden wall. As a result Williams had no misgiving or fear to write a personal letter to Thomas Lloyd at Bronwydd (like others who many years later made personal appeals to Sir Thomas Davies Lloyd and to Sir Marteine) pointing out that, not least, it was a pity as the 'tatoes had been set and …I humbly beg and pray that of your most Highly Onour to send me an answer of his, that Mr Harries the mayor may be satissfy'd without rising any further disturbance, which I shall wait at Newport P.O…….P.S. If a lection will happen to be for the co. of Pemb.I shall be sure if I live to give my Interest with you for the same'.

Rees of Brithdir, following his defeat in the case of Thomas Lloyd brought against him for non-payment of rent, took revenge on John Thomas, one of the witnesses who gave evidence for Lloyd, by evicting him from a plot of land which he rented from Rees. Thomas petitioned Thomas Lloyd and 'prayed for relief' explaining how he was an honest and industrious man who 'had been seized of a severe illness' and could not support his wife and seven children.

Far from being the despotic lords of the barony which some of the pressure groups in the community had alleged, the Lloyds were the protectors of their homagers within the barony. But the protection, patronage and solicitude of the lord towards those who were his dependants, in their hour of need and in the ordinary circumstances of life, called for their allegiance, deference and loyalty. If it is argued that the liberty of the individual was, in any wise, diminished by manorial custom and irksome feudal dues and services, it was also protected by appeal to the lord. In the period 1805-1811, there took place riotous scenes in Llanfyrnach and Nevern. The perennial problems of the enclosure of plots, the erection of 'tai-unos', cutting of 'matts' (without permission) and the like, were easily resolved and harmonious relations restored, between the lord and offending parties, so long as they obtained permission and paid a small, even a token sum, (as an acknowledgement of the lord's rights), kept their plots tidily fenced in, their gardens well tended and their cottages white-washed.

Very often, the Lord Marcher was faced with a dilemma concerning his manorial rights and those of his homagers (who paid their chief rents) in the face of the general enclosure of land. In July, 1810, a gathering of landed proprietors within the barony of Cemais was held at the Serjeants Inn, Eglwyswrw, to consider application to parliament for further enclosure. When this had come to pass about two years later, Thomas Lloyd called a meeting of his 'homagers' at Mountain Hall, Brynberian, to consider their traditional rights (which he had to defend), and to examine the implications of the act of parliament and to prevent any possible detriment to their welfare. The lord of the barony had to exercise delicate diplomacy in explaining the advantages of a more efficient agriculture – improved drainage, irrigation, manuring, fencing, and the like, which would lead to greater productivity and to the prosperity of all. On the other hand, in some cases, cottagers would lose customary benefits: the right to turbary, pannage, the grazing of sheep and cattle, wood for house building and furniture; and these issues and the welfare of the community had to be considered.[9.] What was all-important in the relationship, was the deference and homage paid to the Lord Marcher, his dignity and status, the actual participation in the 'bonhomie' of family celebrations, fox-hunting, free dinners, beery conviviality, and the spectacular pageantry of the periodic perambulation of the barony, which was reciprocated by the latter's benevolence, patronage and protection.

One of the Lord Marcher's privileges, asserted by George Owen of Henllys, was the right to levy dues and tolls on traders and on the goods they sold in fairs and markets. Like the rest of mankind, the traders and inhabitants of the barony strongly resented taxes, especially those imposed upon them within the barony of Cemais. From time to time, they tried to defeat the system by taking their goods and setting up stalls in 'tax free' places outside Newport. As a result, William Owen of Henllys, in the early seventeenth century, submitted a plea to the sheriff of the county to put a stop to this practice. But, there were other reasons too why trading had to be carried on elsewhere: in 1665, the fairs and markets, usually held at Newport, had to be transferred to Fishguard because of 'sickness and plague'. Thus the inhabitants of Newport lost considerable revenue for many years afterwards.

In September, 1714, some seventy burgesses of Newport, including James Bowen of Llwyngwair, Thomas Knolles, Arthur Laugharne, Thomas Phillips of Pentre Ifan (mayor) and the rector of Dinas, with the approval of the Lord Marcher, issued a proclamation which restored a two day fair to Newport '…where the town could profit from the dues on corn and vendables..' However, on account of strong feeling against paying dues and tolls, certain precautions had to be taken to prevent riotous behaviour, and the breakdown of law and order: '…no person was to wear arms, armour or carry weapons (on pain of forfeiture) other than the sheriff and his officers…'The names of traders had to be entered in the 'Tolsy'[guildhall, borough court house] and the accustomed tolls had to be paid, otherwise their goods would be confiscated. Any person found guilty of causing an affray or misdemeanour would be fined and imprisoned, and any person who was 'aggrieved' in the course of trading was to 'repair to the Tolsy...where the Court of pied Powder order [mandate, decision] shall be indifferently [impartially] heard...'

Because of the administrative costs in collecting tolls, these rights were often rented or leased out by the lord for a fixed sum to individual agents, sometimes tradesmen, who regularly attended fairs and markets: Jacob Picton rented the tolls of Meigan fair at the end of the eighteenth century from Thomas Lloyd of Bronwydd for £12 per annum. Very often, 'irregular and unfair proceedings' with regard to tolls were tried in the courts of the barony outside Newport. What seemed to be purely the role of the mayor and burgesses of Newport and the homagers in the country courts, was, in fact, closely bound up with the authority of the lord of the barony. There were complaints of shady dealings in Newport, and these inevitably were brought to the notice of Thomas Lloyd. In October 1801, John Ladd, the mayor was reprimanded by Lloyd for neglecting to hold courts in the town; notices and proclamations had not been made 'in the churchyard' (as was the custom) and Ladd was told in no uncertain terms '...take notice that I do insist upon you that you appoint your jury from the most respectable Burgesses ...Mr Hassall [Lloyd's agent/steward] tells me that you deny him his Right to the Strays and moiety of the Pitchings. You will remember what I told you at Boncath with regard to them and I here repeat that these being always received formerly by the stewards of the lordship of Kemes are also Mr Hassall's right...'

Opposition to the payment of tolls at Newport and in other parts of the barony simmered again over the next decades, and Thomas Lloyd was faced with a petition by the inhabitants of the town in 1843, to do away with them. He replied that tolls were the '..undoubted right of the lord of the barony...and pecuniary consideration does not weigh heavily...' What was important was that the lord's right had to be respected. The lord had never stood to gain much; the mayor had been allowed a proportion of the tolls collected and this concession extended to the 'ale prise', namely the tax on persons brewing or selling ale within the borough.

Such was the discontent that a rival fair of cattle, horses, sheep and other livestock, was advertised to take place at Maenclochog, in May 1843. Thomas Lloyd considered that this move was illegal and tried to stop it. Its sponsors had assured would-be supporters that no tolls would be charged, and it was hoped that all the farmers would be present. Those who were tenants on the Bronwydd estate were placed in an invidious position; they could not openly defy the lord's wishes; their welfare depended so much on retaining his good will. Were they to put in jeopardy their own interests for the benefit of the mayor of Newport and burgesses, and that of drovers, traders and every brand of itinerant huckster who descended occasionally on the town?. Moreover, if rival fairs were allowed, then the trade of Newport would inevitably suffer and its prestige diminish. Keepers of shops and taverns, wood turners, broom makers, coopers, farmers' wives bringing produce to the fair (a general emporium of consumer goods) along with the gap keeper, beadle, constable, stocks-keeper and turnkey would all be affected. It meant the end of a special event in the social calendar: a holiday for farm servants and country wenches who came to enjoy the excitement of the boxing booth and performing bears, dancing below the castle walls, the ribaldry of tapsters and alehouse crones – the 'fun of the fair' would be lost forever[10].

John Hughes, the mayor during that year, had to act as the intermediary. He organised a public petition to Thomas Lloyd. He himself was prepared to remit all tolls allowed to him; and made flattering remarks about Mr. Lloyd who eventually agreed to 'lift' tolls, on condition that it was clearly understood that he, and he alone, had the sole right to them. After all, the 'pecuniary gain' was negligible. It was admitted that all the 'pitchings' [money charged for setting up a trading tent] had never amounted to much: in 1843, the contemptible sum of 12/6d, and in 1876 only £2-9-3½d.

But the problem of the fairs remained dormant but not dead! In the autumn of 1851, a rival fair was a again arranged at Eglwyswrw, instead of at Pencoed farm, where the lord of the barony was entitled to certain tolls. Thomas and William George, solicitors, acting on behalf of Thomas Davies Lloyd advised that the participants at Eglwyswrw would be liable for damages and that the old fair would eventually be deserted. The situation was serious as the names of prominent cattle dealers from distant places like, Llanddewi-Brefi, Llandovery, Newcastle-Emlyn, and even, Swansea, were listed as supporters of the new fair.

Furthermore, the coming of the railway to Carmarthen in the 1850's, and later to other parts of south west Wales, had, in the words of Fitzwilliams, 'freshened up ye Llandysul folks wonderfully' (amongst others) but apart from the various benefits to commerce (and especially to agriculture in the context of this study) 'railways also remodelled the marketing of livestock in Britain by influencing the decline of the fairs'. No longer were dealers bound to the customs and restraints of local magnates living in a make believe world of mediaeval romanticism. The protests in Newport and in other areas of the barony about tolls, dues and archaic usages, were the minor irritations, typical of a new awakening with far reaching effects on economic, political and social attitudes from the 1850's onwards.

In vain did Thomas Davies Lloyd object to a fair proclaimed by '...so called drovers..' to be held in October 1862, and in vain did his solicitor William Griffith George issue a 'proclamation' that such a fair was illegal, because it was '...not held by grant or prescription...' In time, local livestock fairs declined at Newport, as at other places. The rule of the Lord Marcher had decreased and, by the early twentieth century, his role was limited to picturesque and graphic celebrations of ancient glory... The local fair survived until the 1930's, largely as a day of jollification with all the attendant attractions: stalls displaying china, fruit, tin-ware and household goods, coco-nut shies, shooting galleries, roundabouts, chair-o-planes and all sorts of cheapjacks selling their dubious wares to the accompaniment of the fair ground organ, as described so vividly by Dillwyn Miles. The only link with the fairs of former times was the display of beribboned horses paraded by local farmers[11].

George Owen had listed, amongst the rights and privileges of the Lord Marcher all claims to wrecks along the coast of the barony from Cardigan to Dinas Head. But as in the case of chief rents, tolls and baronial courts, there were rival claimants. Some were country gentry, as well as the ordinary poor inhabitants of the coastal regions trying to eke out a living by, sometimes, sordid and illicit means. The winter storms brought a harvest of ship's timbers, cable and anchor, tuns of wine and spirits, barrels of butter, beef, tallow and other commodities. The lord of the barony had to be constantly on the alert: William Lloyd, formerly of Penpedwast, wrote in February 1740, from Monken Hadley to his son-in-law Thomas Lloyd of Bronwydd and Cilrhiwe in Pembrokeshire, a warning letter pointing out that as deputy to the vice-admiral of south Wales, he knew well the coast from Swansea to Cardigan. No one had the right to question the rights of the Lord Marcher '...the Terror and Noise, Bluster and Nonsense, the Power and Number of any adversarious competitions or their Principal can in no way affect our Rights...effectually affected and maintained by our ancestors...' Expressing strong feelings of resentment against all those who challenged the Lord Marcher with regard to wrecks and the like, he advised that all claimants, be they ordinary folk who had pilfered from wrecked ships, or country gentlemen using their 'pretended authority' should be arrested. Due process of law should follow. They were to be summoned to appear before the 'Chief Constable of the Hundred, Constables, Justices and officers of Customs and the Admiralty'. He suggested Bury as a suitable venue: '...a convenient House for Horse and Man's meat; my tenant 'honest Evan' can't fail [to provide] of Fowl and Bacon and a piece of Mutton with Ale from Newport...' It would be advisable to follow strict rules of procedure, such as obtaining affidavits from the customs officials, and that '...our worthy kinsman George Owen...for 2gns...be retained as counsel...I see no reason why wrongdoers or [any] persons who take away goods cast upon your manor without any colour [claim to] of property may not be indicted for Felony...[but added]...with pacific good temper [to] make an example of some petty rogue...' He was not in favour of using the strong arm of the law against all and sundry, conscious as he was of the needs of the local community who had for centuries gathered on the beaches all sorts of odds and ends which were of use to them. There were other humanitarian considerations too, and while the rights of the lord were not in dispute '...when the men [crew] are saved each one has a right to his own effects[goods]...'

The lord of the barony had to act in conjunction with officers of the crown. He had to employ agents on his behalf and pay any incidental expences incurred by government officials. After one wreck off St. Dogmael's in the 1720's, Evan Rees acting for Lloyd of Penpedwast, submitted his account: -

'The High Constable for 12 days attendance - 12s
Thomas James ye constable of Dinas 4 days - 2s
William Owen of Newport............3 days – 1/6d

and added '...I gave to St. Dogmael's people for weighing ye anchor, in drink 15d. I gave 3 shill [-ings] to Fishguard men for bringing ye anchor over from Godwick. I spent myself 10d...' Sometimes, after a shipwreck arguments arose when the captain refused to sell anything other than perishable goods: meat already in bad condition, biscuits and other foodstuffs. And as Rees explained to Thomas Lloyd, he was sometimes lucky to buy salted beef for 1d a pound[12].

In the business of claiming wrecks, the lord had to employ reliable agents to keep an eye on the shores of the barony which was so distant from the lord's mansion houses of Bronwydd and Cilrhiwe. Consequently 'wreck cautions' were displayed all along every beach, giving stern warning against any breach of the lord's prerogative and any threat to his claims. There had to be close co-operation too, between the lord's representative and the Custom House at Cardigan. The matter of ownership and rightful disposal of items cast up on the shore caused disputes, for example: Quantities of 'Balk' had been cast up on the shore at Newport and no one had come forward to claim it. Following another great storm in November, 1833, the 'Zephyr of Belfast' had foundered on the Tuscar Rocks. It was 'bunged up with Tallow casks' which were washed up at various points on the Pembrokeshire coast.

Again, in 1833, William Raymond, a vigilant tidewaiter reported to the Reverend Watkin Thomas, rector of Dinas (a Bronwydd living) who had close contact with Mr. Lloyd, that '...an elegant flute with silver keys...' had been found by two quarrymen on the beach at Dinas. It transpired that they had sold the flute to a Mr. Frost, a 'dealer in flutes' at Haverfordwest, who had not enquired too diligently whose property it was. The rector interrogated Mr. Frost, pointing out that Mr. Lloyd of Bronwydd was the true owner of 'wrecks of the sea', and a charge of receiving stolen goods could be brought against him. Frost pleaded that he was innocent and a man of good reputation who traded with the principal gentry of Pembrokeshire: Mr. Bowen of Manorowen, Mr. Allen of Cresselly, Mr. Tucker of Sealyham, Major Harris and Capt. Probert.

Mr. Frost craved the pardon and indulgence of Mr. Lloyd; he had nine children to provide for and had never involved himself in unfair practices. In due course, the rector reported the facts to Thomas Lloyd at Bronwydd. The flute case had been recovered, but the flute itself had been sent to London (ostensibly to be repaired). Mr. Frost was in a real pickle; 'magisterial process' had been set in motion '…all because he had bought for a few pounds a few Pandean pipes…!' Frost, a man of some intelligence, had consulted weighty legal authorities like Burn's Justice and Blackstone's Commentaries which confirmed that the lord of the barony had no legal title to the property in question, but rather than offend Mr. Lloyd (and, perhaps, lose the trade of many of the other country gentry) he was prepared to make restitution. But, nothing more is recorded of the fate of Mr. Frost nor of the silver flute[13].

In August 1834, John James of Veidrgerigog, in the parish of Newport, had found a ship's pump on Traeth Mawr and had sold it privately for £1-5s. Mr. George, the solicitor, was told to investigate the matter, but was not able to obtain any solid evidence to prosecute James in court. There were other instances too: a piece of ship's Balk, about 20 feet in length, was washed up on a rock. The tidewaiter at Cardigan had to be informed, but as it was too difficult to shift it had to be left to its fate. No one profited this time, but occasionally, the lord of the barony as well as the local inhabitants derived some items of use and value from such wrecks: tallow, for example, could be used to make soap and candles and to grease the axles of carriages and farm wagons. Certainly, this applied to the lord's establishment at Bronwydd and elsewhere; a local fishwife might find a piece of wrecked timber worth 1/6d. But, barrels of beef or biscuits were often in such a bad condition as to be utterly valueless. On the other 'hand, cordage, large lengths of balk, yellow pine, a boat complete with oars, a wicker trunk, a ladies hand basket, cartloads of firewood, a bowsprit, a 50 feet long mast, walnut and American elm', as well as a whole array of various items listed as 'salvage' were always eagerly sought after.

In terms of actual monetary value, some of what was cast up, on the shores of the lordship of Cemais, was not considerable. Nevertheless, the claims of the Lord Marcher were symbolic of his power, prestige and social standing, which had to be preserved, as essential elements to reinforce the 'interest' of the lord in the county. There were disadvantages: the employment of agents who depended on tell-tale in formers and neighbour spying against neighbour, and legal questions could arise with disputes between the Lord Marcher's employees and the customs men; the opinion of local attorneys and London counsel had to be sought and paid for out of estate revenues.

As with other aspects of the Lord Marcher's 'rule', there was a latent feeling of dissent which erupted to open challenge by the officers of the excise, as well as, by the general public. Such grumblings took place from the 1840's onwards, a period when Thomas Davies Lloyd was asserting his status, more and more, as Lord Marcher. Claims to wrecks by Lloyd brought him into conflict with Thomas Harries, the local Receiver of Wrecks. Unfortunately, for Lloyd, the best legal opinion clearly advised that he was not entitled to '…things in the water, lagan [goods and wreckage lying on the sea bed], flotsam and jetsam…all of which were Admiralty Perquisites, and that the most that he is entitled to are things which are derelict and which have been left by the sea…' Much to the chagrin of Mr. Lloyd (and many others living on the Pembrokeshire shores) casks of wine and brandy bobbing up and down in the water could not be claimed; and it is rather significant that these items are hardly mentioned in the inventories of items 'thrown up by the sea'!

Thomas Davies Lloyd was unrelenting in pursuing his claims: he distributed printed posters containing parts of a charter granted by Nicholas Fitzmartin and confirmed by Queen Elizabeth; aged witnesses answered his summons to swear that they had handled wrecks in the past for his father and grandfather, the lords of the barony. His solicitor brought ancient deeds and documents to prove that his claims were based not only on royal charter, but on well established precedents. In order to resolve matters, a gathering of Commissioners of the Board of Trade met in conference at Llwyngwair, the home of his rivals, the Bowens, and after much deliberation agreed that Mr. Lloyd had a right to any wreck lying <u>on</u> the beach, and to that alone.

By 1860, the Board of Trade offered to pay the Lord Marcher a fixed sum, arising out of sale of unclaimed wreck, provided that such remained for twelve months in the hands of the Receiver of Wrecks. In 1868, the gross proceeds derived from wreck amounted to £14-13-10d; cost of salvage and other incidental expences came to £10-19-2d, leaving a net profit of 3-14-8d[14].

From now on, the Bronwydd papers are silent on the matter of wrecks!

The 'Governance of Newport'

ii

As the historian of Newport has explained, the first mayor of the town of whom there is any record was Richard Suetman, in his capacity as '...proposito de novo burgo' who witnessed a charter of Nicholas Martin about 1278. Apparently, the office of 'propositus' or 'reeve' had been in existence for many years since the charter granted by the Fitzmartins. After 1500, the chief citzen was referred to as 'mayor' and was chosen by the lord of Cemais from a list of four names of burgesses, submitted by a Grand Inquisition of jurors selected at the Court Leet and View of Frankpledge. In the history of the Lloyds of Bronwydd, courts leet and courts baron played a vital part in their 'rule' as Lords Marcher, and the mayor of Newport (the 'caput' of the barony) was an official of great consequence to uphold and sustain the Lord Marcher's dignity and prestige. The appointed mayor swore on oath that he would exercise his office 'well and truly, honestly and do equal right to poor and rich'. These were noble ideals, but not always observed in practice: some mayors and their officials were negligent, haphazard in their methods or downright dishonest. Indeed, they were a motley crowd. George Owen had complained in 1626, that he had lost more than £300 in rent, tolls and other dues, through the failure or refusal of successive mayors to collect them.

Another problem which appeared, time and time again, was the illegal enclosure of commons, annexation of burgage lands and infringement of the liberties of the crown to the detriment of the Lord of Cemais. Local gentry like Bowen of Llwyngwair and Warren of Trewern had been fomenting disaffection against Lloyd. The choice of mayor often led to jealousy and rivalry, and to rough tactics and violence. When, the barony of Cemais was acquired in the mid-eighteenth century by Lloyd of Bronwydd, local gentry looked with envy at the new Lord Marcher's position, especially, with regard to the appointment of the mayor. In order not to cause friction, George Bowen of Llwyngwair took a diplomatic course by suggesting that Lloyd's nominee, one James Bateman, was to be chosen mayor for the period 1749-50 to be succeeded by David Davies (Bowen's nominee) in 1750-1751. He ended his letter by expressing concern about Mr. Lloyd's 'gout' and added his 'compliments and best respects [to] yourself and cousins...'

But the goodwill was not to last. Not without reason were the local and county gentry alarmed by the claims of Lloyd of Bronwydd. He had revived baronial or manorial courts which, in many instances, had become obsolete relics of the middle ages. They were useful for deciding boundaries, registering identification marks on sheep, preventing the indiscriminate cutting of 'matts' on common land or unofficial enclosure of plots, keeping a wary eye on wrecks and the erection of storehouses and limekilns along the Parrog and elsewhere. But, to claim the loyalty and deference, the vassal's obligation and fealty to an overlord (with serious consequences in the balance of political interest in Pembrokeshire) was more than many could stomach!

In October 1759, rivalry with regard to the appointment of the mayor of Newport led to a disturbance at a meeting of the Court Leet held in the dwellinghouse of David Davies. Things had got completely, out of hand that the poll was adjourned by Lewis David, the mayor at the time. A month later, the names of two candidates were put forward: Lewhellin John William, the younger, a mariner, and John Griffiths, miller. The former was George Bowen's nominee, and received thirty four votes out of thirty nine cast. He was duly declared victor by Lewis David who attested the appointment 'by mark'. A few days later, George Bowen wrote to Thomas Lloyd about the trouble that had taken place in connection with the appointment of the mayor, stating that he had supported his tenants '...a duty incumbent on him...' against Lloyd's choice (John Griffiths, the miller). Bowen went further and questioned the '...ancient rights and privileges of the Burgesses of Newport and the Lord of the Manor, if such there are?' – In a letter to Lloyd and he wrote that he, Bowen, desired to maintain friendship with his neighbours and every gentleman of his acquaintance. '...you may say that you have a right to the nomination of the Mayor thro uninterrupted custom of so doing time out of mind...' and, whereas, a prescriptive right was infallible in the absence of a law or evidence to the contrary '...a long series of an abusive custom and unwarrantable proceedings cannot, in my humble opinion, destroy the words of a very ancient charter...it is in your power only to bring this matter to an amiable decision, or to a determination by law; the choice shall be yours. I've only one to wish the former, and in that hope I rest...'

The former cordial relations were now at breaking point. Bowen signed the letter formally 'Yr. Obedient and Humble Servant', none of the polite pleasantries of previous correspondence, save a P. S. 'My wife's best Compliments and my own attend yr. Lady and family...'[15]. No doubt, Lloyd's increasing influence was causing alarm throughout the length and breadth of the barony, above all in Newport itself. While matters had been fairly quiet during the dual ownership of the barony, in the days of Elizabeth and Anne Owen at the beginning of the century, things were changing – Lloyd was an avid purchaser of land; he was making greater and greater claims to dues and tolls; he was enclosing more and more acres, he could increase rents and there was always the possibility of discovering mines and minerals on his increasingly larger estate. As has been suggested, his political influence would also be enhanced.

In August 1761, recurring disputes about the choice of mayor of Newport had to be settled in an action at the General Sessions sitting at Haverfordwest. Thomas Hinton or Henton and Llewellin John Williams, mayors during the years 1759-1761, were called to answer on what grounds they had held the office. This resulted in an unpleasant dispute between George Bowen and Thomas Lloyd; and, because Bowen had persistently queried Lloyd's right to choose the mayor (according to ancient tradition, it is true) it was only proper for Bowen to produce any evidence, he had against Lloyd. Bowen had to admit that he was not in possession of any '...rules and documents...' But the dispute dragged on for some years. Hinton was accused of '...unsurping the office of mayor...' and Thomas Lloyd could not avoid becoming embroiled in the fracas. In the spring of 1764, when John Griffiths (the Bronwydd nominee) was mayor, the burgesses passed a resolution that '...Thomas Lloyd, Esq. lord of the manor allow persons to inspect rolls, records, charters and papers in his custody, power and possession re the boro of Newport, and that in the meantime all proceedings in this cause to stay...' Such items of evidence were to be examined by Richard Knethall, gent. David Lewis, gent. and Willam Thomas, gent. This was an added indignity to the Lord Marcher; the audacity of the burgesses to question the authority of the lord of Cemais was beyond belief!

Patronage and the corresponding deference of the lord were the key elements in the frequent disputes which took place, especially those about the choice of mayor. In fairness to Bowen, Llwyngwair, he had no personal ambitions to become mayor. By 1781-82 another Thomas Lloyd had succeeded to the barony, and in order to build bridges between opposing sides, Bowen suggested (in a letter to Thomas Mathais the foreman of the jury) that his name, and those of David Davies (the old mayor) and Jacob Picton be included in the list as candidates. He added '...that Jacob Picton, Mrs. Lloyd's tenant and friend, should be mayor'. If everything went well, according to his suggestion, he would give the jury 'ten shillings in drink...otherwise not a farthing of the 10s [was] to be given to the jury to drink as I don't wish or want to be Mayor but only wish it may be kept, if Mrs. Lloyd pleases, among the freeholders, landholders and inhabitants of the town and parish of Newport...' Jacob Picton was consequently elected mayor and held the office from 1782-1784[16].

With regard to the right to hold baronial courts, impose chief rents, tolls and the like (facets of the 'rule' of the Lord Marcher) the response and compliance of tenants, homagers and the entire community of dependents were inevitably affected by economic, social and political factors. The Lord Marcher claimed to be the 'fount' of authority; he had his functionaries: the mayor, burgesses of Newport, stewards, bailiffs, and other officials. Complaints and grievances had to be heard, and, very often, the lord had to possess the wisdom of Solomon to decide between rival factions and the intrigue and malice of 'parish pump politics'. This was the case in the election of the mayor in 1826 and later in 1837, when he proposed his nominee against that of the court leet. From 1826-28 there were two mayors Thomas Williams of Dolrannog (nominated by the court leet) and William Wigley (appointed by the lord) and in 1837 the lord of Cemais and his officials were compelled by writ to appoint a mayor, Thomas Williams, out of three names put forward. Not only was there rivalry between Bowen of Llwyngwair and Lloyd of Bronwydd, but also between the warring factions within the town itself. This was particularly evident in the years 1823-1843. Because there was, sometimes, no agreement about matters relating to the administration of the town, appeal was made to Mr. Lloyd at Bronwydd, for example, the corporation pound was in disrepair in 1823, and the question arose who was responsible for restoring it – the parish, the mayor and corporation or the lord of the manor?

An estimate had been obtained from David Salmon of Coedwinog, Nevern, and the total cost was £5 for cartloads of stone from the mountain @ 9d a load, a 'lighter' [a large open barge] of flagstones from the 'Quarry', stones from the Beach, labourers and gateposts. Who paid in the end is not known, but it most likely that all bills arrived sooner or later at Bronwydd or Cilrhiwe.

Rival candidates for the office of mayor continued to be a source of aggravation to the Lord Marcher. This was particulary the situation in the 1830's and 40's. Added to the problems concerning the mayoralty was the unrest of burgesses who claimed their right to fish the river Nevern 'irrespective of what the lord might think', amongst other demands. There was intense competition too, between the various factions – to have control of the tolls and dues and all sorts of 'vails' on the side, to hold office from that of mayor

1.

2.

3.

4.

5.

6.

7.

8.

10.

9.

11.

12.

13.

14.

15.

16.

17.

18.

19.

20.

21.

23.

22.

TO THE GLORY OF GOD
AND
IN EVER LOVING MEMORY OF
SIR MARTEINE OWEN MOWBRAY LLOYD. BART.
25TH LORD MARCHER OF KEMES.
ONLY CHILD OF
SIR THOMAS D. LLOYD. BART. 24TH LORD OF KEMES.
BORN FEB. 8TH 1851 - DIED APRIL 4TH 1933 - AGED 82 YEARS.
"IN WHOM IS NO GUILE."

HE WAS A CAPTAIN IN THE PEMBROKESHIRE YEOMANRY, CAVALRY.
A DEPUTY LIEUTENANT FOR CARDIGAN, CARMARTHEN AND PEMBROKE.
A STEWARD OF THE NATIONAL HUNT COMMITTEE FROM 1918-1922,
AND M.H. FOR OVER 50 YEARS.

ALSO IN MEMORY OF HIS BELOVED WIFE
KATHARINE HELENA,
DAUGHTER OF THE LATE ALEXANDER DENNISTOUN OF GOLFHILL.
BORN JULY 6TH 1857 - DIED MARCH 25TH 1937.

24.

25.

26.

27.

28.

29.

30.

31.

32.

33.

34.

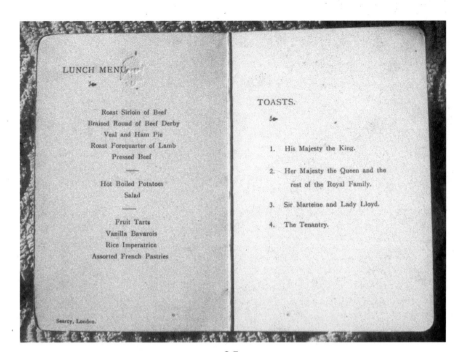

LUNCH MENU

Roast Sirloin of Beef
Braised Round of Beef Derby
Veal and Ham Pie
Roast Forequarter of Lamb
Pressed Beef

———

Hot Boiled Potatoes
Salad

———

Fruit Tarts
Vanilla Bavarois
Rice Imperatrice
Assorted French Pastries

Searcy, London.

TOASTS.

1. His Majesty the King.

2. Her Majesty the Queen and the rest of the Royal Family.

3. Sir Marteine and Lady Lloyd.

4. The Tenantry.

35.

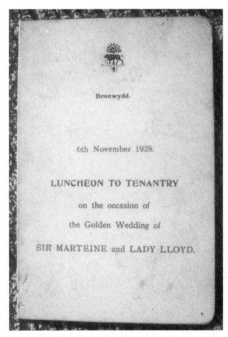

Bronwydd.

6th November 1928.

LUNCHEON TO TENANTRY

on the occasion of

the Golden Wedding of

SIR MARTEINE and LADY LLOYD.

36.

37.

38.

39.

Ground Plan of Brunwydd

Legend:
- (hatched) 18C and earlier
- (white) 1853 - 1856 additions

Porch

Baronial Hall

Main Staircase

Dining Room

Drawing Room

Smoking Room

Little Dining Room

Butler's Pantry

Tower Room

Bell Tower

25 ft.

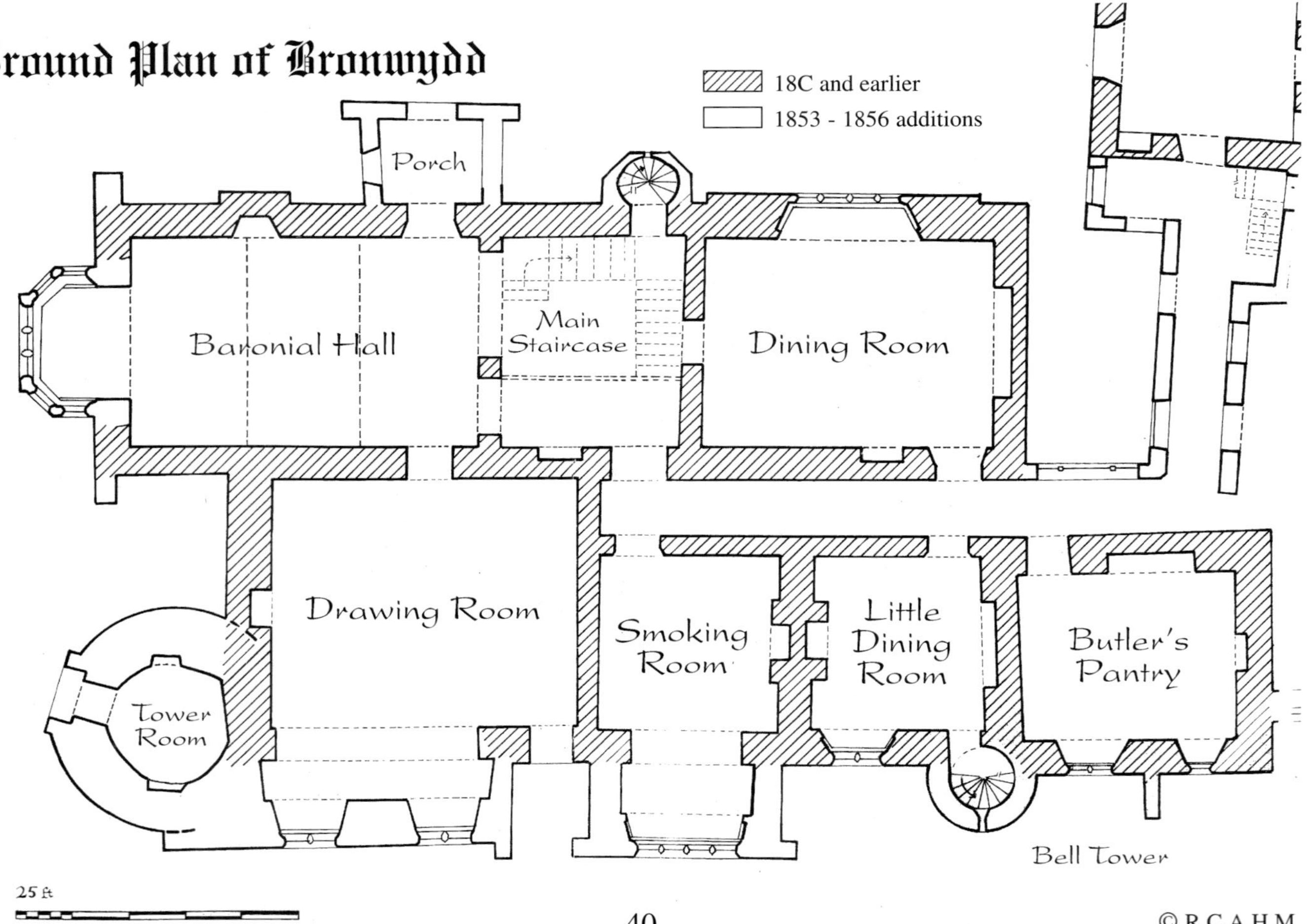

40.

© R.C.A.H.M.

downwards, to cultivate the good favour of the lord of the barony and participate in the petty pageantry of an ancient, albeit run-down township.

At worst, the situation was at times a corrupt gangland scene – plots and counter plots. John Havard had 'money paid down for the mayorship', and bitterly resented his rejection. In 1832, the Reverend Watkin Thomas drew up a petition to Thomas Lloyd in favour of William Harry or Harries of Trecadifor, 'an honest man and likely to support the interests of the lord of the manor.' Neither was elected because John Owen, a rival and untrustworthy character had managed to get his name put forward. He had been dishonest in acquiring parcels of land for himself without paying; he had forged Thomas Lloyd's signature and had falsified certain legal documents. In spite (or through) his shady dealings he held the office of mayor in 1833-1834. He tried to meddle in public affairs when John David Hughes was mayor in 1834-1835. Thomas Lloyd had regarded him as '...being rather an illiterate person...'

There was a genuine concern amongst many of the inhabitants that their holdings might be taken from them by the lord of the manor. Some claimed a prescriptive right to them and were happy to pay chief rent, but only that. Through Edward Rees (mayor in 1838-1841) Thomas Lloyd was informed of the feelings current in and around Newport, and he very tactfully advised Lloyd not to show any 'spirit of revenge in his breast' by demolishing all fences put up by those who over a long period had worked hard on their gardens and cottages. Rees wrote to Mrs. Lloyd at Bronwydd and informed her that, in spite of the hostile and vindictive feeling in the parish against paying church rates, many were ready to paint the church at Newport. Moreover, there were great possibilities for the town and the community. In view of the plans afoot to develop Fishguard harbour, Thomas Lloyd should attend the meetings of Newport Harbour Board to raise at the highest level, in parliament itself, the claims of Newport to have '...a packet station and a harbour of refuge...' there. The case for Newport should be canvassed through Trinity House and 'the under writers and merchants at Lloyd's Coffee House'. In fact, Rees went as far as to express '...the sanguine hope of a new town on Rhos Dinas by the name of Tre-Llwyd [Lloyd's Town],...' He referred to Rees of Brithdir (a persistent trouble maker) as a 'crotchey old character...but would that his son and wife were blown sky high...!

When John Owen died in March 1846, the mayor John Harries commented in a letter to Thomas Davies Lloyd '...I hope in future that the Homagers of Newport may be more pliable for I well know that John Owen only did sow discord between landlord and tenant on the Common of Newport...' He was also aware of the controversy in the town with regard to having 'the fairs and pitchings toll free'. Not only that, he was trying to feather his own nest by suggesting to Thomas Davies Lloyd in October, 1845, that he was willing '...to collect all the pitching [toll] that can be got in the fairs,... and I shall be most happy to be appointed to the office of Mayor...' Within a few weeks his wish was granted. In addition, he was allowed a generous portion of the tolls.

For the time being, ill feeling died down in spite of the discontent about tolls and pitchings after Thomas Davies Lloyd paid his first official visit to Newport, the 'caput' of his barony. The inhabitants had been won over by 'his suavity of manner' with the result that the 'commoners' had become 'tractable and conciliatory..' One commentator summed up their feelings thus '...There was a time in the old feudal wars when the people were obliged to fight for the Lord of the Manor, [and] if this were necessary they were ready to shed their blood for the heir [T.D.LL.) of Bronwydd...'[17.]

It has become clear that Newport, like many small municipal corporations throughout the land, was governed by a small and close obligarchy or vestry. Honesty and efficiency in the administration of the town were sadly lacking. Deference to the lord of the barony and further down the social scale, from mayor to the lowest flunky, bred dishonesty, flattery and servility. And while the Lloyds of Bronwydd could be proud of a long tradition of magnanimity towards the inhabitants of the town of Newport and the lordship of Cemais, it has to be remembered that they were dealing with a largely uneducated and illiterate class of people. The mayor in 1759-1760, was Lewis David alias Lewis George who could not write and most likely could not read. In 1845, those who had any claim to govern the town comprised a mixture of boatmen, 'captains' of small craft, porters, shoemakers, weavers and labourers. The idea of democratic rule was incomprehensible to many, if not to most of them, and the choice of a competent chief citizen very limited.

The passing of the first parliamentary Reform Act of 1832, led to the setting up of a Commission of Enquiry into the state of Municipalities in England and Wales. Newport was not exempt. This placid backwater was stirred and all its abuses, anomalies, corrupt practices were brought to the surface.

The Commissioners of Enquiry into municipal corporations wanted answers to many questions: the limits and boundaries of the town, the terms of its charters; its constitution and its officers –mayor, bailiff, aldermen, burgesses, and the nature of their responsibilities, the town's civil and criminal jurisdiction, its population and their occupations, and its source of revenue.

The total number of burgesses in 1833 was 420; the mayor was the head constable who received no salary except certain tolls and one shilling upon the admission of each new burgess, and at the end of his period in office became an alderman. The town had no civil or criminal court, and no gaol.

Clearly, there were glaring irregularities, especially with regard to the appointment of mayor and the nature and extent of his powers, as well as his function as head constable. By what authority he carried out the functions of magistrate like his predecessors in the past had not been made clear. An act passed in 1535, had laid down that 'no person shall have any power or authority to make...any Justice of the Peace...except by Letters patent under the King's

Great Seal in the name of and by authority of the King's Highness and his heirs...' George Owen had conveniently ignored the statute, and the irregularity had been condoned by successive Lords Marcher over the centuries. Between April and September 1835, the mayor and burgesses had to make answer to the Home Secretary, Lord John Russell – upon what grounds did the borough of Newport claim exemption from contributing to the county rate? Was this claim based on a charter or on an act of parliament? Was there a borough treasurer? How and where were criminals and offenders in matters of public concern examined, sentenced and imprisoned? To these and a multiplicity of other questions there was no satisfactory answer.

Never before had ancient customs and traditional loyalties been challenged. The rule of the Lord Marcher and the influence of other gentry (like George Bowen of Llwyngwair) who manupilated the system for their own ends, by buying votes for their own nominee as mayor and against the Lord Marcher, was shaken to its foundations.

As happened so often in the history of the Lloyds, expert legal advice had to be sought; the ancient charters were studied; the jurisdiction of courts leet and courts baron were examined in relation to the legal system of the land; writs of 'quo-warranto' from the courts of Great Sessions in Pembrokeshire were quoted. The status and authority of the mayor, acting on behalf of the Lord Marcher, raised further question: could he issue distress warrants when rent was in arrear? Mr.Lloyd '...was desirous of granting leases on parts of the enclosed common particularly to some of his friends there...' The opinion of counsel, Robert Vaughan Richards, caused dismay: there was no charter regulating this borough (specifically, with regard to the appointment of the mayor as a Justice of the Peace and the exercise of his power in a legal capacity, even allowing that, as first citizen, he was expected to 'do equal right to the poor and to the rich'). The custom of swearing in the mayor at Quarter Sessions or before two justices of the peace could not be upheld. With regard to any debts arising from the sale of goods, non-payment of rent, trespass, throwing open enclosures and the like, Mr. Lloyd was entitled to seek redress through a civil court '...not as Lord [of Cemais] but as landlord...' like every other citizen of the realm.

The borough remained unreformed by the Municipal Corporations Act: the archaic anomalies remained; the old rivalry between those who were for the lord, and those against him (intermixed with new radical sentiments) continued; nepotism, bribery and favouritism were to survive for the rest of the century. But the burgesses were formidable fighters and quoted ancient precedents: the mayor had held the office of justice of the peace from time immemorial. In 1848, John Harries, the mayor (a Bronwydd favourite) had 'committed a vagrant to the House of Correction at Haverfordwest. Moreover, three vagrants described as '...Rogues and Vagabonds for having maliciously broken several windows...' were sentenced by the mayor to two months hard labour. This action had ruffled the feathers of the county magistrates who considered proceedings against John Harries for 'false [wrongful] imprisonment'. They conceded that, in times past, mayors of towns had ordered people to be put in the stocks but not to prison for felony; and, quoting Blackstone and other learned authorities, the mayor (of a town) or 'prepositus, custos and conservator pacis' had only quasi-legal duties to maintain good behaviour and prevent lawlessness. In 1848, however, the mayor of Newport was not a Justice of the Peace, but '...human memory and custom might construe his action as that of a Justice of the Peace but he [John Harries] has not acted judicially...'

Because the status of the town had not been settled by the Municipal Corporations Act, disputes and disaffection rumbled on for years. Wherever Thomas Davies Lloyd was at his home Bronwydd or in London or travelling abroad, sooner or later the problems of Newport were referred back to him. In 1861, pressure was brought upon him by John Harries of Spring Hill and the Court Leet to use his influence to obtain a Common Council for the town. Once more dusty deeds and documents were brought out and examined; the old arguments were used, ad nauseam – the traditional privileges of the burgesses, the unique status of the Lord Marcher, and so on.

This time Mr. Roundell Palmer, QC. replied that the answer to all their questions and arguments was, No! The constitution of the Corporation could not be altered except on the authority of the Crown and under acts of parliament relating to municipal corporations. But, there was more: the effect of a new charter would be to bring Newport within the provisions of the Mucipal Corporations Reform Act, and under any amended charter Mr.Lloyd's power to appoint the mayor would not be confirmed, but would, on the contrary, be wholly taken away. Mr Lloyd could apply to Parliament for a special act, but was advised not to '.....as I think that there would be no chance of the application succeeding....!'[18.]

During the next few years several events, both locally and nationally, were to change attitudes in the town of Newport – Thomas Davies Lloyd had been honoured with a baronetcy in 1863 (and entertained high hopes of a peerage) and he was a member of parliament. The matter of tolls and pitchings, dues and other relics of the Lord Marcher's feudal power, were no longer of first importance. There were far greater issues at stake. The inhabitants of Newport were, doubtless, becoming better informed, through the 'parliamentary intelligence' columns of weekly newspapers, preacher's sermon and the drover's tap-room chatter about votes for all, water supplies, proper sanitation, libraries, lighting, cleansing of streets, rubbish removal and all sorts of improvements in towns.

Although Sir Thomas Davies Lloyd publicly advocated the education of the lower classes and their right to vote, he and his gentry neighbours were alarmed by radical moments which threatened to undermine the established order in church and state.

It is not insignificant that the gentry were forced by circumstances to close ranks. They had to bend or break; narrow-minded, ignorant and often corrupt oligarchies could not be propped up any more by the local magnate. There was a remarkable rapprochement between Bowen of Llwyngwair and Lloyd of Bronwydd: in 1870-1872, James Bevan Bowen, MP was chosen as mayor of Newport, described as a 'model land-lord and highly respectable'. Sir Thomas Davies Lloyd was happy to congratulate him, '...three hundred years had passed since a member of the Llwyngwair family had had the honour..'

Notwithstanding, the alliance between Bronwydd and Llwyngwair, the influence in high places of Sir Thomas Davies Lloyd and James Bevan Bowen, the town could not stave off the scrutiny of another Commission of Enquiry into the state of municipal corporations not subject to the Municipal Corporations Act. Sir Thomas Davies Lloyd died in 1877, when the enquiry had only just started. The report (published in 1880) repeated most of what had been discovered in 1835, about the origins of the borough in Norman times, its charters, traditions, and in particular, the rôle of the Lord Marcher, the perambulations, courts leet and courts baron. There was nothing new, except that the mayors seemed to be appointed from a rather different sort of person: the rector of the parish, nonconformist ministers, professional people, such as, Dr. David Havard, MD, retired masters of ships, like, Capt Williams Evans and, even, an MP, in addition to shopkeepers and tradesmen who had special knowledge of the needs of the town.

The mayor continued to receive tolls from the two annual fairs: for a horse 2/6d, a beast 5d, two beasts 4d each, three or more 3d each, one pig 1d. Burgesses were exempt from paying tolls, but paid 2/6 to the jury of the Court Leet on admission. The commons around Newport were about 10 miles in circumference, and the commoners had the right to cut turf, but quarrying stones was illegal as the lord was the owner of the soil. The manorial courts dealt with disputes relating to the rights of turbary, pasture, strays and the like, as it had done for centuries. Sir Thomas Davies Lloyd took no steps to enforce tolls, and those on cattle had been discontinued by him. The mayor still took his oath at Quarter Sessions, but could not act 'judicially' as a magistrate. However, he was permitted to take depositions concerning paupers and sign passports by 'right of delegation from the Foreign Office'.

Sir Stephen Cave, MP, chairman of the Commission, reacted very unfavourably to a witness statement that 'Sometimes the mayor exercised jurisdiction and sometimes not!'.

Thomas Davies Lloyd was informed by the Commissioners that '...as there were county magistrates, sitting within the borough every two months, there was no point in keeping the mayor.' No committal of vagrants to prison had taken place since 1838; the mayor and burgesses had nothing to do with the appointment of magistrates.

Among other criticisms of the administration of the borough, of which the office of mayor was central, it was observed that there was no public audit of accounts and the mayor had no jurisdiction to grant licenses to public houses. The prestige of the Lord Marcher was further dented when the Commissioners, especially the chairman Sir Stephen Cave, dismissed his baronial claims and the antediluvian 'privileges and immunities' of Newport, as granted by ancient charter. A 'mandamus' (a judicial writ from the King's Bench division) in 1838 was quoted, recognising the corporation of Newport as an existing body and compelling them to fulfil duties limited under the charter and the ancient customs of the town. Sir Thomas Davies Lloyd did not live to see the Municipal Corporations (Unreformed) Bill come before parliament. Sir Marteine had now to fight on behalf of Newport, the status of the mayor and his own, (according to tradition) unique position as Lord Marcher. He submitted a petition to the Lords Spiritual and Temporal, for the retention of the ancient privileges of the borough when the Bill came before parliament. Repeating arguments which had been put forward so many times before, and realising that he was fighting a lost cause, the steward of the barony, William Griffith George, admitted that the borough had no local funds nor property, and that the 'only thing they wanted to retain was the right to appoint a mayor by the Lord Marcher of Kemeys…a unique privilege for the appointed mayor and the Lord Marcher,[and] highly prized by his ancient family..' Other prominent Pembrokeshire figures gave their support, for example, William Davies, MP for Pembrokeshire in a speech before the House of Commons and Lord Kensington urged that the claims of the Lloyd family ought to be respected and its loyalty to the Liberal Party should be considered. The late Sir Thomas Davies Lloyd had sat as a Liberal member of parliament and it would be a '…great blow to Liberal county gentlemen to see a Liberal ministry despoiling their Liberal friends…' There was so much in favour of respecting and retaining the status quo: corporation meetings lessened litigation; the mayor sat as a JP. and thereby, had a moral influence on the inhabitants, provided arbitration in local disputes and '…as there is [as the mayor has] no control over criminal matters it is harmless.. as an interesting relic of antiquity….'

And so it remained for the time being, - Levi Griffiths, of Mauritius, was installed as mayor in 1899 (in the absence of Sir Marteine Lloyd) by the deputy-mayor, John Williams, Cross House, a chemist. Public spirited inhabitants, like Capt. William Davies, who established the Town and Parrog Improvements Fund, held the office. Eminent county gentry like John Wynford Phillips (later Viscount St. Davids) and Marteine Kemes Arundel Lloyd, Sir Marteine's son and heir, were admitted as burgesses. Mr (later Sir) George B. Bowen, of Llwyngwair, was mayor in 1913-1914. When Capt. Dillwyn Miles was chosen as mayor in 1950, he presented the Lady Marcher, Miss Morfa Withington with a red rose, thus reviving and ancient custom, when the burgesses paid this, a token rent, to the Lord Marcher on the feast of St. John the Baptist.

The custom and ceremonial still continue. Legislation which was passed by parliament at the end of the nineteenth century: the Local Government Act of 1888 and another act in 1894, brought about local government by county and parish councils, the latter replacing the parish vestry. But, the Municipal Corporations Act of 1883 stated that '..nothing in this Act shall be deemed to prevent the election of the Mayor of Newport (Pembroke) as heretofore, or to dissolve the corporation of Newport (Pembroke) or deprive the lord of the Manor or the Burgesses of any tolls, rights of common, or other rights of a pecuniary value...'

Notwithstanding later legislation in the twentieth century, the Court Leet and Court Baron still meet twice a year, and a third court takes place in November, for the installation of the mayor: a quaint and interesting relic of antiquity and of the display and pageantry of long ago, perpetuated by the presentation of a red rose: a symbol of ancient allegiance and loyalty.[19.]

The Lost Peerage

iii

George Owen of Henllys had claimed that '...the Martins were Lordes of parliament by the name of the Lords of Cemais...' The Lloyd family of Bronwydd were, no doubt, aware of many of the glamorous traditions attached to the Lord Marcher and the barony of Cemais, especially after Thomas Lloyd acquired the whole of it in the 1750's. It was, however, not until many years later that the full significance of the lord marchership became of paramount importance to them and most of all to Thomas Davies Lloyd. He was strongly influenced by the intellectual and cultural movements of the time: antiquarianism and romanticism, as expressed in art, architecture, genealogy, literature and other aspects of 'Victorian' culture which he had come across at Harrow and at Christ Church, Oxford where John Ruskin was also an undergraduate. Claiming as the Lloyds did, descent from the Welsh princes and Norman knights, they wished to retain their place and status in society.

The prestige and values of the landed classes who had ruled the countryside for centuries were being eroded and even attacked by the influx of those who had 'new wealth' from the 'dark Satanic mills' of business and industry. These newcomers had the money to purchase land and thereby, to possess the key to social advancement and power as expressed publicly in the 'county' offices of magistrate, sheriff, deputy and lord lieutenant, and with the right support, as members of parliament. These 'advenae' knew little of custom and inherited beliefs. They were bankers, lawyers, owners of slaves in the plantations of the Indies, excise men and others who traded in gold. But, although they had money and had bought land from Welsh gentry (albeit impoverished) of ancient stock, they lacked the insignia and mores of gentility. They concocted armorial bearings, crests and shields, mottos, fancy names and other trimmings. Thomas Lloyd in the 1830's and his eldest son Thomas Davies Lloyd in mid-century, knew how the Buckleys of Llanelli had started off stirring cauldrons of home-brewed ale. The Bath family of Alltyferin, had felt the scorching heat from molten metal in the furnaces of Landore. The Harfords of Falcondale,were Bristol merchants and bankers. Fitzwilliams, owner of the Cilgwyn estate, and a brilliant lawyer, had adopted in 1849, a grand surname instead of plain Mr.Lloyd Hall, (like the Wilkins family, Breconshire sheepfarmers and mercers who through social metamorphosis became the De Wintons of Maesllwch Castle) The Leach family of Corston had been excise men and officials of the Board of Inland Revenue, a lucrative stepping stone, and many others could be mentioned.

In the 1830's.Thomas Lloyd of Bronwydd undertook an investigation into the claim made by his ancestor George Owen, to a seat at Westminster as Lord of Parliament. William Smith, of Cardigan, the cartographer and compiler of pedigrees, drew up a detailed family tree of the Lloyds of Bronwydd. Ancient charters and royal grants were copied and studied. One John Coley, was commissioned to examine the deed of bargain and sale of July 1542, where by Sir John Touchet sold the barony of Cemais to William Owen of 'Maesgwenith' in the county of Monmouth. The purchaser's rights and privileges had to be made clear; and in addition, a copy (made in 1592) of an ancient charter granted by William Fitzmartin to the town of Newport, and witnessed by 'illustrious knights: John de Arundel, Jordan de Cantiton, Robert Fitzowen, William son of Gwrwared, then constable, David Fitzowen, Henry Coit and William Howel ab Eivan Meredith, clerk..' was translated by John Coley in 1833. Maps and surveys of the barony were drawn by Arthur Thomas of Carmarthen and Thomas Lloyd's kinsman Col.Owen Lloyd of Cardigan. But, the whole process of investigation into the 'lord of parliament'case had to wait. For the time being serious matters relating to the administration of the estate were more urgent than a long lost title.

It was in the 1850's that Thomas Davies Lloyd decided to make his claim to become 'Lord of Cemais'. It could be argued that he was obsessed by the 'peerage mania'- to use Professor Cannadine's phrase. But unlike other aspirants for distinction, honour and rank, Davies Lloyd was not a rich man and his estate was small even by Welsh standards. More over, any political influence would be limited to Cardiganshire, a poor agricultural county on the west coast of Wales. He had, however, an ancient title – 'Lord Marcher of Cemais' and he was steeped in glamour and like some others, delusions of family grandeur. His steward and attorney, William Griffith George, was instructed in 1858 to brief Messrs Clayton and Cookson to examine the purchase deeds of the barony by William Owen from Lord Audeley. Intricate points of genealogy, the exact nature of a peerage by tenure and the entanglements of inheritance law, judgments and precedents had to be unravelled, especially the title of honour as 'lords of parliament' of the two, William Martin (father and son) at the beginning of the fourteenth century. The barony of Martin had fallen into abeyance between the heirs of William Martin (the second baron) who was succeeded by his sister Eleanor de Columbers, and James Audeley, a nephew, at the time of his death in 1325. The minutiae of what may be termed the Lloyd of Bronwydd Peerage case are beyond the scope of this study. But, the fault line was the claim that Thomas Davies Lloyd was the lineal descendant of Sir Nicholas Martin whose sons are mentioned above. Mr Lloyd argued that a grant to the barony (and to a peerage) must be presumed from the fact of possession. Obviously, questions would be asked – did William Owen exercise the right to sit in parliament as Lord of Cemais.? Had the peerage of Kemes been drowned in that of Audley for one hundred and seventy years before Mr.Owen came into possession of the barony? If so, it could be assumed that the title connected with Cemais had been forgotten, as had happened in the case of the earldom of Devon, and other earldoms.

Sir John Bernard Burke,Ulster Herald, was approached. He drew up a petition and was of the opinion that a claim for a peerage would perhaps, assist Mr Lloyd in obtaining a baronetcy. This was dismal news. Even the grant of a baronetcy in 1863, could not assuage his discomfiture. The Berkeley Peerage Case was quoted: Thomas the fifth earl had left an only child, Elizabeth, who married Richard Beauchamp, 12th earl of Warwick and 'upon this lady the barony of the Berkeleys should have devolved'. This was considered to be completely analogous to the Cemais case.

Lloyd's supporters argued that the peerage passed with the barony, and the inference was that the tenure of 'Kemes' (Cemais) conferred the dignity of baron on those who possessed it and that consequently, the dignity was held as of right. Privately, in a series of letters from 1863 onwards, Thomas Davies Lloyd solicited various politicians and members of the government by promising his allegiance in exchange for their support. He had held most of the county offices; he had been created a baronet and then succeeded to be elected a Member of Parliament .

It was a chance to present his case once more. In 1868 a petition was submitted to the Queen, to which he received a formal and anodyne response that his request would 'receive careful consideration having regard to the public interest'.- The public interest!?

Sir Thomas had held the ancient office of 'Knight of the Shire' with its connotations of Christian values, chivalry, honour along with all its 'display' and pageantry. In his mind's eye at least, he had ridden victoriously from the polling place girded with his sword like the knights of old to fight battles for his electors. Therefore, there was no doubt at all about his contribution to the 'public interest'. In addition, he had held all the 'county' offices as magistrate, high sheriff and deputy-lieutenant of Cardiganshire and Pembrokeshire. As a member of parliament he had spoken on public platforms and at Westminster.

His record was by no means undistinguished. Sir Thomas had been in favour of the Reform Bill to extend the franchise to a wider public. Although he was a devout churchman he had pleased nonconformists by voting for the abolition of the church rate and the disestablishment of the Irish church. He argued that universities should be open to everybody irrespective of class or creed, and the education of all in the community was an ideal to be aimed for.

Over the years he had been convinced (in spite of earlier reservations) that voting should be by ballot because the 'expression of opinion was free as the air one breathes...yet it was not a panacea for all electoral evils...' No longer could landlords regard their tenants'votes as their own. Nevertheless, 'the bonds of centuries united the country gentleman with his tenants and dependants which no parliamentary reform could destroy'. But in spite of his stand on many burning questions of the day, many in Cardiganshire had doubted his political sincerity and his equivocation on certain matters. He was a gentleman, aristocratic in every sense, educated, with a 'sharp intellect' and had espoused radical causes. But it seemed strange then that he had become a Liberal in politics when his fellow landlords were all Tory. And why had he given   support to the 'Tory house of Campbell' [Cawdor of Golden Grove] in Carmarthenshire? Was it all part of his grand strategy to obtain a peerage?- not that this was so reprehensible in a world where the 'ethics' of patronage, manipulation and diplomatic manoeuvre in high places have prevailed long before, and since![20.]

With his parliamentary career behind him, for the time being, he continued his campaign for a seat in the House of Lords. There was so much in his favour: the house of Bronwydd was highly respected and Sir Thomas was popular on account of his ecumenical outlook towards nonconformists, his patronage and his benevolence (along with that of his forebears). He was held in high esteem in the barony of Cemais. Those of a traditionalist frame of mind were for the lord, notwithstanding the rumblings of some disaffected radicals – as described already.

It remained therefore, to rouse the support of loyal 'homagers' not forgetting the contacts he had with fellow parliamentarians, even Mr Gladstone, himself.

In April 1871, the jurors of the Court Leet, held at College in the village of Felindre Farchog, were most enthusiastic in their support of the Lloyd peerage claim in the form of a 'presentment' which Mr George, the steward, was asked to submit to Mr Gladstone. With the bold confidence, self assurance and conviction of legislators in one of the oldest legislative bodies of the realm, these worthy souls wished to inform Mr.Gladstone of the very cogent reasons (if he was not already conversant with them) why the peerage ought to be revived! In the past, extant peerages had upon occasion been interrupted by a female heir; the revival of the title 'Lord of Cemais' was 'closely related with the constitutional history of the Empire' and 'was supported by a large number of people in South Wales' and because of Sir Thomas Davies Lloyd's political record as a Liberal the inhabitants of the Principality had 'no national representative in the House of Peers'.

The opinion of leading constitutional lawyers was again sought, and, one, J.B. Phillips of the temple, in his reply pointed out the 'insurmountable difficulties' of claiming a peerage based on descent from the 'Martins of Kemes'. The best course would be to argue from the point of view of 'the political expediency of such an honour' as there were no Liberal peers in Wales. This argument would have more weight with Mr. Gladstone than '…any formal petition from the inhabitants of Newport who would be looked upon as mere dependents and could not be considered in any way as the exponents of the views of the inhabitants of the Principality generally!'

In a letter to Mr. Gladstone in April 1872, Sir Thomas Davies Lloyd repeated all the arguments already listed in this account: descent from Rhodri Mawr 'an illustrious Welsh prince' and from Martin de Tours who had accompanied the Conqueror to these shores and whose name was engrossed on the Roll of Battle Abbey. The award of the barony of 'Kemes' and the privileges granted to the Lords Marcher were recounted in detail (indeed, a veritable lesson in Welsh history for the benefit of the Prime Minister!) In addition, his political and public services in parliament and in the community in which he lived and his position as landlord over vast acreages should count in his favour. A grant of a peerage would meet with 'universal approbation'.

For the next five years of his life, Sir Thomas submitted more petitions: to the Attorney General, Queen Victoria and the Committee of Privileges of the House of Lords. The eminent judge Sir James Fitzjames Stephen, in a very lengthy opinion, found serious problems: nothing in the 'Baronia de Kemeys' or in other evidence adduced, showed that the Lord of Kemeys were barons by Tenure. Even if it could be proved that a barony might be held 'in capite of the king by a commoner who may have owed 'suit and service' to the king's court before the existence of the House of Lords in its present form '… it would be found almost impossible to support such a claim in the present day…'If however, Stephens continued, it could be proved that Sir Thomas was the heir male of the ancient 'Lords of Kemeys', summoned by writ to sit in Parliament as a peer and actually so sitting became a hereditary peer, he did not see why Lloyd should not obtain the title. Possession of estates and the exercise of the privileges of ancestors would facilitate the claim, but proof of actually sitting as well as, proof of descent from the person to whom the writ of summons (to the parliament) was addressed, was essential.

This was disconcerting news, but Sir Thomas remained confident. His claim was sound; he would achieve his ambition; he would save the dignity and honour of his ancestors. In what transpired to be his last endeavour, he commissioned the services of Edward Walmisley another leading counsel. But, he lost once more. All the arguments had been sifted like fine grain. The questions vital to the case had not been answered satisfactorily: there was no proof '…that any possessor of the Lordship Marcher of Kemes was ever summoned to Parliament in right of such lordship as Lord Kemeys…' The claim of a barony [rank. title] through descent and by inheritance had remained in the Audley family and was in abeyance. Most hurtful of all (to Sir Thomas) was that '…the much vaunted descent from William Martin was based on shaky foundations; his connection with the Lordship of Kemeys had never been proved….[and could Sir Thomas] prove either the origin of the Barony or even the accuracy of the Pedigree??..'No!

None other than Sir Charles George Young, Garter King of Arms, had been consulted and in a letter to Sir Thomas' solicitor, wrote that his client was 'in error with respect to any pretensions he has [enclosing the result of his investigations] so that he may be relieved from the ideas he at present entertains or a useless attempt to establish any claim…'.

Sir Thomas Davies Lloyd died on the 21st July, 1877, and for the time being, the peerage claim was abandoned. No doubt, he was a very disappointed man and his ambition, pride, and what one may describe as his 'ancestor worship' had been dealt a fatal blow. Suprisingly, in spite of the detailed research, profound scholarship, prudent advice and not least, the enormous expense involved, the Lloyd family clung tenaciously to the traditions cherished since the days of George Owen of Henllys. The weighty tomes of Burke on the Peerage, Baronetage and Knightage of the realm, as well as other genealogical reference books, continued to record what was now being regarded as fanciful. J.Horace Round (as mentioned already) and other participants in the peerage case had demolished the time honoured tradition believed in by the Lloyds of Bronwydd.

When Sir Marteine Lloyd inherited the estate and title as second baronet, his immediate concern was with the administration of the estate. The matter of the lost peerage had to remain dormant for some time. But following his marriage to Katherine Helena Dennistoun, who, as has been noted, claimed descent from Scottish kings and European nobility, antiquarianism, genealogy, mediaeval pageantry and heraldic display became an important preoccupation at Bronwydd. George Owen's claims about the rank and title of the Lord Marcher once more came to the surface in family conversations and were embraced by Lady Lloyd as one of her main antiquarian interests.

Sir Thomas Davies Lloyd's parliamentary career and his efforts through his political friends to acquire a peerage had not been forgotten. As a prominent baronet in west Wales, it might be possible after all, to gain a seat in parliament. A sally into the political arena was worth a try, and might even succeed.

With a general election pending in 1885, Sir Marteine Lloyd, by now disillusioned with the sympathies of the Liberal party- the 'Land for the People' ideology, the disestablishment of the Anglican Church in Wales, Home Rule for Ireland – was attracted to the Conservatives. 'Habitation 636', a cell of the Primrose League had been founded at the Salutation Hotel in Newcastle-Emlyn and attracted many of the 'Tivyside' gentry including Sir Marteine. Their battle-cry was the protection of religion and monarchical government against the forces of atheism and republicanism.

Encouraged, no doubt by over zealous friends and Lady Lloyd's enthusiasm (often for lost causes) – in this instance, the possibility of a seat in the House of Commons which might lead to a peerage – Sir Marteine was induced to be adopted as the Conservative candidate for the eastern division of Carmarthenshire, with its headquarters in Llanelli. His adoption meeting was an occasion of violent demonstrations, general mayhem with broken windows and bloody noses – the mob crying 'Go home, Go home...' with curses and obscenities added to abusive slogans against the game laws and the eviction of tenants- the entire menu of radical protest. Needless to say, Sir Marteine lost to the Liberal candidate, David Pugh of Manoravon, Llandeilo, who had a majority of two thousand five hundred in a poll of some six and a half thousand. Not only was Sir Marteine Lloyd's debut on the political stage a fiasco, but it also marked the end of the hegemony of the landowning classes in the mainstream of national politics. What was left to him was the possibility during the next decade, of becoming a county councillor or, at worst, a member of its poor relation – the parish council! Sir Marteine was elected to the Cardiganshire County Council in 1892, and with his uncle the Reverend Rhys Jones Lloyd represented the community on the School Board, the Board of Guardians and the local bench of magistrates, where their services were given freely and conscientiously for many years.

The accession of King Edward vii in 1901, brought in an age of sumptuous entertainments, processions, uniforms, decorations and symbolic spectacle of every kind. Lady Lloyd, notwithstanding cost and expense, indulged her tastes to the full. She had the advantage of a wider cultural and social background (in many ways unlike the earlier Lloyds of Bronwydd). She mixed with high society in London and other fashionable centres. Her generosity and hospitality, as the lady of the 'Lord Marcher of Kemes' and of her baronial castle in remote Cardiganshire, prompted articles in the fashionable journals of the day. Bronwydd, her new home...admittedly very modest in comparison with very grand Scottish houses, still evoked memories of her early life in Scotland. And she was prompted to delve deeply into the history of the Lords Marcher into whose family she had married. What was their standing, nationally, with the coronation of King George v about to take place in June 1911? This event reminded Sir Marteine Lloyd and his family of an old tradition that the Lord Marcher always had the right to carry a 'silver harp' in the coronation processions of former times. Lady Lloyd took up the idea with gusto, and if it was not possible to participate in the ceremony, then was it not their due to be allowed two seats in Westminster Abbey, one for Sir Marteine and one for herself? Many hitherto, new arguments were found: the first Lord Marcher had at one time, dwelt in Newport castle; he had three hundred retainers who were in attendance on him; he held contests of bards within the castle walls and presented the winner with a silver harp. Like many other claims this was an amalgam of ancient lore, bizarre antiquarianism and 'Gothick' fantasy.

Distinguished Welsh lawyers of the day, Sir Samuel T. Evans, W.Llewellyn Williams, KC. and the eminent Pembrokeshire scholar, Dr.Henry Owen of Poyston were solicited for their support. Appeal was made to the highest authority in the land, the Duke of Norfolk, Earl Marshal and the eighth Officer of State who had sole charge of royal celebrations. Mr.George, the solicitor and steward of the barony, pleaded with Sir Marteine, to discontinue the claim: 'fees would be thrown away' The Earl Marshall wrote in reply...that he had no power to allocate seats at the Coronation as those were reserved for personal friends of the king and for special categories of citizens. The carrying of 'the silver harp' was merely 'family tradition', and there was no evidence that Sir Marteine's ancestors had ever exercised such a right![21.]

During the years 1911-1921 Sir Marteine and Lady Lloyd were drawn deeper and deeper into, what might be called, the mirage of the Bronwydd peerage campaign. Early in 1914 notable peerage cases were heard before the Committee of Privileges of the House of Lords which related to the claims made by Viscount Gage and Sir Robert Bouchier Wrey, Bart. to the baronies of Dynaunt, Fitzwaryn and Martin. Lord Gage claimed the title to the Martin barony through two attainders in the Audley family and the right to inherit through the female line from William Martin, summoned to Parliament in 1325, and as the seventh in descent from Martin de Tours, who it was argued had been granted the territory of Cemais after the Norman Conquest. That was an arrogant assertion, according to the Lloyds of Bronwydd, as Sir Marteine Owen Mowbray Lloyd, 2nd. Baronet, was by right of tenure, Lord of the Barony of Cemais. Sir Robert Bouchier Wrey's case, for the revival of the barony of Fitzwarine [-yn] was based on the barony of Cemais having fallen into abeyance, after William Martin's death, between his heirs: his sister, Eleanor de Columbers and his nephew, James Audeley. The barony of Fitzwaryn, had descended through an heiress to the heir of Bouchier many years later, another branch of the same family. The Lloyds were convinced that the barony of Cemais (not Martin) had continued successively in several generations of the Audley family, and then (it was emphasised) by right of inheritance to Owen of Henllys, the ancestor of Sir Marteine Lloyd. Sir Marteine and Lady Lloyd were aghast that the arguments put forward on behalf of Viscount Gage and Sir Robert Bouchier Wrey (especially the Martin element in the case) were the very ones made by Sir Thomas Davies Lloyd a generation earlier, and dismissed out of hand. A letter was sent from Bronwydd to Sir John Simon, the Solicitor General, asking why the Gage claim had ever been allowed to be heard by the Committee of Privileges in the first place. Lady Lloyd took up the cudgels with

Fox-Davies, and in one reply to her remonstrations and her interpretation of the evidence she presented, he replied by telegram in March, 1914: '..Never a rag of a chance for peerage because though descendants you were never heirs..'

In spite of the pressures of the time: the outbreak of the Great War in August, 1914, and the devastating blow to Sir Marteine and Lady Lloyd with the death on active service in 1916, in the first battle of the Somme, of their only son and heir, Marteine Kemes Arundel, Lady Lloyd continued with the peerage claim. She crossed swords time and time again with Fox-Davies, even, implying that he had used the Lloyd pedigree to support the Gage case. The Bronwydd muniments had indeed, been lent to the College of Arms, but Fox-Davies vehemently resented the innuendo and replied to Lady Lloyd '…on the contrary the real truth is that, as to the later generations, you have appropriated Lord Gage's ancestors…[and added with undisguised irritation]…however, if you are consulting Garter [King of Arms] he will be able to explain things to you. I confess I apparently, have failed. Yours truly, A.C. Fox-Davies'. By 1921, W.Llewellyn Williams was again approached to give his opinion, as he had done with regard to the 'silver harp' in 1911. Writing to Sir Marteine Lloyd in December, 1921, he confessed that he could not understand nor explain how William Owen had obtained a title, particularly as his son, George Owen, had stated plainly that his father 'had purchased' the barony of Cemais from Lord Audley. Moreover, there were problems with the Lloyd of Bronwydd family tree, and, assuming that 'Kemes' was a lordship marcher, how was its status affected by the Act of Union of 1536?

Llewellyn Williams was of the opinion that lordships, like that of Cemais, were converted into manors with small privileges. And so, the matter remained; the peerage and the title 'Lord Cemais' belonged to history. Feudal rights, the payment of tolls, the perambulation of the barony, followed by a concourse of dutiful homagers, had become relics of the past, except one annual custom: the choice and installation of the mayor of Newport by the Lady Marcher of Cemais, in a unique and picturesque ceremony[22].

Later in the 1920's, Lady Lloyd consoled herself by gathering material for her book. 'The Lords Marchers of Kemes' which was published in 1930. Sadness and nostalgia had blighted the lives of Sir Marteine and Lady Lloyd in their old age. Her book was an act of 'pietas' in memory of an ancient family, of ancestors (be they real or imaginary) of noblesse and worth. The controversy relating to the origin of the family, the crevices and cracks in long pedigrees, the prolonged litigation over many years and the arguments bandied about by genealogists and lawyers did not damage in any way the high esteem with which the Lloyd family of Bronwydd were regarded. Tenants, 'homagers' of the barony, the burgesses of Newport, chapel deacons, church wardens, clerics and nonconformist divines knew little of the peerage case nor of any doubts about pedigree and lineage. The communities who knew the Lloyds of Bronwydd looked up to them as an esteemed ancient family; the squire of Bronwydd was the 'Lord Marcher of Kemes' like his ancestors before him; he had a special place in society, as well as his duties, and in none was he found wanting. The family had genuinely believed, as an article of faith, that they were descended from Martin de Tours, from the Audeleys and (quite correctly) from George Owen, who had put it all down in black and white so many centuries ago. In any case, they were the inheritors of what George Owen had contrived; and, 'de facto', if not, 'de jure', a tradition of status, power and responsibility with its ceremonial, etiquette and ritual, in which the Lloyds took a delight in and responded generously and with magnanimity towards those who came their way.

Towers and Turrets

i

It was pointed out at the beginning of this account that Bronwydd was originally known as 'Tyddyn (tenement, homestead) llain y Bronwydd' which had been acquired by 'Philip Brwyn of Ffoshelyg, gent.' In 1562. In a deed of July, 1591, the house and lands are described as 'the capital messuage (dwelling house and outbuildings} and lands called Plas Bronwydd'. This was the residence of the Reverend Thomas Lloyd, MA. Rector of the parish of Llangunllo: a 'plas' or squire's hall or residence.

Once can only conjecture that 'Plas Bronwydd' at this time, was like many other small gentry dwellings in the Teifi valley and throughout the length and breadth of Wales: a farmhouse-type building for example, Plas Aberporth, Bronhydden, Ffosesgob, Gilfach, Pantgilgan, Coedstre-isaf, Old Waunifor, and many others.

As Dr. Peter Smith has shown, they were modest dwellings surrounded by 'all the apparatus, the barns and beast houses, the muck and the mire inescapable in a working farm'. Over the centuries, with expanding acreage, increasing rents and changing fashions, many of the Welsh squires' modest farmsteads were enlarged. More commodious residences appeared on the landscape: heavily built 'double-pile houses, plain in style, with tall square chimneys, high pitched roofs with stone tiling, two stories and an attic, supported by massive oak timbers'. The best of them was probably, the nearest equivalent to an English manor house.

The inventory and valuation (made in May 1663) of the cash reserves, household and farm stock left by Thomas Lloyd of Bronwydd, show that he was a farming squire of quite considerable wealth. In 1670, according to the Hearth Tax Returns, the house was assessed for eight hearths, and was one of the largest in 'Tivyside'. Of course, there were many larger houses in Wales. In Glamorgan, for example (a rich county compared with Cardiganshire) there were eight houses with more than twenty hearths; in Pembrokeshire, thirteen with more than ten and, in Carmarthenshire, the Earl of Carbery's house at Golden Grove could boast of fifty, while its nearest rivals had only eighteen hearths apiece.

It is reasonable to suppose that the mansion house of Bronwydd was further extended in the eighteenth century. Nicholas Carlisle in his '*Topographical Dictionary of the Dominion of Wales*' 1811, draws attention to Bronwydd as '... the seat of the late patriotic Colonel Lloyd who gallantly commanded the Teifiside Volunteers and afterwards, the Fishguard and Newport Fencibles, is in this parish ...' It was important historically and Samuel Lewis, in his '*Topographical Dictionary of Wales*' 1833, describes Bronwydd '... the seat of Thomas Lloyd, Esq ... (as) ... a handsome mansion, beautifully situated on the summit of an eminence richly clothed with wood...'[1]

After his father's death in 1845, Thomas Davies Lloyd, like many other squires throughout the land, set his heart on rebuilding Bronwydd. Since the Napoleonic Wars, many new mansions had been erected and others completely restored. As mentioned already Thomas Davies Lloyd, an ambitious Welsh squire had hob-nobbed with dukes, earls, marquises and baronets at Christ Church, Oxford, and elsewhere. He had married in1846, Henrietta Mary Reid of Watlington Hall, Norfolk – a lady with aristocratic connections. For his part he claimed descent from Norman barons and their descendants who were 'Lords Marcher of Kemes' and peers of the realm. He was determined to establish his own position in society and to have royal recognition of the status of his ancient and esteemed family. His home therefore had to be a symbol of its owner's influence, privilege and power.

According to a plan of the Bronwydd demesne, drawn by Arthur Thomas of Carmarthen in 1834, one can clearly discern the pleasure gardens, walks, carriage drives, groves of trees and every feature of the handsome mansion described by Samuel Lewis. The double pile residence and its domestic offices were sited away from the farm building, stables and coach houses, as well as from the smells of piggeries and 'beast houses'. It was the home of the Lord Marcher, the focal point in a demesne (allowing for the home farm, woodlands and game preserves) as well as other properties in neighbouring parishes, amounting to over twelve hundred acres. The entire estate which extended further into north Pembrokeshire, Carmarthenshire and Glamorgan, in total, extended to some eight thousand acres. But, the mansion house was old fashioned; commodious for country dwellers, admittedly, but lacking in taste, refinement and style becoming a gentleman of parts, breeding and sophistication.

Irrespective of cost and finding the cash to pay for his plan, Thomas Davies Lloyd was determined to rebuild Bronwydd in a style befitting the rank and dignity of the Lord Marcher. Moreover, as it seemed to him, there could not be any possible impediment to prevent his acquiring, eventually, a seat in the House of Lords. At all costs, his home had to reflect the grandeur of the barony of 'Kemes'. Bronwydd, as it was, reflected the plainness of a dissenters' conventicle. Thomas Davies Lloyd was attracted by the novel ideas of the Gothic Revival; he had been a contemporary of John Ruskin at Christ Church, Oxford; he had experienced the ecclesiological reforms of the Oxford Movement after 1833. A remarkable change in the buildings in and around Oxford had taken place, and more dreaming spires, churches, castles, towers and turrets were to be seen throughout the land. Indeed, Thomas Johnes of Havod had pioneered, fifty years earlier, in reviving the Gothic style of architecture in Cardiganshire. Lloyd was, without doubt, familiar with other devotees of the 'curious, the medieval and antique': Horace Walpole's novel and surprising

Strawberry Hill, Sir Walter Scott's immensely influential house at Abbottsford, in a Scottish 'baronial' style, full of curious and antique artifacts of every kind (and Scott would have been well known in Cardiganshire mansions not only on account of his literary works, but also because one of his sons had been educated at the Lampeter Grammar School of the Rev. John Williams, the classical scholar and later, the first rector of the Edinburgh Academy) and, the 'ecclesiastical fantasy' of Fonthill, built by William Beckford, author and cultured eccentric. All these new mansion houses were topics of comment and conversation in polite circles and reflected the current aesthetic and cultural values which Lloyd and others of his class aspired to. Such considerations have to be borne in mind when one asks why Bronwydd, Newport Castle (and later Llangunllo church) were rebuilt in a particularly flamboyant and distinctive style[2].

After Thomas Davies Lloyd's marriage in 1845, and, before the rebuilding commenced, arrangements had to be made for the accommodation of his mother Anne Davies Lloyd. Temporarily, much of her surplus furniture was moved to the neighbouring mansion of Gernos or Mount Gernos, as it was also known, during December 1847 to January 1848. Fortunately, an inventory was compiled (by the trusty agent and steward John Daniel Jones) which gives some idea of the contents, value and more importantly the number of rooms in the old house:

Drawing Room – Two Large Square Tables, £4-5s; Three Hair Bottom Chairs (Mahogany), 7s-6d; One Elbow-do, 5s; One Mahy. Stand Tea Caddy and Cupboard United, 5s; One Large Green bays (Baize) Screen, 1s-6d; One Footstool, 1s; Onc Carpet, £1-5s;

Pictures in the Drawing Room, - The Earl of Dartington's Hounds, 4s; The Highland Chieftain, 6s; Byron's Dream, 6s; Britton Ferry, 2s; Sea View, 5s; The Castle of Cilgerran, 2s; Dutch Figure (Old Woman), 2s.

Dining Room, - Two Sofas and Covering, 28s; One Hair Bottom Stool, 5s; One Sofa Table, 8s; One Painted Stand?; One Set of Salmon Colour Moreen (stout woollen/cotton material) Window Curtains and Pair of Pins, (rods) 16s.

Pictures in Dining Room, - Portrait of T. D. Lloyd, Esqr. 2s; do. of Rowland Hill, 2s; do. of the Duke of York, 2s-6d; do. of Napoleon, 1s; do. of the Duke of Wellington, Riding, 2s-6d; Picture of a Woman Feeding Pigs, 5s; Print, Fair Religion and her Lovely Train, 5s; The Holy Family, 1s-6d;

Breakfast Room, - Two End Tables?; Mahogany Bookcase, 25s-0d; Painted Escritoire, 5s; Hair Sofa, 5s; Three Mahogany Hair Bottom Chairs, 15s; Two Mahogany Elbow Chairs, 21s; One Small Mahy. Table, ?; Salmon Colour

Window Curtain, ?; Drugget (woollen over carpet/cover for floor or table) 5s; Large Oak Desk, 10s;

Pictures in Breakfast Parlour, - 7 Hunting Prints, £1-4s; 'Shall I Go?' (T.D.Ll) 1s; Mysie Happer, 1s; The Church of Llangunllo, 1s; The Vicar and Moses, 1s; The Welsh Curate, 1s; The Ruined Castle, 2s; Samuel, 1s-0d; Oval Picture, (Subject Unknown), 2s; Small Looking Glass, 15s; Painted Inkstand, 2s.

R. J. Lloyd Esqr's Bedroom, - 1 Bedstead and White Dimity Curtains (Note-There is one Bedstead of the late Mrs. Thomas at Bronwydd they are to be exchanged); 1 Painted Cupboard with 3 drawers, 12s; One Set of Mahy. Drawers lined with Cedar, 10s; One Old Mahy. (chest of) Drawers with Centre Cupboard (3 drawers wanting), 1s; One Feather Bed, Bolster and Pillow, One White Quilt and 1 Coloured Quilt, One Welsh Blanket, One Window Curtain, 60s;

Mrs Lloyd's Room, - One Mattress (Flock), One Feather Bed, One Welsh Blanket, One Indian Covering, Coloured Quilt, One Old Quilt, One Iron Bedstead (Military), One Feather Bed, One Bolster and 2 Pillows Window Curtains (Salmon Colour), One Old Mahy. Drawers, 30s.

Middle Bedroom, - Crib Mattress, One Bolster, Five Welsh Blankets, Three Old English do, Five White Counterpanes, One Quilt (Marcella), One Rug, One Old Quilt, One Set of White Bed Curtains, Two Old Window Curtains, One Painted Chair Seat with Horse Skin, 1s; One Shower Bath, Two Mahy. Elbow Chairs, One Painted Stand.

Mr George's Room, - One Woollen Mattress, 5s; Two Feather Beds, £4-10s; One Welsh Blanket & One Large English do, 7s-6d; One Pillow, 5s; One White Quilt, 3s-6d; One Painted (Chest of) Drawers, 5s; One Mahy. Desk of Drawers, 10s; One Shower Bath, 10s; Two Mahy. Elbow Chairs, 5s; One Painted Stand, 1s-6d; Bed and Window Curtains, Carpet.

Mr. Owen's Room, - One Feather Bed; Two Welsh Blankets; One English do; One Marcella Quilt; Two Pillows: One Woollen Mattress, 4s; Bed and Window Curtains; Mahy. Desk and Drawers, 18s; Mahy. Wardrobe (Old Fashion) 15s; One Large Painted Box, 3s; Mahy. Drawers (Four) 15s; Carpet.

Garret, - Painted Wardrobe, 15s; Two Quill Beds and 1 Bolster; Two Welsh Blankets; One Old English do; Two Old Quilts; Old Oak Carved Chest, 3s; Two Tin Fenders, 2s; One Deal (chest of) Drawers, 10s; One Mahy. Elbow Chair without seat, 1s.

Stair Case, - One Eight Day Clock, 20s. Passage, - One Old Stand (Stoves).

Butler's Pantry, - Painted Cupboard Bedstead; Feather Bed; Four Pillows; Two Welsh Blankets; Two Old White Counterpanes; One Large painted Cupboard, 10s.

Back kitchen, - One Large Cupboard (Old) 5s; One Large Old Table, 2s-6d.

Cellar, - Three 18 gallon Casks; List of Silver and plate; 4 Long Candlesticks plated – to be valued; 12 Large Forks silver to be returned; 12 Small Forks, 6 Tea Spoons, 1 Mustard Pot, 2 Butter Ladles, 1 Gravy Spoon, 6 Dessert Spoons (all of silver to be returned).

Thomas Davies Lloyd was aware that the rebuilding of Bronwydd in a grand style meant that the old house had virtually, to be gutted. Naturally, he had consulted architects and builders, and at this stage, he prudently arranged that the existing house, its contents, outbuildings, live and dead stock should be valued for insurance purposes. In January, 1849, the valuation was as follows:

Mansion House - £2000; Household goods, linen, plate, watches and trinkets - £750; Musical and mathematical instruments - £75; Pictures and Prints - £50; China, glass and looking glasses, £70; Utensils, live and dead stock, - £115; Barn and granary, - £40; Stock of grain, - £35; Work horses, stable and hay loft, - £50; Cart house, blacksmith's shop and kennel, - £50; Coach house, - £20; Live and dead stock, - £80; Carpenter's shop, - £5; Contents thereof, - £5. (plus odds and ends) in all, about £3,500[3].

Lloyd could chose from a wide choice of architects to design what would appear in time, as an entirely new building. Very well known persons, like Sir Charles Barry, William Butterfield, Anthony Salvin, A.W.N. Pugin, Sir G. Gilbert Scott and Sir Jeffry Wyattville were in favour of revived Gothic and neo Tudor styles, and they had designed public buildings of national importance. The latter had been responsible for the new mansion of Golden Grove for Lord Cawdor in 1827, and Gilbert Scott was to re-design Cenarth Church some years later. Possibly, because of the high fees charged by such eminent and much sought after architects and their reluctance to undertake what was more suitable for lesser practitioners, Thomas Davies Lloyd turned to those who were already well known in the Teifi valley. Richard Kyrke Penson (1815-85) was an obvious choice: a surveyor for the county and like Lloyd, a member of the Cambrian Archaeological Association. He was a Fellow of the Society of Antiquaries, a water colour artist of some repute and one who could easily present his clients with attractive sketches of the designs he had in mind for their 'restored' and dolled-up houses, and (in some cases) the churches and parsonages within parishes of which they were patrons. He was commissioned by Thomas Davies Lloyd to create a baronial mansion at Bronwydd, as well as Dynevor Castle for Lord Dynevor, and the modest Llidiardau in Llanilar. Penson was in sympathy with the ideals of the Gothic revival, even to the extent of building the lime kilns at Cilyrychen, Llandybie, in the 'Gothic' style![4]

Fortunately, the accounts relating to the building of Bronwydd, have survived, a comparatively rare occurrence in the history of many country houses. As will be seen, they provide a detailed analysis of the materials used and their source, the number and nature of the various craftsmen and skilled workmen employed, the wages earned, transport methods and the like.

R. Kyrke Penson prepared coloured sketches of a baronial castle whence the Chevalier Bayard might have ridden forth, to joust and to hunt, to do battle against infidel and tyrant, and to rescue hapless damsels in distress. Such a house had, also, to radiate an air of dignified repose, jovial hospitality, with feasting in the great hall and the yule log crackling in the fireplace. Bronwydd was an example of full-blown romanticism – a mixture of styles – Norman, Gothic and Tudor – with towers and turrets, battlements, crenellations, machicollations, loopholes: all the fearsome devices for defence against attack. Gargoyles, grotesque symbols of medieval folklore, oriel windows and half timbered projections, fanciful weather vanes and other elaborate ornamentation were added.

Penson's task was to convert a plain (albeit dignified) house into a mock mediaeval castle. From a roof plan, and the demesne map, the original house faced towards the south, with the rear pile projecting a few yards to the west. Clearing the site, around the old house, commenced in the early summer of 1853. Carts and waggons began to arrive with loads of stone, bricks, lime and gravel. By the autumn, a symbolic foundation stone was laid at the foot of what became later the belfry, which abutted on the great square tower. Coins and other topical memorabilia were deposited in a casket underneath. The work was in full swing by November, and a contract had been signed with Messrs. Thomas Roberts and Wiliam Jones of Brecon. The original estimated cost of rebuilding Bronwydd was about £3,280, but, as it turned out, the final cost was reputed to be more like £10,000. As the work proceeded, costs rose by the day. Within a year of starting the work, William Jones was declared a bankrupt and many suppliers of materials and workmen were not paid. One William Evans of Capel Drindod, Aberbanc, had not received one penny of the £16 for haulage during the first few months, and he refused to do any more work for the contractors unless Thomas Davies Lloyd became guarantor of all the amounts owing to him. And he was only one of the many persons who were not paid for work done at Bronwydd. Because William Jones had been declared bankrupt he could not continue in the partnership. Claims for breach of contract, counter claims and all sorts of legal difficulties followed, much to the aggravation of Thomas Davies Lloyd. Additional costs by the summer of 1855, half way through the work, had amounted to about £3,500, and long drawn out proceedings against Jones's assignees in bankruptcy added to the problems.

John Daniel Jones, acted as clerk of the works and regularly submitted bills and accounts (relating to every aspect of the work done at Bronwydd) to R. Kyrke Penson, then resident at Ferryside, a few miles beyond Carmarthen, who charged fees of 5% for his professional work. Thomas Roberts too, was in financial trouble and at one stage was in debt to about fifty labourers, hauliers (one of the latter being Mary Griffiths of Blaenllan, Coedybryn) and odd job men drawn from about ten miles radius of the mansion. Skilled craftsmen had not been paid and the prospect of ever completing the 'new' mansion of Bronwydd looked very remote indeed. Discussions took place between Davies Lloyd, John Daniel Jones and Kyrke Penson, as well as, with William Griffith George, Lloyd's solicitor. An obvious solution was to dismiss Roberts. He was not considered satisfactory, but any other agreement could not be made 'until the matter with Roberts had been settled' and he could only be discharged for 'want of skill or for not doing the business (the building) in a workmanlike manner'[5].

It is astonishing that Thomas Davies Lloyd ever considered that such a project could ever be achieved. He was desperately short of money and parts of the estate had already been sold, namely Nantlledfron and other holdings in the parish of Clydai, to John Colby of Ffynone, for £2,900. He had to borrow from about sixty persons throughout the social spectrum: thrifty and hardworking craftsmen and artisans, farmers, shopkeepers, dissenting ministers, minor squireens, £5,000 on mortgaged property from Miss Bowen of Llwyngwair and various sums of money ranging from £50 to a £1000. Most of the creditors were from the neighbouring parishes of Llangunllo, Troedyraur, Llanfair Orllwyn, Llangeler and the towns of Newcastle-Emlyn, Cilgerran and Newport – places where the 'good name of Lloyd of Bronwydd' was held in high regard. Mr Williams, the druggist, Newcastle-Emlyn, lent £500, the Rev. J. P. George £600, Miss Lucas £1000, a prosperous farmer like Daniel Evans, Trecagal, Bangor Teifi, £300, and Miss Jones, Pengelly and Mr. Davies, Cilfallen (a small genteel house above Cwmcoy) lent £600 and £700, respectively. In fact, the capital and the interest on these capital and loans (a sum of £17,141) had not been paid as late as 1872-73!

In spite of problems with the contractors, the raising of money and a constant flood of bills to be met, the work continued. Since the commencement, carpentry, masonry, plastering, glazing, bell hanging, ironmongery, cleaning extras and furnishing had reached a total cost of about £3,600. The original estimate of Jones and Roberts was wide of the mark and half way through, it was thought that 'say in round form' the sum of £6,000 @ 4% would be required to complete the building of Bronwydd. Various stratagems, in addition to borrowing from local people were considered: the sale of Rhippinllwyd and other properties would raise some £4,000 and would alleviate the situation. By

August 1855, and two years after the first stone was laid, it had cost almost £6,000. The dismissal of Thomas Roberts meant raising almost another thousand pounds by way of compensation to him.

In spite of these difficulties, Thomas Davies Lloyd, like Thomas Johnes of Havod, indulged himself in a 'world of Romantic creativity'. After a short stay at Gernos, his mother, Anne Davies Lloyd went on a prolonged tour of the continent, and returned to spend the rest of her days at Cilrhiwe, were she died in 1888 in her ninety-fourth year. Thomas Davies Lloyd and his wife Henrietta had to take up residence at Velindre House, in the village of Velindre 'Shincin', so as to be within easy distance to be consulted and to keep an eye on the rebuilding of Bronwydd[6]. While Lloyd's family and domestic arrangements were temporarily satisfactory the actual completion of his new home was going to be a real nightmare. With costs increasing daily, an up-to-date analysis made in May 1855 showed that the original estimate was too low, reflecting the incompetence of the contractors who also acted as quantity surveyors and, not least, a certain degree of uncertainty with regard to the final plan on the part of Thomas Davies Lloyd.

Materials were obtained from a wide area: stone for building came from Blaengwinllan, a local quarry and from Gwarallt y Faerdref on the Alltyrodyn estate in the parish of Llandysul. Blue slate for 'flagging and coping' was carted from Cilgerran, bricks from Cardigan, Carmarthen and New Quay while 'Bath freestone' had to be brought from the west of England. The latter was transported by sea from Bristol to Cardigan and Carmarthen. One bill mentions a consignment of 90 tons @ 9/- per ton, with a landing charge of £24-12-6d. After the coming of the railroad to Carmarthen, it was brought in large blocks to the station, trimmed to manageable sizes by craftsmen on the spot who lived in cabins or 'lodges' on railway sidings and were given an allowance for their maintenance: food, fuel and the like.

Masons were responsible for the initial trimming of the freestone. The process of 'sawing and sculpting', with the final decorative embellishments was carried out *in situ* at Bronwydd. The rate charged by the hauliers for carting the blocks from Carmarthen, was 9d per foot length of block stone and about a dozen hauliers were employed to carry stone and timber to the building site. Other items may be quoted as indicative of costs and haulage charges at the time, for example, David Lloyd of Penpwll, Saron, was paid 7d per hundredweight for a load of 15½ cwts. on one occasion. Lime had to be transported from the limekilns of east Carmarthenshire, such as Crwbin and Cilyrychen, Llandybie. Some local timber was used but 'Baltic timber' was imported and carted to Bronwydd from Cardigan. Iron and lead items could be obtained from blacksmiths in the locality but copper had to be brought from Llanelli, and the 'works' further afield. Horsehair, for lath and plaster partitions inside the house, was obtained from stables in Newcastle Emlyn and local women were employed to fetch it from time to time. The Bronwydd cart was constantly in demand for bringing materials, such as, bricks and tiles from Cardigan, Carmarthen and New Quay, with John Rees of Pengallt farm in charge.

During the building period, Bronwydd was a hive of activity, with about sixty to seventy persons (including a few women) on and off the site, in July 1854. They can be classified broadly as follows,-

Occupation	No.	Daily Wage	Native of ...
Carpenters/ Foreman	8	1/3d – 3/0 - 3/4d	Cenarth, Cilgerran, Henllan, N.C. Emlyn, Pont Seli ...
Bath stone Masons/Foreman	8	3/8d – 4/6d	6 Brecon, 2 Carmarthen
Walling masons Setter	12	2/0 – 2/6d 3/0	Local
Bath stone Sawyers	2	1/8d – 2/4d	Local
Labourers	12	1/2d – 2/4d	Bangor Teifi, Brongest, N.C Emlyn, Pentrecagal
Hauliers/ Stone & gravel	3	3/0 – 3/6d per day	Local farmers and tenants
Stones from 'Top' & Cunllo quarries	6	1/6d – 2/6d per load	Local farmers and tenants
Lime	7	11/6d – 14/6d per load	Local farmers and tenants
Blacksmith	1	Depending on each item	Local farmers and tenants
Plumber	1	Depending on each item	
Plasterers	10	1/0 – 4/2d	?
Painter	1	3/6d	?

Other items mentioned in the accounts are Elias, Penmount, who 'with his horse turned the mortar machine' at the rate of 3/6d per day. Amongst the other non-skilled workmen were 'the mortar boy' who earned 1/5d per week, and reliable trustworthy persons who had special duties, like Samuel Jones of Alltgoch, whose responsibility was to go to Newcastle Emlyn to 'change money' to pay the workers, and James Rees, who, for 6/2d went to Ferryside, presumably, to take copies of the accounts, discuss problems and exchange information about the progress or otherwise (?) at Bronwydd with Mr. R. Kyrke Penson. Because some of the workmen lived a long distance away from Bronwydd, they lodged in local farms and cottages, in hay-lofts and barns, or possibly, in 'lodges' and 'cabins' in the vicinity of the mansion. Perhaps they shared with coachmen, grooms and stable lads, lofts and attics usually used to accommodate out door staff.

A few special craftsmen employed during the building of Bronwydd, had to come a very long way (considering the means of transport at the time) and travelling and lodging allowances were paid to them. Isaac Dando of Brecon, one of the free-stone masons was on one occasion paid 16/2d – a sum which also included 'working the mortar mill' when he was not occupied with decorative carving. James Rees received £2-7s for travelling to Pembroke, Newport in Monmouthshire, and to Bristol, and this amount covered his coach, railway and steamer fares, while his subsistence allowance for seven days was fourteen shillings. David Jones another 'freestone sawyer' together with his work mates received 9s for their coach fare to Carmarthen, 2/6d for a tea kettle, 1/6d for a teapot and 6d for cups and saucers for their own use at the quayside.

By the Summer of 1855, and within a year of the completion of the rebuilding of Bronwydd, the old house had almost disappeared. The south western façade had been transformed; the outside outer ashlar walls had been added. The main tower to the east stood solidly with its battlements and bell tower adjoining. The whole structure – belfry, oriel window and the round tower to the west, reminded one immediately of the Rock of Cashel, the ancient capital of Munster, the twelfth century cathedral and Cormac's chapel. But Gothic windows and arches, half timbered projections, florid carved and pierced stonework, further added to the glamour attached to the stately home of the Lord Marcher of Cemais[7].

The entrance porch to the north was in a more restrained style and was approached by a short flight of steps flanked by a low wall of pierced stonework. Above the doorway was a Gothic arch and in the centre of the tympanum above, a carving of a boar tied to a holly tree (a motif derived from the arms of George Owen of Henllys) which reminded one of Thomas Davies Lloyd's ancestry. His religious sensitivities were proclaimed in the motto – 'I Dduw bo'r Diolch'. And again above the front door were carved the words 'Welcome Stranger- God Speed the Parting Guest' to reassure the visitor with greetings of good will for his stay and to bid him every blessing on his journey.

Further inside, one came to a small lobby and then to the main panelled hall, which served as a library, audience and recital room. One of its striking features was the vast mediaeval fireplace, and opposite, a number of bookshelves containing works on a variety of subjects – foreign travel, standard works on farming, horses and hounds, animal medication and devotional works, which were very important in the rule of life of the 'Good Colonel Lloyd' and Mary, his wife – the Sermons of Jeremy Taylor, the Diary and Journal of Archbishop Laud, the Prayers of Dr. Samuel Johnson, not to mention the writings of Welsh authors like Griffith Jones, Daniel Rowland and the sermons of a neighbour, the Calvinist Ebenezer Morris of Rhydlewis. In describing the books in the Bronwydd library, another important feature which ought to be mentioned is the contents of the muniment room (where that was sited in the house has never been established) with its vast collections: ancient charters, pedigree rolls, the works of George Owen of Henllys, estate papers and the like which had been treasured for several centuries. Judging from the arrangements of the rooms, the arches, door cases, windows with elaborate tracery and the carved stonework everywhere, the old house had been transformed beyond recognition. The dining room was on the north side, as was often the case in country houses, the withdrawing room on the south side to catch the maximum sunlight, and then, the morning room, the little dining room, smoking room and the butler's pantry at the base of the stone spiral staircase to the bell tower. In addition to his daily duties the butler tolled the bell to summon farm workers, grooms, gardeners and others to their tasks and daily meals in the servants hall. Outdoor staff had to walk considerable distance and the Bronwydd bell (of about two hundredweight) could be heard for miles across the countryside. One of the labourers had to walk about four miles from Rhos Penboyr to be at his work place by 7.a.m The green baize door separated the main reception rooms of the house from the servants' quarters –the kitchen, out-kitchens, larders, pantries, servants' hall, the visiting coachman's snuggery and, of course, the housekeeper's room and the butler's pantry – two employees who were at the peak of the staff hierarchy.

The interior of the mansion had been 'Gothicised' with the usual features of good taste in that style: pointed arches to doorways, alcoves, recesses, most of which bore pious and chivalric mottos, epigrams and Biblical quotations, for example: 'Deus pascit corvos' (God feedeth the ravens), 'Wine that maketh glad the heart of man', 'Eat thy bread with joy and drink thy wine with a merry heart', 'Nisi Dominus aedificaverit domum..' (Unless the Lord build the house..). 'L'homme propose mais Dieu dispose' (Man proposes but God disposes) amongst others. The roof itself was tiled in a geometric pattern; the main triple chimney stack was decorated with Christian crosses in marked relief, and individual pinnacles along the irregular roof line, supported metal pennons which were pierced with the initials of various members of the Lloyd family.

The house, perched on a hilltop, made a dramatic impact on the visitor, and this was experienced from the south lodge and the massive entrance gates. On each side, the tall pillars supporting the gates also held two leaping wolves facing each other: a heraldic motif derived from the arms of Selyf, Lord of Cilycwm. The drive had been contoured and designed to provide a new and changing vista as one passed masses of rhododendrons and azaleas, carpets of daffodils and lilies, amongst many other varieties of shrubs and flowers, each bearing exquisite fragrance and colour in its season. The drive ended on a wide terrace where the house stood; a spacious lawn, with a tall sundial and flowerbeds, as well as a tennis court flanked the right hand side, as one faced the mansion. Further up, on the slope overlooking the terrace, a small pavilion had been built to accommodate the Bronwydd brass band, which performed there on special occasions. Towards the southwest, two narrow terraces, parterres, borders and a proliferation of choice roses, which adorned the walls, led ultimately down to the dell where the 'American garden' had been created. The latter was an innovation in the 'English garden' where plants from foreign parts brought into special prominence the squire's botanical taste and discernment. Towards the north, and still to the left of the main terrace, a little gate led to a very special enclosed garden, surrounded by a prim laurel hedge. Here was the dogs' cemetery, complete with marble head-stones to commemorate generations of corgi, spaniel, setter, amongst many others of less distinguished lineage, each with its unique identity: Fido, Tramp, Spotty and Nell and every faithful creature which had given joy and pleasure to its owner. Lower down the 'Bronwydd' or 'the wooded slop' there was a special spring, renowned for its therapeutic water; its remarkable healing properties had long been known. Sir Marteine's butler used to go down to the well every evening before dinner, to draw water which he carried in a silver ewer back to his master. Around the spring, a quaint and protective 'antique' wall had been built, with a simple gothic arch enclosing a significant headstone (an in keeping with the architecture of the house) bearing the Biblical quotation – 'Cyfod ffynnon, cenwch iddi – Num.xxi.17 (Spring up O well; sing ye unto it), recalling the joy of the Israelites when Moses found them a well during their wanderings in the desert.

Before the building of Bronwydd was finally completed, it seems that certain changes were made to the original design: a two light window was installed in the round tower, and the 'present windows converted to narrow lights'; the three parapets of the square tower were to include arrow slits with a string of, albeit, blocked machicolations beneath. Final touches had also to be added: all 'Bath stone' work outside and inside the 'new house' had to be cleaned; two coats of soap an alum (mineral salt consisting of double sulphate of aluminium and potassium, etc.) wash were to be applied to all the outside freestone work. All stone carving had to be completed according to drawings; a 'stack chimney' with 'Top (quarry)' stone and 'Bath (stone) quoins' had to be completed, and all old pointing was to be raked down and replaced with 'fresh flat pointings'.

There were also several matters which needed attention inside the house: the passage along the base of the 'Bachelors' House lying against the outer kitchen' was to be tiled; the entrance to the wine cellar had to be finished and 'a pipe was to be connected to the beer cellar'. The 'Bath stone' balustrade in the 'Archway' between the Two Halls and stairs into the wine cellar had to be added. Outside, ridge crests, a weathercock on the top of the round tower with 'flags' (vanes) over different gables, were added to the building. David Jones was to be paid £148, payable in fortnightly installments of £22, for putting up and pulling down the scaffolding, and the mention of a few items can be added to show how the new completed Bronwydd was completed: a mahogany seat for the water closet; (it would seem that there was only one!); David Davies, the blacksmith from Maesllyn, sent in his bill in January, 1856, for six 'bonnets' to chimneys —9/6d, altering front hall grate – 12/-, mending pantry fender 2/-, 10 eye bolts with screws, 40 hooks and 5 bars – 6/-, mending fire irons 6/8d, 'spent three days making pan in grate to air the rooms' – 12/-. Mr. Clark, the 'carver' in wood and stone was responsible for the work in the dining and morning rooms, as well as the chimneypieces, but, alas, there is no information about what it cost. New furniture was carted from Cardigan and Carmarthen, where the items had been brought from fashionable London stores.

The exterior and interior was completed by June 1856, and the various rooms and the extent of the house can be visualised from a survey made some years later:-

Ground Floor

Stairs and Entrance Hall	Butler's Pantry
Main Hall	Lavatory
Dining Room	Housekeeper's Room
Drawing Room	Kitchen and small room adjoining
Morning Room	Servants' Hall
Small Dining Room	Footmen's Bedrooms

First Floor

Bedrooms (named as follows),-

Cheltenham – bathroom & dressing room	Lichfield
Pambroke	Cilrhue
Newcastle	Carnarvon
Orielton	Kemaes – bedroom, dressing room, bathroom

Attic Floor

Spare Room	Laundrymaid's Bedroom
Tower Room	Maids' Bedroom
Tower Landing	Old Schoolroom

According to the Census Returns for 1871, the occupants of Bronwydd were Lady Henrietta Lloyd, her son Marteine O.M. Lloyd, Mr.Hutchings, a private tutor, cook, house, laundry, dairy and kitchen maids (seven in all) together with a butler, footman, coachman, huntsman, groom and bailiff – a total staff complement of fourteen – the same number as in the old Bronwydd in 1851. In the early 1900s David Jenkins, the Llandeilo architect, carried out the following improvements:-

Heating Apparatus (Central Heating?)	£286 - 12 - 2
2 New WCs and lavatory, tank, cisterns	83 - 11 - 10
New house drainage	29 - 5 - 0
Hot plate chest and copper boiler in kitchen	23 - 8 - 8
Architect's commission and expences	32 - 9 - 6
Painting	88 - 15 - 0
Repairs	67 - 19 - 5
	612 - 1 - 7

By the mid- 1920s a telephone had been installed

Purists in architectural taste have criticized the mixture of styles, the irregularity of outline, its towers, turrets, battlements, corbels and lofty chimneys, as bizarre and eccentric. Nonetheless, it was a product of its age, a landmark in the countryside, and an imposing pile built as a monument to the glory of a distant past, a proud heritage and a social order which was meant to last for centuries[8].

When he inherited the Bronwydd estate and the Lord Marchership of Cemais, Thomas Davies Lloyd came to realise the long distance between his family home at Bronwydd and the castle of Newport, the ancient 'caput' of the barony. He was also familiar with the history of Newport and that, in ancient times, the barony had been ruled from the castle ever since William Martin had built it in 1191. The castle had played an important part throughout the centuries: Nicholas Audley, another Lord of Cemais had lived there and, such was its importance that he was ordered by King Edward iii, in 1370, to strengthen its fortifications incase of an invasion by the French. During the revolt of Owain Glyndwr in 1409, it had suffered damage, and towards the end of the Tudor period (like many other castles) its rôle in defence had come to an end. By

1583, it was described as '... in utter ruyne and decay and hath been so for a long tyme and is not valued at anything in the rent rowles..'. It was used for many purposes: as a place of detention for petty rogues and vagabonds, and as barns and storehouses. In 1594, one of the towers was used for '...keeping of the Lordes houndes' and became known as '...the Hunters' Tower'.

By the end of the eighteenth century, topographical writers and artists like Sir Richard Colt Hoare and Henry Gastineau portray the castle of Newport as an ivy clad ruin, romantic, picturesque and a striking feature in the landscape. It had probably been plundered by local inhabitants; its stones used for building houses and cottages in the town, as had happened at Cilgerran and Newcastle-Emlyn. Burgesses had, sometimes, gathered there, in one of the under-crofts for meetings of the court leet. But it did not seem to have any future. In medieval times its demesne extended as far as Bury (Berry), and had once belonged to Lloyd of Bronwydd (through marriage into the Ford family of Bury) but the latter and all its land had been sold in 1786 to George Bowen of Llwyngwair. As has been made clear in this study, Thomas Davies Lloyd had great ambitions to become the Lord Marcher par excellence, 'Knight of the Shire' and 'Lord of Parliament'. Part of his plan was to acquire the old castle of Newport as the Lord Marcher's Pembrokeshire home. He was not deterred by the unpleasant fact that the castle was a ruin[9]. Lloyd's romantic imagination foresaw the castle of Newport rebuilt and refurnished, with ancient armour and trophies of the chase, finely woven tapestries hanging from its walls, its ramparts re-echoing to the revelry of banquets, the buffoonery of jesters, minstrels and the fulsome praise of bards.

Negotiations for its purchase were set in motion. The castle and Bury had descended from George Bowen of Llwyngwair to the Reverend David Griffiths, the 'Methodistical' vicar of Nevern, who had built a new mansion house at Bury in 1811, called Berry Hill. His son David George Griffiths was in financial straits by the 1850's, and the castle of Newport and the land around it were put up for sale. The ruins of the castle were not considered to be worth much apart from its picturesque attraction to artists, antiquaries and travellers interested in relics of olden times. The Castle Mill, however, was deemed to be of real value: the town's burgesses were bound by custom to grind their corn there, and the moat adjoining the castle served as a millpond, fed by the brook Afon y Felin. There were also, a few acres, which were rented out. But Thomas Davies Lloyd was only interested in the castle ruins and a little land around it - to ensure privacy and to provide for a small pleasure garden.

The real problem was finding the purchase money. The rebuilding of Bronwydd was going to be a drain on his meager finances in addition to the many other schemes he was engaged in. The sum of £700 had been mentioned between him and Mr. Williams Griffith George, his solicitor. In May 1852, a whole year before laying the foundation stone of the 'new' Bronwydd, Lloyd had met Mr. James Salmon, a Newport builder, to examine the ruins of the castle and to estimate what it was worth. Discreet approaches, concerning possible loans, were made to various persons. Rumours circulated that the castle ruins, the mill and several acres of land might fetch about £1,500 in a public sale. David George Griffiths had been the nominal owner, but had mortgaged his estate to the Reverend David George. The latter promised to lend Thomas Davies Lloyd the sum of £600, and his brother the Reverend John Picton George, a further sum. Already, a Mr. Williams of Cardigan had promised a loan of £500 @ 4½% interest, which had been deposited at the National Provincial Bank of England at Aberystwyth. Miss Bowen had been approached in the hope of borrowing £1,400 but '...no reply had been received...'!

Meanwhile, the Reverend David George had to consult his agent David Thomas of Gellyorlas 'as to the price to be offered at the sale', and Thomas Davies Lloyd was encouraged to find that George Bowen of Llwyngwair had made enquiries '...if a relation of his should purchase the Castle and Mill at Newport, whether Mr. Lloyd would purchase the castle and grounds ...' a suggestion, which was accepted, provided it was at a fair price. Subsequently, the sale took place in September, 1853; the whole property was knocked down to Miss Bowen (Martha Margaret Bowen, Cotham Lodge,? - Newport) for £1,775.Mr Bowen of Llwyngwair wrote to Thomas Davies Lloyd on 17 September to inform him '...that you might have the Newport Castle and lands at the same price for which they were knocked down to Miss Bowen'. Because Lloyd only wanted the castle, he was only prepared to offer £300 for it. By February 1854, and after a great deal of negotiation, the sale of the castle and grounds was completed and it became Lloyd of Bronwydd property for the sum of £700[10].

In due course parts of the castle were restored as a private residence from plans made by R. Kyrke Penson the architect employed at Bronwydd. The actual conversion was carried out by James Salmon, who continued to work there, on and off, until his death in August 1871. Extensions and improvements were made from time to time, and by 1900, David Jenkins, the Llandeilo architect, had devised a new water supply and drainage system. Periodically, the castle was let to wealthy industrialists and nouveau riche magnates on a short-term basis: those who wished to enjoy (in baronial surroundings) the salubrious air and glorious scenery of this part of Pembrokeshire.

Newport Castle, thus became a comfortable and dignified home worthy of the status and title of Lord Marcher of Cemais, and from its towers the baronial flag fluttered when the baron and his entourage visited his 'caput'. It was a formal expression of lordship and a statement of power. The accommodation at the castle was considerably less than that of Bronwydd, and consisted of –

Ground Floor: Hall, Drawing Room, Dining Room, Nursery, Butler's Bedroom, W. C.

Upper Floor: Four Bedrooms, Dressing Room, Servants' Bedroom, Bathroom and W.C.

Basement: Butler's Pantry, Kitchen and Scullery, Larder, Lobby

Towards the end of the nineteenth century the 'castle and offices' at Newport were valued, for insurance purposes, at £1,000.

To complete his building projects Thomas Davies Lloyd restored the 'Old College' at Felindre Farchog in the parish of Bayvil. According to tradition, the original building had been built as a school by George Owen of Henllys, but he had died before the new institution had been properly endowed. Dr Charles states that this old building had degenerated into an inn by 1739, and was used, sometimes, as a meeting place of the court leet of the 'Barony of Kemes'. In keeping with his claims, as Lord Marcher, Thomas Davies Lloyd, wished to revive its ancient status and make it an edifice befitting the role and as part of the 'display' of the lord of the barony. According to a survey made by the Royal Commission on Ancient Monuments in 1925, there were traces of stone mullions and carved features suggestive of its great age. Above the door was a stone plaque with the inscription 'Llysdy Arglwyddi Cemais 1559-1620'. One large room with its headroom, reaching to the roof, had a coved timber ceiling, and here homagers and suppliants came to plead (before the lord or his steward) their 'presentments', namely, the complaints and problems which affected them from day to day. With the decline of courts leet, courts baron and the rule of the Lord Marcher, this courthouse was abandoned and rented out to a tenant, whose duties were to look after the place. In recent times it has been sold as a private dwelling and fortunately, still stands as a relic of the rule of the 'Lords of Cemais'.

The old house of Cilrhiwe, in the parish of Llanfihangel Penbedw, was another Lloyd family home. It was here that Anne Davies Lloyd spent most of her very long life, and perhaps, so as not to disturb her quietude, no attempt was made by Sir Thomas Davies Lloyd to rebuilt the house. It is thought that it dates back to the seventeenth century –a double pile two-storied house with an attic, and assessed in 1670 with eight hearths. Commodious and well built, albeit in a plain style, the interior contains a broad Jacobean staircase, with balustrades and finials, rising from the hall to the upper stories. The old parlour is fully panelled, as is, also, one side of the hall. It remained the property of Sir Marteine Lloyd of Bronwydd until 1911, when it was sold along with the Cilrhiwe estate lands. Fortunately, it is still occupied and preserved as a good example of the vernacular style of former times[11].

One feature of baronial rule was the periodic custom of the perambulation of the boundaries of the barony, like the beating of the bounds and the marking of the limits of land claimed by many communities. In the history of the Bronwydd family, the 'perambulation' was a public assertion of the 'rule' of the Lord Marcher. The prestige and power (claimed and exercised with vigour by George Owen of Henllys) seems to have diminished before the lordship was acquired by the Lloyd family of Bronwydd. The Bronwydd deeds, for a few generations before the barony became Bronwydd property, are relatively silent with regard to any exhibition of power displayed by the lord. But with the marriage of Thomas Lloyd of Bronwydd to Ann Lloyd of Penpedwast in 1739 and the purchase of the remainder of the barony in 1751 the situation changed. Lloyd was determined to exercise his power and to demonstrate this by celebrating periodic perambulations claiming chief rents and holding courts baron and courts leet. But, as will be seen the 'perambulation' became an exercise in expensive pageantry and a grand spectacle to enhance the credit and reputation of the Lloyd family. Moreover, it gave the populace within the barony and the residents of the town of Newport, an opportunity to show their loyalty and to enjoy the largesse handed out on these occasions, the jollity, merriment and general festivity shared by all.

In June 1759, eight years after acquiring the entire barony, Thomas Lloyd succeeded in finding an elderly witness to testify to what the customs had been many years since. No written record of any perambulation had survived. However, one George William of the parish of Ambleston (well outside the barony) was prepared to declare on oath, that he was eighty eight years of age and clearly remembered a perambulation of 'sixty three years ago' (1696) and '…could recall every stopping place along the route…that Owen of Henllys was then Lord Marcher, and cattle from Maenclochog being impounded, and…how trespassers for coming and going within the Boundary of the Perambulation were dealt with at College (Felindre Farchog)…being an adjournment of the Court Leet…' George William signed his statement 'by mark'. According to this single witness, what had taken place was simply a 'perambulation' or 'walking around' the perimeter of the barony for the purposes already mentioned. Miscreants were dealt with on the spot – for trespass, enclosing plots, cutting 'matts', allowing animals to stray, building 'tai-un-nos' and the like – by the Lord Marcher and his jury (usually twelve or more loyal homagers). These matters became an ever-recurring problem and had increased by July 1777 when another perambulation took place[12].

By the early decades of the nineteenth century the septennial perambulation developed into a more formal prestige celebration. Thus, for example, in July,

1813, Thomas Lloyd, the Lord Marcher, James Davies, the deputy steward of the barony, the Rev. David Harries, clerk (in Holy Orders) 'one of His Majesty's Justices of the Peace in and for the county of Pembroke' assembled at Mountain Hall, Brynberian. One Thomas Philip swore an oath to lead the perambulation along the 'ancient boundary of the common within the Barony of Kemes' as he saw it perambulated 'about thirty six years ago and afterwards eighteen to twenty two years ago'. Indeed, by now there were well established precedents according to Thomas Philip, and what the aged George William had vouched for in 1759.

The lord and his officials participated in the ceremony by 'carrying banners aloft, with the barony's flag foremost'. But, there were hindrances and minor irritations on occasion. On arriving near a place called 'Plygytrench and along the trench to Fleming's road…banners were dropped because a Mr. Greenish challenged the land below the said road as the private property of Sir John Owen, Bart. of Orielton…' Greenish claimed that he had held the land for thirty years and that he had papers to prove that adjacent land belonged to the Grove estate (Hafod Grove/H. Glandwr?) of Mr. Colby. After heated exchanges, Greenish was told to produce such papers to Mr. Lloyd within fourteen days '…and he refused whereupon the Lord Baron and the Homagers made up their minds to have the case stated for Counsel's opinion..' Mr James of Vaynorfach, who was born at Vagwrgoch, in order to clarify the situation, stated with regard to the years claimed by Greenish that '…there is no more than seven or eight years all told..' But, there was further trouble '…when Col. Scourfield's tenants said that the great part of what was walked as common, formerly part of Mynydd Du farm and as Martha, Mynydd Du had said, that stones had been placed thereon as marks when Col. Scourfield and Mr. Hassall had agreed..' As there were no threats and the parties had reached a compromise the perambulation continued peacefully. Banners were raised once more, along '..a line between Kemes and Maenclochog..' and, eventually after several stops the procession reached Clynymaen and adjourned until eleven o'clock the next day.

The second day proved to be more eventful: an encroachment by James Thomas, was broken into by those in the perambulation, and apparently, without a scuffle a breach was made in the hedge and possession was made of the Poor House (?) and garden. Other enclosures, dwellings, 'turf houses' or 'peasants' cotts were occupied, but a 'ffald' (parish pound or enclosure for stray cattle) was ignored as '..it was not considered an enclosure..' In some places, nuisances were observed and complaints made against some occupants of cottages when they infringed the rights of others to the commons.

What appears clearly from time to time is that the perambulation was as much of an assertion of the lord's rights as an opportunity for many aggrieved commoners to have their own rights ratified and confirmed by the Lord Marcher. Sometimes buildings had been erected across the boundary line, and the procession had to go through 'kilns and cow houses' near Troedyrhiw

115

cottage, the 'poor house' below Brynberian bridge and through a garden to the left of the door of a 'meeting house'. There were many similar instances of incursion into the barony and in many cases, where the exact boundaries were, had long been forgotten[13].

The practice of perambulating the boundary continued regularly in the years 1817, 1822 and 1829. The perambulation followed on the adjournment of the court leet and court baron, although it would appear that individual presentments could be dealt with by the lord himself when he was present. In May, 1817 Thomas Lloyd was there in person to resolve any problems while the steward James Davies carried out the formalities such as, swearing in thirteen jurors, reading out the names of complainants and the like. The dispute with Greenish continued, and there was no indication at all that he intended to produce papers (if he had any) in support of his claim against Thomas Lloyd. The latter had once more to rely on the oral testimony of elderly inhabitants on the commons, to ascertain the route taken by previous perambulations. Martha Lewis, Mynydd Du, swore on oath that '..about forty years ago she saw a perambulation..' when Mr. Lloyd of Cwmgloyne was present, and 'that Rowland Williams of Eglwyserrow-[wrw] and his wife had brought victuals and ale ... and those who carried the banners this day *went the same way..'* In spite of the periodic perambulations, which had taken place since 1759, enclosure of land and building on it still continued up to the last perambulation in 1882 in spite of the vigilance of agents and stewards, and strict injunctions from the Lord Marcher.

But, as well as a means to consolidate the rule of the lord, an element of pageantry, ceremonial and public jollification becomes more prominent as the years went by. At the head of the procession, the 'pioneers' marched, stopping at various points on the route to examine boundary marks and 'to fix stones on doubtful sites marking the boundary'. Social involvement and community merry making, not only provided some diversion and relief in the humdrum lives of the peasantry, but also, acted as a means of defusing many of the tensions of the day. One can imagine the bonhomie in country taverns and inns when the procession arrived, the stirring sounds of the brass band, the calling of drinks all round after traversing many a mile of rough country, the doles handed out and the 'vails' earned on these occasions: for example –

	£ - s - d
'Ale for the jury at Mountain Hall	8 - 10
Expenses for (? Owen) Lloyd and self at Eglwyswrw	11 - 6
Ale for Band at Castle Inn, Newport	3 - 0
Paid for two 'pioneers' 3 days @ 1/6 each ...	9 - 0
" one 'pioneer' 2 " " "	3 - 0
Ale for 'pioneers' at Castle Inn, Newport	8
" and pence to the boy from Tafarnybwlch ...	6

Cash to Mr. Owen Lloyd towards his expenses   3 - 6

Bill for Ale to pay Band, etc. at Mason's Arms ...   1 - 0 - 9

When Thomas Lloyd of Bronwydd, died in 1845, his son and heir Thomas Davies Lloyd was serving with the 82nd Regiment of Foot in Canada. Taking advantage of his absence abroad, and at a time of 'Rebeccaite' unrest and other incidents of social upheaval, further encroachments were made on the commons of the barony, and unclaimed wrecks were plundered 'because there was no one to represent the lord...' There was so much looting and the danger of violence between rival gangs (not to mention the loss to the lord and those who might have an honest claim to goods and property) that Joseph Watkins of Cwmeog wrote to advise Mrs. Ann Davies Lloyd that 'walking the mountain' (as well as other measures) was urgent. One item was singled out, namely, five acres or more, worth £7-5s a year at Whitechurch (Eglwyswen) had been enclosed without having the titles to its ownership 'presented' at a court (baron). After remonstrating with the offending parties, Watkins reported that they all agreed, except two, to pay chief rents. Local homagers, loyal to the Lord Marcher expressed the hope that '..the Lord of the Manor will walk possession...the sooner the better..'[14]

In June 1846, after Thomas Davies Lloyd's return from Canada he considered the perambulation of the barony to be of first importance. Thomas George, the steward, had notices printed of a perambulation to take place on 1st July, with a special 'adjourned' court at Mountain Hall '..when and where the respective Homagers are required to attend and whence the Procession will commence immediately..' As in previous years, the proceedings began with the swearing in of the jury and homagers.

Starting from Eglwyswrw, the Lord Marcher's 'Progress' (it was now becoming a very formal and grand event) set forth to go round the whole barony, which lasted for four days.

Wide publicity was given in *'The Carmarthen Journal'*, *'The Welshman'* and *'The Pembrokeshire Herald'* to the Lord Marcher's descent from Martin de Tours, the suzerainty of the Lords of Kemes from Norman times and their rights confirmed by '..Royal Charter contemporaneous with Magna Carta, the bulwark of the British constitution..' The claims of the Lloyd family of Bronwydd were unassailable: to chief rents, to their authority executed through baronial courts and to the allegiance of the inhabitants. The populace responded with enthusiasm; they came in crowds, the halt and maimed old and young. Banners fluttered in the breeze; church bells rang from parish to parish, calling the people to join in the celebrations, to show their respect and not least, one suspects, to express solidarity with the 'status quo'. The Bronwydd Brass Band led the procession into the town of Newport, playing the stirring tune 'See the Conquering Hero Comes'. Welcomed by the Mayor, Aldermen and Burgesses and the 'whole assemblage, which had crowded on each of four days', they testified their unfeigned loyalty to Thomas Davies Lloyd.

A Court was held at the castle (a symbolic act as the castle was still in ruins); a jury and burgesses were sworn and a perambulation of the town and surrounding commons followed. At six o'clock a sumptuous dinner was served at the Castle Inn, with J. Harries, the mayor, presiding. On the mayor's right sat Thomas Davies Lloyd with the Rev. William Thomas on his left. Full justice was done to the entertainment, and loyal toasts to the Queen, Prince Albert, the Royal Family, the Army and Navy and to the established Anglican Church, and as the account continued, the mayor called for '…bumpers (large measures) of wine to toast the distinguished visitor Thomas Davies Lloyd, Esq. of Bronwydd…' The highest respect and admiration of the community to the Lord Marcher, his extensive landed possessions and concern for those less fortunate were extolled in the speeches that followed.

In reply, the Lord Marcher gave a resume of his career so far: his service to the Queen in foreign climes, his never ending love for his native Wales, and especially, the cordiality he had received from his brother Welshmen during the perambulation. He emphasised his concern for the continued prosperity of the ancient borough of Newport. And, with further toasts to his mother, Anne Davies Lloyd, the 'grand dinner ended with eclat'. But the celebrations continued well into the night. On the castle mound, a huge bonfire was lit, along with tar-barrels on the bastions of the castle. A profusion of rockets and other fireworks illuminated the sky 'casting a magnificent light over the town and neighbourhood of Newport', according to a press account.

This event, on Friday, 7 July 1846, may well be regarded as Thomas Davies Lloyd's debut on the stage of British politics. The glamour of being the first citizen in a west Wales backwater was gratifying and very enjoyable; the acclamation of a tail wagging (and largely) uncultivated and ignorant populace, were gestures to be accepted graciously. But, no doubt, Thomas Davies Lloyd had a higher ambition; the campaign to become a 'knight of the shire' and 'Lord of Parliament' was about to be launched[15].

Perambulations were regularly held from now on. They followed the same pattern and took the same route; courts baron and courts leet were held to uphold the quasi-judicial role and importance of the lord of the barony, in spite of the constant breach of custom and challenge to his authority and what appeared to the lord as the acrid and malignant intrigue of radical elements. The perambulation of 1853 commenced at Eglwyswrw; courts were held at Mountain Hall; presentments were heard, and when all was settled, the jollification began. The 'very efficient' Bronwydd Band led the procession. Here and there, copious draughts of 'cwrw da' were drunk and, after a long trek, a copy of the ancient charter was presented to the mayor at Newport. This was more than a symbolic gesture but a re-affirmation of the town's rights and privileges since the days of Nicholas Martin. The status of the town had not been seriously damaged after the Royal Commission of 1835, but a renewed attack was always possible, and, indeed, came about in the 1880's as has been described.

Another perambulation took place in July 1860. Herdsmen and shepherds, yeomen farmers and petty traders, freeholders and gentry assembled on Brynberian bank. About seventy loyal homagers bearing banners attended the court in the open air, which was compared to '..that granting of the Great Charter of England by king John to his barons at Runnymede..' Allowing for the somewhat hazy interpretation of the signing of Magna Carta in 1215, the event was intended to emphasise the continuity of the rule of the Lord Marcher. Oaths of allegiance to him were sworn. The feudal theory of the lord's rights over land, the barons holding land of the king, the place of vassals and serfs in the hierarchical pyramid was re-enforced. The corresponding duties, obligations and services owed by the lower orders, in exchange for dependence on and protection from the lord, formed the basic structure of social anatomy.

Emotion and sentiment were added, when the young heir to the barony, Marteine Owen Mowbray Lloyd (a little boy of nine years of age) took part in the ceremonies for the first time. On the left breast of the jurors, Mr. George, the Steward and the Rector of Newport, he (aided by his mother and governess) pinned rosettes as their badge of office. In response they bowed in obeisance, and affirmed their allegiance then and for the future. The perambulation ceremony continued with the swearing in of the new official 'Markers of (the) Boundary' and then, the procession re-formed in strict order with a retinue of markers, flag bearers, pioneers who were fully 'armed' with mattocks and spades, jurymen, horsemen and officials of the barony carrying halberds, followed by a throng of pedestrians. On Brynberian bank, the '...flag was taken through the window of one house and out through the other..' such was the attention to detail with which the ceremony and the integrity of the boundary were observed. Other developments are significant. At the gate leading to Llwyngwair, James Bevan Bowen, Esq. met this motley feudal militia: a gesture of amity and goodwill between families, which had been formerly rivals for pre-eminence in the affairs of Newport and the barony. Moreover, the throng included clergy of the established Episcopal church and nonconformist ministers – all prepared to bury their doctrinal and political dogma and eager to pay '..homage to the man they delighted to honour..'

By the time Newport was reached the procession was a mile long - horsemen, gentry, carriages, donkey carts and the '...young heir on his Lilliputian pony..' The Lloyd family carriage was taken up to '. the newly erected hall of the castle...' where Thomas Davies Lloyd addressed those assembled in a speech which provides the key to his interpretation of past history and to his own social and political ideology. Not without a degree of simulated modesty, he asserted that he was unworthy to have any claim on any one present. They, his audience, were all gentlemen of independent means (referring to the county

119

gentry and freehold farmers) who had left home and harvest at a critical period of the year (mid July). Nevertheless, and to loud cheers, he claimed that '..ancient custom is on my side..there was no constraint on any one…but we are all tied together by bonds of mutual interest…not of yesterday's growth but accumulated for centuries…their fathers and forebears had showed loyalty, and in this matter-of-fact nineteenth century the age of chivalry is not over.. (and with regard to the Lord Marcher's rule within the barony)...its vitality is that it carries out the great principle of self-government, the very basis of our institutions…' the foundation stone of which was a benevolent gentry and aristocracy of merit to whom a dependent and deferential gwerin owed its allegiance. These sentiments were to be repeated later when he was a Member of Parliament at Westminster. That so many people showed their support to the Lord Marcher on perambulation day is not surprising. These events were of considerable economic benefit to the community –additional employment, provision of goods and services, increased trade in shops and taverns and not least, the largesse handed out to the poor and needy according to the following list of payments (one example from many)

John Harris, Newport (as Steward) .... £45 -	1 -	1 ½
Margaret Harris, Serjeant's Inn, Eglwyswrw	2 -	4 - 11
R.Watkins, Eglwyswrw, 67 yards 'Cadis'		
(coarse cloth/ribbon).........................	5 -	7
Rachel Phillips, Newport, porter (type of beer) to flagmen	3 -	0
John Harris for Ale	1 -	1 - 10
John Griffiths, 4 days attendance, peramb	4 -	0
James Williams, attendance at perambulation ...	0 - 16 -	0
Stephen Phillips, 4 days attendance as flag bearer	14 -	0
David Bateman, 4 days labour @ 5/- a day	1 - 0 -	0
Wm. James, 4 days as pioneer	12 -	0
Jn. Peregrine, 4 days as pioneer	12 -	0
Dd. Jones, Mt. Meline for showing commons, 4 days	12 -	0
Thos. John, " " "	12 -	0
Jn. Griffiths " " "	12 -	0
Samuel Jn. " " "	12 -	0
David Stephens, pioneer	12 -	0
Jn.Watts, Tw Bach, Meline	12 -	0
Thos. Bevan, (for) ale, spirits, etc	4 - 5 -	1
Jn. Rees, Surveyor	8 - 18 -	0
Eliz. Hughes, Royal Oak, ale to Band, etc	8 -	6
D. Seaborn, Draper, Oil cloth and Ribbon	12 -	0
H.Morgan, 2 days attendance	3 -	0
Jos. Williams to jurors, band etc	15 -	11
Sarah Frances, Ship Aground, workmen, at Dinas Church	5 -	0

Various labourers	10 -	0	
Ale, etc	10 -	2	
John Davies, Llwyngwair Arms	11 -	6 -	1
Mary Rees, Cwmgloyne Arms	1 -	7 -	6
David Hughes, Tavern y Bwlch	18 -	6	
Dd. Williams, Bank Pencelly for taking care of flags			
@ 2/6 per day	10 -	0	
Total, with certain deductions 1/-	£50 -	11 -	1½

Over all, the expense of the perambulation had greatly increased during the years and even, Lady Henrietta Lloyd expressed concern. The bills for breakfasts, dinners, suppers, gallons of port, grog, ale and spirits, together with the cost of horses, ostlers, labourers, flagmen, material for banners, ribbon for bunting and the like, showed that all and sundry were profiteering; it was time to look closely at the cost of the perambulations. To take only one example from many the 'flagman' one Stephen Phillips and the 'good persevering walkers' had to be supplied with suppers, bed and breakfast at various hostelries all over the barony. Phillips was 'of tee-total habits', yet the amounts claimed for him seemed too much. Lady Lloyd gave instructions to Mr. William Griffith George to question John Daniel Jones of Hawen, Rhydlewis, (who supervised the event) about certain amounts charged for in the dozens of bills, which came to Bronwydd. In reply Mr. George explained '…with regard to Mr. Stephen Phillips' teetotal drink I can only say that [was] all he had during the perambulation. Why Mrs. Rees (an innkeeper) should charge 2/6d I do not know unless he had during the week several crusts of bread and cheese and she may have thought it right to stick on a little on that account or perhaps she thought that sixpence for the inn-keeper's profit not out of the way – what was the size of the bottle? When I examined and signed the bill, it did not occur to me as being above the usual price. I did not know at that time the value of Peppermint per bottle otherwise I should have had an explanation of Mrs. Rees. You are aware we endeavored to act as economically as we could and I had hoped that our expenses would have been less than on former occasions…Wm. Griff. George…'[16]

Irrespective of cost, the perambulations for the years 1867 and 1875 were marked by greater ceremonial and pageantry. It will be recalled that Sir Thomas Davies Lloyd had been honoured with a baronetcy in 1863; he had been a Member of Parliament, and was angling for a peerage (privately if not publicly). Press reports of the perambulation of 1875, the last one for Sir Thomas, gave full blown coverage of the Lloyd 'ancestry' from Martin de Turribus and other illustrious Norman barons to George Owen of Henllys, and thence to modern times. As in previous years, the perambulation started off from Eglwyswrw, where a large concourse of people had assembled. Farmers on horseback and pedestrians were present 'by the hundreds' some of them wearing fancy costumes and carrying banners to greet Sir Thomas Davies Lloyd, Baronet, Lord Marcher of Cemais, and his entourage - Marteine O.M. Lloyd, the Rev. Rhys Jones Lloyd, Miss Jones Lloyd (his daughter) and Sylvanus Howell Lewis, Esq. of Brookfield near Bronwydd. Following the usual custom the Bronwydd Band played 'See the conquering Hero Comes' and that with great effect under the baton of Samuel Jones. This added much to the enjoyment of the celebrations. Following the usual route the procession was led, in strict order of precedence, by the steward, the surveyor of the barony, along with another functionary in the hierarchy —the woodward, one James Rees, and officer likened to the 'Keeper of the Royal Woods and Forests'!

At the head was Mr. Thomas John of Castell '…a veteran pioneer of the barony, eighty four years of age … who had taken part in no less than seven perambulations..' The Bronwydd band took its prominent part as on previous occasions, and looked resplendent in its new livery: red capes and blue uniforms with gilt buttons. Another innovation was the Band Flag bearing the motto 'Church and Queen' a clear signal to those adherents of radical, anti church and Liberationist factions. A whole variety of other flags were carried by 'Flag Bearers' dressed in scarlet tunics. The blue baronial flag proclaimed in bold white lettering 'The Barony of Kemes, County of Pembroke, Sir Thomas Davies Lloyd, Bart., Lord of the said Barony'. Tenants and homagers on horseback, as well as the crowd 'padding the hoof' followed, each with banners emblazoned with homespun slogans: 'Na symud mo'r hen derfyn a osododd dy dadau' (Do not move the old boundaries set by your forefathers), 'Hir hoedl i Arglwydd Cemais' (Long life to the Lord of Cemais), 'Success to the Lord of the Manor' and, at least, one in Latin, 'Veritas, via vitae' (Truth, the way of life) – all expressing loyalty to the Lord Marcher and to the Crown and Constitution. There was special mention of a local 'Knight of the Thimble' on his diminutive mountain pony bearing his standard 'The baron of Kemes for Ever'!

The 'pioneers', that sturdy band of loyal retainers, were dressed in new scarlet tunics with silver buttons and, as in previous years, carried halberds and mattocks but adorned for this occasion with rams' horns, flowers and other bizarre frippery. There was no shortage of 'cwrw da' and an unlimited supply of victuals of every kind, so that all present could enjoy themselves to the full in an atmosphere of cordiality, merriment and goodwill. Churchman and dissenter, radical and Tory appeared, outwardly at least, to exist in perfect accord. Tensions were to erupt from time to time, but were subsumed in the goodwill between different social classes; the centuries old loyalties had not yet felt the full onslaught of political and social change.

Here and there, along the route of the perambulation, courts baron and courts leet were held perhaps by this time, more of a symbolic gesture of influence than of the reality of power – an occasion of theatrical display, jollification, laudatory poetry and rhetoric, reaffirming the time-honoured attitudes of benevolence and deference. Fully aware of the political and social climate, the

Cardigan and Tivyside Advertiser added that all who were present at the perambulation '... had assembled to see that the Lord of the Barony had not been despoiled of any of his legitimate possessions, from which it may be safely be augured that their own rights and the defence of Wales would be stubbornly defended if cause arose...' in the amalgam of praise for the Lord of Cemais, his benevolent paternalism, love of homeland, and by implication, an attempt to smother discord and unrest, the account of the 1875 perambulation concludes with a 'patriotic' call for unity, both nationally and locally:

'... Though far from our mountains and valleys we roam
Still she [Cymru] is our mother, still she is our home
Then never let discord, ambition or pride
The 'undeb' [unity] of Cymry [the people] unwisely divide
But, let us, whatever our future may be
Dear Cambria be ever most mindful of thee ...'

The last perambulation of the Lord Marcher took place in 1882; the movement for parliamentary and local government reform was gaining momentum; the pageantry and 'display' indulged by the Lloyds, as Lords Marcher, was one of the casualties. Tradition was to give way to new forms of government and to democratic rule which dismissed the customs of the mediaeval past into the realm of fancy and the dim memories of long ago[17].

Family Celebrations

i

A gentleman's position and status in the community were reflected in the pattern of his social activities. Family events (examples of which will be described in the following pages) were meant to be celebrated in great style and with lavish display, so as to mark the stages in the family's continuity for many generations. Not only, were the marriages, christenings, coming of age of the eldest son and the death of the squire, important in the annals of the family but also, in the life of the estate and its tenants. Celebrations connected with these major events gave an opportunity to re-affirm old loyalties and to cultivate the good favour of the future squire. In the case of Bronwydd and the Lloyd family, details relating to domestic events and celebrations are very rare until the nineteenth century, when local newspapers recorded what was taking place at the mansion itself, as well as in the other large country houses of the county. The birthdays, especially of male heirs and their coming of age as future squires and landlords, were occasions of great rejoicing. With reasonable good fortune, the estate would survive. The lives of country folk: tenants and cottagers on the estate would continue unaffected as it had done for generations.

When Marteine Owen Mowbray Lloyd came of age on 27 February 1872, the celebrations were muted because the family was in mourning for his mother, Lady Henrietta Lloyd, who had died a few months previously. The intention had been to mark the occasion ' one of the most magnificent demonstrations that had happened in south Wales of sincere affection and appreciation of Sir Thomas Davies Lloyd as landlord.'

In spite of the sadness of the family, tenantry and neighbours were united in their decision to observe the young heir's birthday for, at least, two reasons: deference and respect towards the Lloyds, and as a gesture of hope for cordial relations between the landlord and his tenants in the future. They looked forward for fair play, equitable rents, no evictions, sympathy and compassion in times of distress, bad harvests and the like. Moreover, there were other bonds between landlord and tenant: respect for the Crown, the Constitution and the Established Church, on the one hand, and the continuation of the amicable toleration and patronage of dissenting 'causes' (chapels and meeting houses) here and there on the vastly scattered Bronwydd estate, on the other.

On the morning of Marteine O. M. Lloyd's birthday, about five o'clock the neighbourhood re-echoed with the discharge of forty guns from the bank overlooking the mansion house, and, '. simultaneously the Bronwydd Band struck up an inspiring air, continuing their music at intervals throughout the morning'. At eleven o'clock, a special service as held at Llangunllo Church, and '. the sacred edifice was crowded with tenantry and friends of the family.'

124

The officiating clergy were the Rev. Rhys Jones Lloyd, Troedyraur, John Price Jones, Newcastle Emlyn, and John Sinnett of Bangor Teifi, amongst others from the Emlyn Deanery. The service, as far as the Litany, was in Welsh (a reminder that the Lloyd family of Bronwydd did not despise the language of their ancestors). The 'Venite' was sung to a setting by P. Fussell, and the Te Deum to a Gregorian chant, the latter showing that the musical taste brought about as a result of the Oxford Movement had, by this time, infiltrated into the Teifi valley. Further light is shown on the liturgical nature of the service: the anthem sung was 'Arise, shine for thy Light is come', by Sir George Elvey, organist to William IV and to Queen Victoria, at St. George's Chapel, Windsor. The sermon, delivered by the Rev. Henry Jones, St. Dogmael's was on 'the apt text': 'and if children, then heirs, heirs of God, and joint heirs with Christ' [Romans VIII 17], which emphasised the nature of the divine and earthly order and the obligations of each and all within it.

The birthday celebrations continued with a dinner provided for the Cardiganshire tenants of the Bronwydd estate at the Cross Roads Inn, near Henllan. A 'silver hunting horn with a gilt bell and mouthpiece (costing six guineas and supplied by Messrs Kohler and Sons, London) was presented to the young heir. The gift was '…introduced to the company by Mr. James Rees, builder, of Look About, near Bronwydd, who inaugurated it by filling it to the brim with whiskey…' With a few appropriate remarks he drank to the health and happiness of Mr. Lloyd. The horn was then passed round to all present, filled again and again, and '. quaffed amidst the hearty cheers and heartfelt blessings for the heir of Bronwydd.'

Marteine Lloyd replied that it had not been possible to invite the tenants to Bronwydd on account of '. the deep family affliction.' (and in some Victorian houses at least a year had to pass before the household returned to normality, in terms of hospitality, entertainment, dress and behaviour at public worship after a family bereavement). The young heir was expected to behave as a Christian gentleman, and he was discreetly reminded of this when Mr. Thomas Jones, of the Bronwydd Arms, near Carmarthen, son of John Daniel Jones, the agent to the state, presented a Bible to Mr. Lloyd, while Miss Howell of Glaspant and the Rev. William Rees of Llangunllo gave him a copy of the 'Imitatio Christi' by Thomas a Kempis.

Similar events were held throughout the barony of Cemais, at Eglwyswrw, Newport and elsewhere. Local 'poets' rose to the occasion ready with their pens to extol the squire, as the bards of old had done throughout the centuries. In rustic verse, John Daniel Jones expressed the loyalty of the community and loudly acclaimed the good name of the Lloyds of Bronwydd: -

"Cydunwn gyda'n gilydd
Roi 'cheers' mewn llawenydd
I Marteine Owen Mowbray Lloyd
Ac enw gwych y Bronwydd.

Hir einioes dedwydd ddyddiau
Mewn llawnder byddo'i drigfan
A chaffed fyw r'un fath â'i dad
Yn serch y wlad yn gyfan

Mae'n disgyn o hen achau
Lin o lin o'r fath orau
Boed iddo yntau ddedwydd fyw
Dan nodded Duw ei dadau ...[1]

Weddings within gentry families were an occasion for ostentatious display, especially, if a good match had been arranged, with a generous portion or dowry by the bride's father to fill the coffers of the bridegroom's estate; or an alliance with another gentry family of, at least, similar (or better still) superior rank in the social hierarchy. It was hoped that the birth of a male heir in due course would ensure the continuance of the line and the estate. Sometimes a veil had to be discreetly drawn over the origin of the bride's wealth, if it had been derived from trade and commerce or some 'vulgar' and plebeian activity.

Whereas the Lloyd family of Bronwydd had, over many centuries, intermarried with Welsh (and mainly Pembrokeshire heiresses), as mentioned earlier in this account, Thomas Davies Lloyd married in 1846, Henrietta Mary Reid, a lady who could claim aristocratic Scottish connections, as well as, with the English, Oakeley clan of baronets: a union of special significance to the Lord Marcher of Cemais. Sir Marteine O.M Lloyd married in November 1878, Katherine Denistoun (see p29). The wedding took place at the church of St. Michael and All Angels, Helenborough in Scotland. Admission to the church was by ticket and 'many applications had been turned down, such was the interest in the event'. The account in the press described in detail the flower arrangements in the church, the dresses of the bride, the presents received and so on; the bridal journey to Edinburgh station, and thence, the 'progress' by rail to Hales, near Cheltenham, and other stops, so as to arrive at Bronwydd in 'about ten days time'. Eventually, they arrived in Carmarthen, and 'the couple stayed with the Morris cousins' at Coomb, Llangain. Then, on the last day, they travelled to Llysnewydd, Henllan, for lunch. At Henllan Bridge, forty tenants greeted Sir Marteine and Lady Lloyd on horseback, all wearing white rosettes, and where 'they were liberally provided with 'cwrw da'. By the time the couple arrived at the Bronwydd Lodge, some fifteen hundred people had gathered, many carrying banners bearing messages of welcome. The carriage was drawn by 'hundreds of eager hands from the lodge to the front door of Bronwydd', with a 'picked bodyguard carrying javelins and halberds' as escort. The crowd carried banners with words of welcome; feasting and merriment followed in the 'baronial hall' at Bronwydd, and a dance was arranged for the servants and their friends which lasted until the early hours of the morning.

Elsewhere in the barony, especially, at Newport, the marriage of Sir Marteine was celebrated with a long procession comprising the burgesses and inhabitants of the town. Patriotic and benevolent societies took a prominent part, the Loyal Kemes Lodge of Oddfellows, the Ivorites, Good Templars and local Band: each organisation wearing its special regalia and waving banners with slogans proclaiming the virtues they believed in. The Foresters, for example, propagated the doctrine of 'mutual well-being according to the ancient order of things', with the slogan 'Adam and Eve were the First Foresters – Unitas, Benevolentia et Concordia'.

Notwithstanding the pious mottoes and Biblical precepts, boldly displayed on banners and the 'cwinten' (see n.) ale-houses like the 'Llwyngwair Arms' and the 'Angel' were declared 'free houses' where beer, porter and 'fiery spirits' were freely available. At Cardigan, Dinas, Eglwyswrw and Felindre Farchog, the marriage was celebrated with great rejoicing and William Bennet of Dinas, received special commendation for 'supplying 38 gallons of Benzolene at wholesale price'. Farm servants and yokels gathered furze and faggots from the hillsides, which, with petroleum oil and 'Stockholm tar' they used to feed the bonfires. Mrs. Anne Davies Lloyd of Cilrhiwe entertained a large party 'with the best in food and drink'. Following a centuries-old tradition, local bards recited 'englynion', and those present sang to the accompaniment of harp and 'crwth'. In the autumn of 1878, collections were made throughout the barony to provide a 'testimonial' to Sir Marteine on the occasion of his marriage. Perhaps, it was natural for tenants and dependants in the neighbourhood of Bronwydd to feel more indebted than those further afield. As the following figures show the people of Newport and Dinas seem to have been stingier in their response: -

Cardiganshire	- Aberbank and district	£50	- 17	-	6
Carmarthenshire -	Penwch nr St. Clears	25	- 11	-	0
Glamorgan	- Llandeilo Talybont	9	- 17	-	5
Pembrokeshire	- Eglwyswrw	15	- 5	-	6
	Newport and Dinas	7	- 4	-	1
	Llanfyrnach	6	- 14	-	6

Was this because the inhabitants of Newport and Dinas were divided in their loyalty to the two traditionally rival houses of Bronwydd and Llwyngwair? Was there a strong and latent radical element in these places – the Rees, Brithdir, faction – against what some might regard as the overweening influence of the Lord Marcher? One never can tell![2]

Very rarely, and possibly owing to special circumstances, the marriage ceremony was held in a private house, the permanent residence of the bride, and in the company of family and close friends. Nevertheless, information was given to local newspapers, because the family concerned would have been the principal landowners in the area, with a community of dependants: farming tenants, cottagers, carpenters, joiners, masons, blacksmiths and artisans, whose livelihood and general well being were closely linked to the 'plas'. On 27 January, 1875, the wedding took place at Pentre (the home of the Saunders Davies family) of Thomas Morris (eldest son of William Morris of Coomb, Carmarthenshire) former MP for the Carmarthen Boroughs, and Alice Elizabeth Ann, only daughter of James John Lloyd of Bronwydd and Susan Maria Anne Saunders Davies of Pentre. The ceremony was held, by special license, in the 'magnificent drawing room' at Pentre, where Miss Lloyd had spent most of her life. A table was converted into 'a temporary altar covered with velvet of the grandest description with lace trimmings, upon which vases of hyacinths added colour and fragrance to the setting'. Gilt chairs were arranged for the guests and the attendants were the young ladies of Bronwydd and Pentre. On a lesser scale than a public wedding there were only two officiating clerics, the Rev. Rhys Jones Lloyd of Troedyraur, and the Rev. Alfred Barker of Sherfield Hampshire. In the absence of a pipe organ, the hymns and wedding march were played, in a 'most masterly manner on the grand forte-piano by Miss Saunders Davies. The wedding 'breakfast' followed in the 'noble dining room', with a special wedding cake by Bollands of Chester. The menu was as follows –

    Hot -   Turtle and Oyster Soups: Mutton Cutlets and Oyster Patties:
              Roast Woodcocks and Asparagus

    Cold -   Turkeys, rolled and plain; Chickens, Pheasants, Partridges, Pies
              (of every description); Rolled and Pressed Beef; Rolled Veal
              and York Hams; Tongues, Oxford Brawn; Savoury Jellies;
              Lobster and Chicken Salads; Ornamental and Clear Jellies

    Sweet -   Creams, Tipsy Cakes, Gateaux, Meringues and Pastries;
              Pineapples, Grapes

    Wines -   Madeira, Champagne, Port, Claret

In the evening a 'grand dinner party' (followed by a concert) was held at Pentre. The 'Mount Gernos Band of Brothers (the Messrs. Tyler of Gernos) sustained the principal parts'. Wedding presents were laid out in '… Mrs. Saunders Davies's private boudoir, to be examined and admired by all the guests'. A lengthy list of all the gifts was published, as was customary, in the local newspapers. Because this wedding was a family and estate celebration, Mrs. Saunders Davies had, already, entertained on New Year's Day 'all the men and women working on the Pentre estate, with a sumptuous repast of beef and plum pudding washed down with an unlimited supply of the strongest 'cwrw...' brewed (on the premises) for the occasion. Fireworks, bonfires, and the like, as has been noticed already followed as part of the general merry-making during such celebrations[3].

In this account of Bronwydd and the Lloyd family, it has become clear that Bronwydd (like some other country houses, even, to a much greater extent) could be described in Professor Mingay's phrase as 'the theatre of hospitality'. In addition, to quote 'The Cardigan and Tivyside Advertiser'. on every occasion when there is a day of rejoicing at Bronwydd, the inhabitants of the surrounding countryside, both on the estate and outside its confines rejoice with them, because not only is the family a distinguished one but a very popular one throughout the country...' These works re-echoed the evidence of the Liberal politician, W. Llewelyn Williams, before the Land Commission, that there was nothing more remarkable than the loyalty expressed by the community to the old Welsh families (especially in the face of political, radical and social change).

The occasion referred to was the wedding, in August 1921, of Miss Joan Henlys Lloyd, the youngest daughter of Sir Marteine and Lady Lloyd, to Col. Philip Saxon Gregson-Ellis of the Grenadier Guards, the only son of Col. and Mrs. Gregson-Ellis of Bryndyffryn and Plas Clough, Denbighshire. The ceremony took place at Llangunllo Church, which had been decorated by Goodyears, Bond St. London. The choir of St. Peter's church, Carmarthen, directed by the organist S.J. Mundy FRCO sang the service. Bishop John Owen, along with the Rev. E. Owen Jones of Llangunllo and local clergy officiated. The bride's attendants were the daughters of the Earls of Lovelace, Lisburne, Lord Percy St. Mair and Don Julio de Bittencourt of the Chilean Legation. A local 'prima donna', Madam Teify Davies, made her debut amongst the aristocracy with a rendition of 'A song of Thanksgiving', and 'an old and valued servant' Mr. Thomas Beazley, was one of the ushers in the company of distinguished members of the nobility. True to the hunting and sporting tradition of the family, an arch of 'otter poles' was formed by members of the Hawkstone Otter Hunt, led by the Master, Major David Davies, Llandinam.

The long list of guests included the names of the prominent gentry and nobility of the realm. The Prime Minister, D. Lloyd George and Dame Margaret (amongst many public figures) were, however, unable to be present because of other engagements. Sightseers from miles around came with banners and other emblems bearing messages of goodwill. The children of Aberbanc School founded by the Lloyd family were given a celebration party[4].

The lifestyle of the gentry was notable for lavish entertainment of guests at parties associated with particular events: the seasonal feasts and festivals of the Christian year, rent days, special occasions in the annals of the family, like coming-out balls, the presentation at Court of daughters, the visit of a famous figure, and such as those mentioned already. If tradition can be relied on, a 'fête champetre' was held at Bronwydd, in 1780, to honour Sir William Jones (1746-1794) the eminent philologist and authority on Hindu law. And another 'fête champetre' was held in June 1810, to celebrate the birthday of King George III. Regarded as a 'most splendid entertainment' the 'fête champetre' was a spectacle much in vogue in the great houses of the nobility, but the ill-fated Eglinton tournament of 1839,completely spoilt by a freak rainstorm, rendered such a costly event both risky and unfashionable. The indoor equivalent to the 'fête champetre' was the 'bal masque' when the participants wore fancy dress, bizarre costumes representing legendary and historical characters, cupids, 'druids and country swains'. Other events centred round musical and dramatical performances with the gentry taking the main parts. Invitations were sent throughout the county, and Bronwydd and Pentre were well known for the generosity and lavish display provided by the owners of these houses[5].

A 'Grand Ball' was held at Bronwydd in January 1882, (the first since the death of Sir Thomas Davies Lloyd in 1877) to celebrate Sir Marteine's year of office as High Sheriff of Cardiganshire. Two hundred invitations were sent out, and over a hundred persons were present. Rooms were lit with wax candles, and the architectural features of the house lent themselves admirably to the floral motifs depicting the valour, chivalry and noble character of the family. A contemporary journalist described this grand and 'mock medieval' event when '...the groined roof of the library put one in mind of the olden days, when illustrious barons and their retinue met each other, with a boar's head at the high table.' Guests were graciously received under a grand canopy over the front entrance steps which were 'richly carpeted in to the library which was fitted up as a reception hall for the occasion ... a hundred Chinese lanterns, fifty wax candles ... seasonal greenery holly and mistletoe, and hot house plants' adorned the rooms. The drawing room was re-arranged as a ballroom '. lit with gold candelabra...' The Carmarthen Quadrille Band provided the music, ranging from the current fashionable dance tunes to ancient Highland Scottish Reels'. A firework display on the terraces below the mansion '. lit up every angle of the noble building.' The guests included the Lord-Lieutenant of the county, Col. Sir Pryse-Pryse-Pryse of Gogerddan and his party, the principal gentry of the three counties of Cardigan, Carmarthen and Pembroke and Scottish relations of Lady Lloyd, descended from the kings of Scotland, who had been specially invited to '. add luster to the occasion'.

Dr. Mark Girouard asserts that eating and drinking, was the very essence of having a party. A party was not good unless it involved gorging and getting drunk! The following list gives some indication of the nature of the hospitality offered for supper on the night of the High Sheriff's party in January 1882: -

Supper - Oysters, Mayonnaise, Salmon, Soufflé of Lobster,Prawns in Aspic, Pigeons à la Princess, Supreme of Chicken, Cutlets Medallion, Terrine de Fois Gras, Ducklings, Lamb, Ham Glacé, Fillet of Beef a la Jadiniere, Hunter's Beef, Turkeys a la Royale, Ox Tongues, Raised Game Pies, Roast Chickens, Veal and Ham Pies, Béchamel Fowls, Forequarters of Lamb, Lobster Italienne, Anchovy Salads, Croquante of Oranges, Empress Meringues, Gateaux Francaises, Chocolate Tarts, Berlin Tarts, Liqueur and Macedoine Jellies, Raspberry Creams, Pine Creams, Charlotte Russe, Trifles, Tipsy Cakes, French and Venetian Pastry.

Dessert - Oranges, Pine (apples), Apples, Tangerines, Figs, Almonds, etc.
Ices, Strawberry Cream, Lemon Water.

Apart from this gargantuan supper there was, in addition, a 'Refreshment Buffet' for the guests during the dancing. 'Tea, Coffee, Ices, Cake, Biscuits, Claret Cup, Lemonade, etc, Soupe Julienne', were available.

In the press account, there is little mention of the wines, spirits and other alcoholic beverages, but one can be fairly certain that the Bronwydd cellars were fully stocked at this time. That the guests enjoyed themselves, not wisely but too well, is most likely and corroborated by H.M. Vaughan's comments on the 'deep potations' of some of the gentry he knew. It was not uncommon for gentlemen of good position to appear tipsy in the ballroom, at dinner parties, hunt and other celebrations. Indeed, a story is told how the Bronwydd carriage, on returning from a party at Pentre, capsized on a sharp bend of a narrow country lane. Sir Marteine was one of the occupants. Fortunately, no one was injured. When the coachman apologised the next day for the mishap, Sir Marteine reassured him that he had no recollection whatsoever of the incident![6]

In the annals of the Lloyds of Bronwydd, and towards the end of a chronicle of family celebrations the Golden Wedding anniversary of Sir Marteine and Lady Lloyd, in November 1928, turned out to be the last memorable social event at Bronwydd. In spite of the financial constraints on the Bronwydd estate, as on many others also, Lady Lloyd was not deterred by the advice of John Evans of Cardigan (the agent) to exercise economy. She was determined to celebrate in great style, and considered it an obligation. 'We owe it to our tenants and our neighbours to have a little flash.'

131

Dinners and parties were held throughout the barony of Cemais, as had been the case for many generations. In a large marquee at Bronwydd, some three hundred tenants and friends sat down to luncheon. 'the well known firm of Seary and Transley of Sloane St. London' carried out the catering. Alderman John Evans, JP. acted as Master of Ceremonies. In eloquent speeches, the noble and illustrious ancestry of Sir Marteine and Lady Lloyd, the country and sporting pursuits of an ideal squire, the charities supported by Lady Lloyd, and, not least, Sir Marteine's knowledge of Welsh, the language of his fathers, were given prominence. He was a 'rural Welshman' and the Bronwydd tenants were 'part of the family'. 'Shoals of congratulatory messages' arrived from afar: Lord and Lady Kylsant sent their good wishes by 'radio telegraph' from the ship 'The Olympic' and a neighbour Capt. Davies of Glenview, Llangunllo, did likewise from somewhere in mid-ocean.

The town of Newport was decorated as for a 'celebration of national importance' and tea parties and treats were given to the children. Thomas Thomas, Y Gwaunydd, a local rhymester composed verses in honour of Sir Marteine and Lady Lloyd:-

"Dathlu'r ŷm briodas euraidd
Lady a Sir Marteine Lloyd
Ni chaf eiriau all fynegi
Deimlad pawb o bob rhyw oed
Am eu haelionusrwydd gwastad
Heb ddiffygio drwy y lle
Haeddant barch am eu hymddygiad
Gan drigolion gwlad a thref.

Mae Sir Marteine yn rhagori
Ar holl fonedd gwych ein gwlad
Yn ei roddion at bob achos
Parod yw yn ddi-nacad
Hefyd Lady Lloyd mae hithau
Gorff ac enaid o'r un chwaeth
Yn llesoli pawb o'i chwmpas
Dyna'i phleser a'i hoff waith

Yna wedi gado'r ddaear
Caffont fynd i'r Nef i fyw
Byth mewn gwisgoedd gwynion disglair
Moli'r Oen yng nghwmni Duw ...."

Other worthies of the town of Newport, like Mr. E. R. Gronow, expressed his greetings in homely verse. The Rev. D. G. Phillips, rector of the parish added further tributes, and a local dissenting minister, the Rev. Ben Morris of Ebenezer Chapel, spoke in Welsh, because Sir Marteine and Lady Lloyd were Welsh (unaware of Lady Lloyd's Scottish connection). Mr. Morris had been born on the Bronwydd estate and spoke on behalf of himself and the Ebenezer church congregation. The official proceedings came to an end with a speech by Sir Evan David Jones, JP. DL. MP of Pentower, Fishguard[7].

Gentry preoccupation with status, dignity and display extended to the mode whereby, the death of the squire or a member of his family was observed. In some instances, the death of the local squire could be a calamity: the loss of the leader of the community and the unifying force in a hierarchical social structure, which had existed for centuries. A country house funeral could be a formidable affair, and a state funeral is the closest modern equivalent. The deceased lay in state, for relations, tenants and the local public to come and gaze at the corpse, as a show of respect. The ceremonial and ritual had to be observed scrupulously with acts of 'pietas' reflecting the obligations of each social degree and rank.

Inside the mansion, clocks were stopped, doorknockers muffled, stair banisters draped and the whole place seemed to be shrouded in black. The aged and infirm were given lengths of black cloth to make 'mourning scarves' and dozens, if not hundreds of black robed mourners followed the cortege to the church and to the deceased's final resting place. Although customs varied from place to place, the funeral procession was arranged in groups according to their station in society: peers, baronets, knights, esquires and gentlemen, along with a sprinkling of professional men, such as, lawyers, doctors, estate agents and the like. The kinsmen of the late departed carried the family banner, crest, and coat of arms or hatchment and on a cushion the badges, medals and other insignia of honour of the deceased. The hatchment was hung up in the church where the family worshipped, sometimes in perpetuity – all part of the pageantry of death.

Since early times, the commemoration of kings, elaborate tombs had marked chieftains, warriors and the famous, and, by the eighteenth century the family vault became fashionable amongst the gentry of the lower Teifi valley, as in other parts of the country. Rhys Lloyd of Bronwydd, in the early 1600's was content to be buried in a simple shroud, without any pomp or ceremony. But later, the family constructed a vault in the churchyard, at the west end of Llangunllo church[8].

Reference to a few Bronwydd funerals (as in the case of weddings, grand balls and the like, already mentioned) shows how lavish and dignified ceremonial was observed. Lady Henrietta Lloyd, who died on 5 November 1871, was buried in '… a new and spacious vault, because the old vault had only room for one more occupant' according to 'The Tivyside'. There was a very large cortege with mourning carriages extending for a mile; the funeral was conducted in a 'most solemn manner' and there was universal sadness. The bells of St. Mary's Church, Cardigan, tolled all day as a token of respect. 'The poor have lost a kind and considerate friend in their hour of need, and one

133

who showed sympathy with them in their troubles' – such was the sense of loss in the community.

Six years later, in July 1877, Sir Thomas Davies Lloyd, Bart died, in 'the noontide of his life'. The cortege left Bronwydd at twelve noon on Friday, 27 July and contemporary accounts describe exactly, how carriages carrying the Revs. W. Rees, Llangunllo, John Sinnett, Bangor Teifi, and T. Rogers of Llanfihangel-Penbedw, went first, followed by those of Dr. Thomas, Newcastle-Emlyn, and Dr. Powell of Rhydlewis – 'the late Baronet's medical attendants'. The hearse was heavily draped and drawn by four black horses, plumed, their hooves blackened, with Bronwydd servants as bearers, walking alongside. In the Bronwydd carriage which followed were the immediate male relations: the new baronet and heir, Sir Marteine, and the deceased's brothers the Rev. Rhys Jones Lloyd, Capt. Owen Lloyd, together with the Rev. Nigel Greesly. Then came the carriages of Mr. Thomas Morris of Coomb, Messrs. John and Reginald Lloyd, and Mr. Sylvanus Howell Lewis of Brookfield. The Kilrhue (Cilrhiwe), Pentre, Llysnewydd, Noyadd Trefawr and the carriage of Col. J. R. Howell of Pantgwyn were prominent. In the procession the Bronwydd family servants followed, and finally, some forty carriages of other county gentry with a vast concourse of people – 'gwŷr traed' (on foot) who had come from miles around to pay their respects to the deceased, and also, to participate in this 'solemn and dramatic spectacle of death'.

Sir Thomas Davies Lloyd was buried alongside Lady Henrietta in the new vault his body in three coffins: of lead, cedar wood and the outer one of oak. made by the estate carpenters and fitted with silver gilt handles by Messrs. Thomas and Evans.Messrs. Davies, also of Newcastle-Emlyn, provided suits and other articles of wearing apparel. In passing, it is noticeable that 'gentlemen only' attended this funeral.

Mrs. Anne Davies Lloyd, born in 1795, died in 1888. She had spent most of her long life at Cilrhiwe, as a typical Welsh lady of the manor: speaking the language, reading her Welsh Bible and taking part in the life and customs of the farming community of the neighbourhood.

Her generosity was a byword in the Cardigan area: in an out-kitchen at Cilrhiwe a whole sheep (together with vegetables) was regularly cooked in a huge 'pair' (cauldron) and distributed to poor folk during cold winter weather. Such, were some of the memories of Anne Davies Lloyd, current in the locality until fairly recently. The funeral cortege started out from Cilrhiwe on a fine June morning on its long journey to Llangunllo: plumed horses drew the hearse and its 'glass panels' was singled out for special mention. The Tyrhos Choir and the Rhoshill Lodge of Ivorites were present, to lead the congregation in singing the hymn, written by the Methodistical Baptist, Dafydd William, Bethesda'r Fro (1720-94)

"Yn y dyfroedd mawr a'r tonnau
Nid oes neb a ddeil fy mhen
Ond fy annwyl briod Iesu
A fu farw ar y pren ….

Blinds were drawn, young and old, the sick and infirm came to the doors of their newly whitewashed cottages to witness the cortege passing through Cilgerran, Llechryd, Cenarth and other villages. And after the obsequies, in Llangunllo church, the coffin was '…buried in the old family vault now closed…'[9]

The pageantry and splendour in the long history of Bronwydd drew to an end in April 1933, with the death of Sir Marteine O.M. Lloyd. Failing health, reduced circumstances, and, especially, the loss of his only son, Marteine Kemes Arundel Lloyd, in the Great War, had all taken their toll. The 'Grand Old Man of South Wales', a Justice of the Peace, Deputy Lieutenant for the three counties of Dyfed, Master of Foxhounds and, above all, the twenty-fifth Lord Marcher of Cemais, left Bronwydd for the last time.

Obituaries in 'The Times', and other newspapers, recalled his social work as chairman of the 'Discharged Prisoners Society', and his concern for the under-dog was such that many an 'old lag had reason to remember with gratitude his fatherly exhortation and kindness'. He was the epitome of the sporting squire: hunting, fishing, breeding fine horses, supporting the United Counties Hunters' Society, the Carmarthenshire Hunt Steeplechase, and proud owner of the Bronwydd Beagles and the Bronwydd Hounds. He was a patron of the United Counties Agricultural Society, and treated his tenants with compassion and generosity (sometimes, it could be argued, with excessive leniency).

Generations of the same families had toiled on Bronwydd land, and looked up to Sir Marteine with respect but without subservience, with affection but without pretence. The funeral took place at Llangunllo on Saturday, 4 April. Donald MacDonald, piper to the Mackintosh of Mackintosh, Cottrel, Glamorgan and Moy Hall, Inverness, led the cortege. The coffin was borne in a farm waggon drawn by 'Dolly' an old mare blinded in the War. The strains of Scottish laments re-echoed over the countryside, as 'nobility and commonalty', to use an ancient phrase, followed the coffin to its final resting-place. The clergy of the Emlyn Deanery, Bishop David Lewis Prosser, civic dignitaries, doctors and lawyers, the Burgesses of the Newport Court Leet, and, not least, the pupils of Aberbanc School, had a place of honour along the route. The choir of St. Peter's Church, Carmarthen, led by the organist, F. Vernon Curtis, FRCO, sang the funeral service, and the Bishop read the committal sentences and Blessing. The ceremony concluded with the vast congregation singing 'O fryniau Caersalem ceir gweled..' and then, departed, with heavy hearts, to the strains of 'The Flowers of the Forest' played by the piper.

Traditional deference and respect had not diminished. All over the barony and the estate, there was mourning: at Newport, the barony flag was flown at half-mast, blinds were drawn in farm and cottage. The charity of the deceased is still extolled, as part of the folk memory of the area. From now on the doors of Bronwydd closed for the last time, never to open again to the Lloyd family. Lady Lloyd moved from Bronwydd to Newport Castle, a less costly establishment to maintain. She died in March 1937, at Lady Carnarvon's Nursing Home, in London, and was buried at Llangunllo[10].

Benevolence and Patronage

ii

The deep personal regard and public respect shown by the community towards the house of Bronwydd, as related already, can be explained in terms of the family's benevolence and patronage. Over the centuries they showed 'good nature, civility, paternalism, benevolence and generosity' – ideals which social analysts from the Tudor period onwards have regarded as the mark of 'true gentility'. The lower orders responded with respect and deference. In some ways, it could be argued that after the collapse of monastic charity at the dissolution of the monasteries, the gentry were the pioneers in this field until the coming of the welfare state.

Of all the 'Tivyside' gentry, the Lloyds of Bronwydd, were for almost four hundred years at the head of their peers on account of their liberality towards good causes. First and foremost, the Lloyds (like the majority of Welsh gentry) were supporters of the constitution: a protestant church as an arm of the state, the two houses of parliament with the sovereign at the apex. Roman Catholicism was anathema denigrated in a virulent 'Paisleyite' cocktail of abuse against Romish idolatry, superstitious practices, the threat from the anti-Christ Pope of Rome, stirred up also, by memories of the Armada, Guy Fawkes, Irish lewdness and alliances with the enemies of the realm - all part of the folklore shared by many of the gentry, the educated and the ordinary people of the land. The attitude of the Lloyds, in particular was a broad tolerance towards the rise of nonconformity, the break with the Anglican church, the growth of radical politics – a philosophy of 'live and let live'.

As owners of the advowsons connected with five parishes, they had a vested interest other than in terms of cash from the sale or lease of the advowson. They were, it is true, expected to keep the churches in good repair and to be concerned with the welfare of parishioners. They acted as virtual owners of these parishes; they could nominate a person of their choice as 'minister' (to use Prayer Book terminology) of the parish: a friend or near relation such as a younger son from one of the 'county' families. It was important to appoint

136

someone of safe theological and political views who was not likely to foster dissent far less discord in the community.

In September 1714, William Laugharne, MA, clerk in holy orders was given the living of Newport (and this is part of the Bronwydd story) by his elder brother John Laugharne of Llanrheithan. Many years later Thomas Lloyd chose the Rev. James Bowen (of the Pentre Ifan and Llwyngwair family) to the same living. And after Bowen's death, Thomas and Anne Lloyd of Penpedwast appointed in 1759, the Rev. John Higgon, clerk MA to succeed as rector of Newport. In this way family ties were forged, political links were strengthened and the squire's influence consolidated. About the same time, the living of Meline was held by the Rev. Watkin Lewes (father of Sir Watkin Lewes one time Lord Mayor of London) an appointment through Bronwydd influence – a further example of family ascendancy and perhaps, open nepotism in an age when there were few educated persons to occupy such positions.

In the nineteenth century Bronwydd patronage continued. Three Bronwydd nominees were incumbents of Newport. The Rev. Llewellyn Lloyd Thomas, Evan Jones and David Griffith Phillips were appointed during the period 1824 to 1904,and their influence was strong in supporting the rule of the Lord Marcher in the sometimes unruly affairs of the town and in the matter of wrecks, as in the case of the 'silver flute'. Clerical pluralism does not seem to have caused any qualms of conscience. James Lloyd of Bronwydd, esq. presented the living of Dinas in 1825 to the Rev. Daniel Bowen, MA of Waunifor, Llandysul, who was also, unashamedly a Prebendary of St. Davids Cathedral, vicar of Llanllwni and rector of Whitechurch and Kemes! Sometimes the exercise of patronage was to favour young men of promise from within the Lord Marcher's immediate domain, for example, the Rev. James Williams, from Penrhiwllan (a village of a mile or so from Bronwydd) was appointed rector of Dinas in 1879 and held it until his death in 1905.

In the history of the Lloyds of Bronwydd, it was a moral imperative for them to support churches and meeting houses (tai cwrdd). To take a few examples-Rees Lloyd of Bronwydd, in 1632, left by will a sum of money towards 'the reparation of Llangunllo church' and like other gentry (from post-reformation times until late in the eighteenth century) a token sum towards '. the cathedral church of St. Davids.' The tower of Cardigan church collapsed in August 1705, and Thomas Lloyd of Bronwydd and James Lloyd of Cilrhiwe donated 5gns and 1gn. a piece. By the end of the eighteenth century Llangunllo church was in a very dilapidated state. This prompted the Rev. John Howell of Penybeili to bequeath £100 to pay for all dilapidations and £21 to the curate, but according to Samuel Lewis, in 1833, the church was rebuilt at ' the sole expense of the late proprietor of the Bronwydd estate, (i.e. Col. Lloyd). In September 1796, he arranged for '. nine Turnpike trust tallies in the Cardiganshire district of the value of £300 to be held on trust for the minister and congregation of the protestant meeting house in St. Thomas' Green, Haverfordwest, and at Keston

137

in the parish of Camrose...' according to the will of his mother-in-law Sarah Jones[11].

His ecumenical outlook inspired him to build at his own expense a chapel at Aberbanc, Henllan, to be known as Capel-y-Drindod (Trinity Chapel). This gave rise to a popular legend. It is said that the Colonel was out hunting on the Cardiganshire coast, and unexpectedly came to a wide chasm. Miraculously, his horse jumped clear, thus saving itself and master from certain death. Consequently according to this bizarre story, the event was regarded as an omen, which led to Lloyd's 'conversion' from his wicked ways. He is supposed to have given up hunting and drowned all his hounds! In fact, Sir Marteine Lloyd in a letter to the 'Western Mail' in May, 1902, wrote – 'Colonel Lloyd was too good a sportsman to drown his hounds, and Sir Thomas Davies Lloyd's father succeeded to the pack of foxhounds which were given up and sold to go to Ireland at his death in 1845...'[12]

Col. Lloyd and his wife Mary were strongly influenced by the Methodist movement and 'Methodistical' clerics like the Rev. David Griffiths, Nevern and David Jones, Llangan, visited Bronwydd frequently. No doubt, Col. And Mrs. Lloyd were alarmed by the spread of Unitarianism (a creed which was deemed to be theologically flawed and had amongst its followers those of republican sympathies derived from the French Revolution) in the Teifi valley. It had its 'causes' at Panteg, above the Cuch valley, Penrhiw in Llangeler parish and further up the Teifi beyond Llandysul towards Lampeter.

The new chapel at Aberbanc was intentionally named Capel-y-Drindod, and in a codicil to his will dated 2 July, 1795, Colonel Lloyd bequeathed the sum of £600 to trustees, the interest from which was to provide the stipend of 'Evangelical Preachers' be they Methodists or Dissenters to preach the 'pure Gospel in the Calvinistic line twice on a Sunday to the maintenance of the Gospel cause in that neighbourhood...' Moreover, he expressed in his will the wish that his widow would 'maintain the Lord's cause there ...' at Bronwydd and in the locality.

Indeed she added to her husband's bequest a further sum of £600 towards maintaining the Christian ministry at Capel Drindod. After her death, the Rev. Maurice Evans, vicar of Llangeler, composed an ode in her memory and in praise of her 'methodistical persuasion' and generosity to neighbours and paupers. He described her as a 'true Dorcas' who taught people how to sew, read and write. She had her private chapel at Bronwydd where daily devotions, singing, praying and Bible reading were observed, -

'Yn ei chapel gyda'i theulu
R'oedd bob dydd yn Efengylu,
Darllen, canu a gweddïo -
Pawb mewn syndod sydd yn gwrando...'

138

Unfortunately, there followed controversy and confusion with regard to the Capel Drindod charity, largely because of mishandling by the Court of Chancery (before the Charity Commissioners were established in 1853). Consequently Mrs. Anne Davies Lloyd of Cilrhiwe provided £600 to purchase additional stock. By 1915, the annual dividend had fallen to £23-6s a year, and Sir Marteine Lloyd contributed one guinea each Sunday to make up the stipend of the minister. In 1923, the ticklish Methodist minister of Twrgwyn, Rhydlewis, the Rev. John Green, threatened legal proceedings alleging mal-administration of the trust funds, so that W. Evans George, solicitors had to inform Mr. Green that Sir Marteine was neither legally nor morally liable for any loss incurred by the chapel trustees over the years. Consequently, the trustees of the day – David Davies, Dole, Llangunllo, David Arthur Davies, Henfryn Mills, woollen manufacturer, and Thomas John Jenkins, surgeon, Henllan, executed a deed in October, 1924 indemnifying Sir Marteine Lloyd of all liability in respect of the Capel Drindod Fund, and the 'cause' continues to derive income from the Bronwydd charity to this day[13].

Lloyd patronage was given to other dissenting chapels, and, regardless of any controversy between church and chapel, tory and radical, squire and tenant, the community lived side by side interdependent on each other. Irrespective of the diatribes of radical politicians like Henry Richard and later, Lloyd George and Tom Ellis, Sir Thomas Davies Lloyd could genuinely claim that he had 'the best feeling towards his nonconformist tenants and neighbours'. Leases of long duration at a token rent were granted to Cana Congregational chapel at Velindre Farchog in the parish of Bayvil; the 'cause' at Horeb, not far from Bronwydd, received generous donations; Sir Thomas Lloyd granted land for 'his friends' to build a chapel at Bryngwenith, with an adjoining cemetery, on Cwrrws bank – a very significant gesture when Henry Richard was making allegations in parliament that Welsh landlords had refused dissenters land to bury their dead.

In 1871, Anne Davies Lloyd of Cilrhiwe allowed a nonconformist minister the use of a dwelling house on her estate free of rent. Hospitality was given to Calvinistic Methodist ministers at Cilrhiwe, when the 'Sasiwn' was held at Cardigan in September, 1876, and there are many instances of Bronwydd generosity: musical instruments and other equipment given by the Lloyd family to chapels and worthy institutions. Indeed, prominent 'Tivyside' radicals publicly extolled the '…the generous, tolerant and kind feelings towards nonconformists which have ever characterised the family of Bronwydd.' – to quote the words of Dr. Lloyd of Newcastle-Emlyn (a prominent nonconformist radical) when Miss Nesta Constance Muriel Lloyd of Bronwydd laid the foundation stone of Bryngwenith chapel in 1883. In a bitter attack on landlords during the East Carmarthenshire election campaign of 1885, when Sir Marteine Lloyd stood as a Tory candidate, the Rev. David Adams wrote an open letter to the *'Cardigan and Tivyside Advertiser'* stating that '. while disclaiming the least sympathy with the present political views of Sir Marteine Lloyd, allow me on behalf of the Congregational Church of Bryngwenith to correct that wrong impression (of being inimical towards Dissenters) – a charge levelled against Sir Marteine'.

As David Jenkins has pointed out, the Lloyds of Bronwydd were not imbued with the 'hauteur' of some gentry families: they regularly attended 'cyrddau mawr' (big preaching meetings) in local chapels, the 'cymanfa bwnc' (catechising festivals), and the Horeb and Bwlchygroes Basket Weaving class. Sir Marteine and Lady Lloyd were always present at the operettas and concerts (produced by the talented Daniel Jenkins) held at the Penboyr C. of E. school at Velindre, in the early 1900s. Their magnanimity towards political opponents was manifest when the Rev. Rhys Jones Lloyd and Sir Marteine gave public tributes at the funeral of Dr. Enoch Davies, Bryn Teifi at Bwlchygroes in December, 1896, one of the most virulent anti-church, anti-tithe and anti-landlord campaigners in the lower Teifi valley[14].

Loyalty to the Anglican Church and antiquarian interest prompted the Lloyds to contribute towards the restoration of historic churches beyond the immediate neighbourhood of the mansion. They were expected to dig deeply into their pockets when churches were restored or built anew. The much publicised 'History and Antiquities of St. David's' compiled by W. Basil Jones and Edward Augustus Freeman in 1857, and later on, Sir Stephen Glynne's reports on ancient Welsh churches aroused (in the more cultured gentry) the urgent responsibility to safeguard the future of the cathedral and the endangered churches of the diocese. After its restoration the church of Eglwyswen was reopened in 1873 and Eglwyswrw some ten years later, both within the barony of Cemais to the designs of the architect R. J. Withers, who had been responsible for the Town Hall at Cardigan, Llandugwydd, Cilrhedyn and other churches in the area[15].

It has to be borne in mind too, that the rebuilding of churches was, partly, a political statement by the 'Tivyside' gentry, with Sir Thomas Davies Lloyd as the principal instigator, in response to the increase in chapel membership (as the Religious Census of 1851 had shown), the clamour of anti-tithe protest, liberationist and church disestablishment agitation. But, the Christian zeal personal piety and moral stance of Sir Thomas and his Lloyd forebears, since the days of Col. Lloyd and Mary, his wife, especially the latter (with her sympathy, inherited from the Williams family of Haverfordwest and Swansea, for the Moravian Brethren) is not, thereby, diminished.

It will be recalled that Thomas Davies Lloyd had been created a baronet in 1863, and was later a Member of Parliament. Whereas, the ancient church of Llangunllo had been repaired and renovated from time to time, it was no longer a place of worship befitting a baronet and a 'knight of the shire', dwelling in his new castellated mansions of Bronwydd and Newport. There were serious constraints, however: his stretched financial situation did not match up to his social pretensions. Consequently, resort had to be made to raise money by 'voluntaryist' methods: concerts, garden fêtes, house to house collections, and as a last resort, loans from well-to-do freeholders, merchants and gentry patrons. And this plan was not to be frowned upon because, as Professor Ieuan Gwynedd Jones has shown, the restoration of Llanrhystud church in the 1850's and others, had been achieved through such voluntary effort. In the 1860's concerts were held at Aberbanc, Cardigan, Newcastle-Emlyn and in other places, under 'the management of Sir Thomas Davies Lloyd, assisted by George Powell of Nanteos, Miss Evans of Highmead, the Rev. Rhys Jones Lloyd and Capt. Jones Parry of Ty Llwyd and by several lady and gentleman amateurs, who with the distinguished violinist Herr Hauptmann … rendered solos on the piano, violin, violoncello and flute.' In 1867, the original estimate for the rebuilding of Llangunllo church was £1000 of which £550 comprised collected subscriptions and a grant from the Incorporated Church Building Society. Sometimes, as happened in the parish of Eglwyswrw in 1883, where Bronwydd influence was strong, and in spite of sectarian affiliations, 'different denominations also contributed towards the rebuilding of the old church of our fathers (hen eglwys ein tadau)' although, it was Sir Thomas Lloyd who was the chief promoter, as Lord Marcher of Cemais[16].

The 'new' Llangunllo church was to be a restatement of the 'mysteriousness' of a medieval church, and, apart from antiquarian considerations, the building had to emphasise the 'spirituality, sacramentalism and ritual' of the church against the arid rationalism of the eighteenth century. As a contemporary of John Ruskin at Christ Church, Oxford, and with his taste for the 'antique', as Lord Marcher, whose ancestors (he thought) had dwelt in ancient castles and had worshipped in the shadows of Gothic arches, he was, also, influenced by Augustus Welby Pugin, amongst other disciples of mediaeval culture. John Middleton of Cheltenham was the architect chosen for the task of rebuilding Llangunllo Church. He had many patrons in 'Tivyside', and was employed in restoring Llandysul, Llandyfriog and Henllan churches where he provided his clients with what they wanted in terms of taste and aesthetics. The restored church of Llangunllo was ready for its consecration by Easter, 1870. David Davies, of Llwyngwern and his neighbour David Thomas, both of Penrhiwllan, had been responsible for the carpentry and masonry. What was virtually the 'new' church of Llangunllo cost some £2000 in all.

In addition to items of liturgical and ritualistic significance, the pulpit was in memory of George Martin Lloyd (1830-1849); the east window was added later in memory of Sir Thomas Davies Lloyd and Lady Henrietta. A small pipe organ was installed in 1893, which was played by Miss Nesta C. M. Lloyd. Perhaps, the most poignant and touching memorial is the west window dedicated to the memory of Capt. Martin Kemes Arundel Lloyd of the Grenadier guards who was killed on the Somme in 1916. It must not be forgotten, however,

141

that the Tylers of Gernos, were close collaborators with the Lloyds; they donated sacramental vessels, adorned with precious stones and, in passing, were responsible for introducing Tractarian usage in the services, such as, the early celebration of the Eucharist, Gregorian chants, a robed choir, clerical vestments and the like. The last recorded act of church patronage by the Lloyds appears to be a gift of land at Pontarddulais in the parish of Llandil-Talybont for a new church in 1910[17].

From the evidence of wills throughout the centuries bequests were made by gentry families to the dependent poor (at the very base of society) in their localities and beyond. In the absence of adequate support before the welfare state the Lloyds were sensitive to the needs of the deprived, and this sympathy was extended to those who had suffered from epidemics, tragic loss of life at sea and in coal mines. Dr. John Jones along with Colonel Thomas and Mary Lloyd had in the 1800s made many charitable donations to the poor in Cosheston, Lawrenny, Lampeter-Velfrey, Whitechurch, Monkton, Mathry and in the towns of Tenby and Pembroke. In the winter of 1815, eleven families lost their loved ones when fishermen were drowned in the coastal waters between Aberporth and St. Dogmaels. The 'Carmarthen Journal' gave wide publicity to the tragedy and Thomas Lloyd of Cilrhiwe, and his mother Mary Lloyd responded with generous donations to the relief fund. With a commercial interest in the maritime trade of Cardiganshire, and personal acquaintance with the 'captains' of small craft and their families, the Lloyds felt duty bound to support the bereaved.

The functions organised by gentry families to relieve suffering were often linked to their social activities: in April, 1869, Lady Henrietta Lloyd organised a Hunt Week concert at Cardigan, the proceeds of which were to be devoted to the dependants of the seamen who had perished when the 'brig Sarah Ann' sank on the Laugharne Sands. The function at Cardigan was described as a very 'moving occasion' with 'the full black attire of the gentlemen' and the 'buffo singing' of Col. J. R. Howell and the solo instrumental contributions of various members of the gentry from the three counties, added to the success of 'such a worthy occasion'. Equally dangerous, with loss of life and limb, was the construction of the railway to Henllan, Newcastle-Emlyn and Cardigan, when Irish 'navvies' (navigators) were often the victims. 'The Railway and Navvies Relief Fund' was formed in the 1880s with members of the Lloyd family of Bronwydd and Cilrhiwe, amongst the main contributors. Many other examples may be cited: at a time of extreme hardship in 1845, about eighty five poor persons in Newport – widows, labourers, fishermen, masons and many more, received free corn from Thomas Davies Lloyd. In 1852, he and Mrs. Lloyd provided woollen blankets to the poor of the parishes of Llangunllo, Llanfair Orllwyn, Llanfair-Treflygen and Llandyfriog, and the account relates that 'they were only carrying out a duty incumbent on them, that it is better to give than to receive.' – a reassertion of the age-old imperatives of gentry benevolence. Sometimes, mishaps which had happened to individuals in the immediate locality met with an immediate response from Bronwydd, in terms of clothing, food, money or medical attention, as in the case of '. a poor woman injured by a steer at Newcastle-Emlyn.'

It is sometimes argued that the gentry, in this instance, were only 'caring for their own' – people on the estate, inhabitants of local towns where family influence and deference were strong and in circumstances where they had a vested interest – but this is not true. Charities in aid of those who suffered far outside the borders of the Bronwydd, and very far from their estate were supported – in 1863, parishioners in Llangunllo, following the example of Sir Thomas Davies Lloyd, collected funds in aid of the Lancashire cotton workers who were unemployed and without means of support on account of the lack of raw cotton from America during the Civil War of 1860-1865. Gentry concern extended to public hygiene, and amongst the more enlightened gentry, Thomas Davies Lloyd was aware of the need for proper sanitation, measures towards public health, humane conditions of work and the welfare of artisans. During an outbreak of cholera in Velindre (Shincin) in the 1850s he supplied large quantities of lime as a measure to 'cleanse' cottages and prevent the spread of the epidemic. And some ten years later, Anne Davies Lloyd was quick to respond to a similar outbreak at Cilgerran, by supplying disinfectants and other forms of relief. With a greater awareness of the lack of hospitals to 'provide for the sick poor' the Carmarthen Infirmary was founded in 1857 through the initiative of gentry like the Lloyds and voluntary efforts by public-spirited citizens. Later, Sir Marteine Lloyd was likewise equally active in working for the establishment of the Joint Counties Asylum (later the St. David's Hospital) at Carmarthen, in the 1880's.

Naturally, a landowner with a large number of tenant farmers on his estate had to take very strong measures when the health of farm stock was in danger. During an outbreak of the 'cattle plague' Sir Thomas Davies Lloyd (using his influence as member of Parliament) called a meeting of gentry and 'responsible farmers' (ffermwyr cyfrifol) at the Court House, Newcastle-Emlyn. There, it was decided to take steps to halt what was, probably 'foot and mouth' disease. Whereas many of the farmers were ignorant of the dangers and some landowners feckless in taking action, Sir Thomas persuaded the Newcastle-Emlyn Union Board of Guardians to levy a rate of 1d in the £ to compensate farmers who had lost animals, with each parish to set up its own committee to deal with the emergency. A punitive clause was added to the scheme, namely, that 'no one was to join the Society (to fight the plague and derive benefit) other than at its foundation.'[18]

An inadequate and unpopular system of poor law relief, the stigma of the workhouse and the penny-pinching overseers of the poor, often led to criticism of the gentry as a class and as an obvious scapegoat for social deprivation.

143

Amongst the most vociferous critics of the economic divide was the Rev. E. Pan Jones (1834-1922) born within the Bronwydd demesne. As a polemicist of national standing, his views were repeated (often in anonymous correspondence in local papers like the '*Cardigan and Tivyside Advertiser*') – the essence of the charge was the very nature of society at the time – the well fed and well clothed privileged classes, in contrast to the aged and invalid poor, without food, fire and clothing, illiterate and ignorant. A recent analysis of the state of the rural poor in Wales in the eighteenth century has shown the high level of poverty of the vulnerable labouring classes and the inadequacy of relief handed out by hostile parish vestries. To the end of the nineteenth century and even as late as 1945, there survived appalling living conditions in the cottages where people lived – 'mud without and misery within'. It could be argued that gentry contributions were paltry compared to the sums spent in the pursuit of 'display' and the conspicuous consumption enjoyed by them. 'Crisis charity' as has been mentioned –'cawl', rounds of beef, meal, and blankets and clothing were very welcome at the time, but hardly sufficient to sustain life in the long term.

Rural poverty was a bottomless pit (and may be likened to third world want) it was hereditary and symptomatic at times of ignorance leading to 'thriftless waste' – a topic that was of concern to Thomas Davies Lloyd. During harsh winters Lady Henrietta Lloyd and her mother-in-law Mrs. Anne Davies Lloyd, did not begrudge gifts of food or Llanidloes flannel, ready made clothing and other essential items to the needy poor. But, according to an old Welsh saying in the Teifi valley – 'Beth a geir yn rhad a gerdd yn rhwydd' (What is obtained freely is soon squandered), and this was true of free gifts from the 'plas'. One serious challenge to be faced by the gentry was the 'education' of their dependants in the habits of thrift, self help and self respect to drag themselves out of hereditary poverty. In December, 1873, Sir Thomas convened meetings of clergy, ministers of the Gospel, church and chapel activists, to provide means 'to succour the afflicted through their joint efforts, alleviate suffering and help widows and orphans.' Provident societies, such as the 'Loyal Glanteifi Lodge of Oddfellows, Ivorties and Rechabites existed to encourage members to save 'for the evil day', to adopt and carry out the maxims of many Victorian reformers: 'Patriotism, Philanthropy, Morality, Friendship, Love, Truth' with biblical precepts thrown in – 'Faith, Hope and Charity'. To show an example, Sir Thomas Davies Lloyd (a baronet, it must be remembered) sought other gentry to follow his example by becoming members of the Oddfellows and other provident societies. Pageantry and display also, attracted people to join in the meetings and hospitality at Bronwydd. Colourful processions led by the Bronwydd band added to the enjoyment and 'esprit de corps'. Clothing clubs supervised and given financial support by Lady Henrietta M. Lloyd were set up to encourage the poor to set aside a penny or more a week, in a fund for the purchase of clothes. The Newcastle-Emlyn Savings Bank was formed in 1878 with the Rev. Rhys Jones Lloyd as Treasurer, assisted by W. Evans George, solicitor, and the well known Methodist minister the Rev. Evan Phillips. With the development and spread of banks, co-operative and provident societies by the end of the nineteenth century, private individual efforts by philanthropist gentry gradually went out of fashion. But care and concern for the deprived continued on a personal and local level. Lady Katherine H. Lloyd, was widely known for kindness to those who were ill and suffering: in December, 1902, she publicly appealed for funds to help 'the hawker Joseph Gwydr (Glass) who was a hundred years old to save him from the workhouse.' and up to the 1920s she was remembered for her gifts of blankets, food and medicine to sick and poor folk, not only in the neighbourhood of Bronwydd but farther afield in the parishes of Cynwyl Elfed, Llangeler and Penboyr. Long before 'care in the community' was ever imagined, Sir Marteine Lloyd promised the old lady of Rhipin, near Bryngwenith, that, in the event of her death, he would see to it that her incapacitated daughter would be cared for[19].

The education of the working class was an important feature of the paternalistic rule of the Lloyds of Bronwydd. Their tenantry and dependants deserved the encouragement to become informed and enlightened. Hitherto, the education of the masses had been limited to the imperatives of Bible teaching: piety, honesty and sobriety, especially the latter to counteract the vicious degrading caused by drink – 'liquid fire and distilled damnation'. To this end, Archdeacon Benjamin Millingchamp and Mrs. Mary Lloyd of Bronwydd collaborated with the S.P.C.K to provide a few hundred copies of Welsh and English Bibles, Books of Common Prayer and Psalters, for the 'Tivyside' public. In March 1836, Thomas Lloyd delivered a 'very moving speech' at a meeting of the British and Foreign Bible Society at Twrgwyn Chapel, Rhydlewis – a remarkable example of ecumenical co-operation. Likewise, twenty years later Thomas Davies Lloyd sponsored the 'Vale of Troedyraur Branch of the Bible Society' in conjunction with local clergy and ministers of other denominations. To many, the libellous allegations of the 'Llyfrau Gleision' (The Report of the Blue Books of 1847) were regarded as an act of treachery towards the Welsh people, and the canard that the Welsh 'gwerin' were bedevilled by ignorance, immorality, superstition and every imaginable vice, must have quickened the conscience of many a country squire –'afflicted by fits of public morality' to use Macaulay's trenchant phrase! Thomas Davies Lloyd and his wife, the Rev. Rhys Jones Lloyd promoted societies for the 'advancement of morality amongst the lower classes' – one such was formed at Aberbanc in 1850. As those who had to administer the Poor Law, sit as magistrates, visit workhouses and deal with feckless and drunken tenants, come to the rescue of battered wives and half-naked starving children, they realised that the situation was desperate. The Bwlchygroes and Newchapel Temperance Society held a meeting on the Frenni Fawr in June 1875; addresses were delivered by 'very distinguished people' and the movement had the support of Sir Thomas Davies Lloyd and Rhys Jones Lloyd[20].

An idealist, Lloyd had been the 'prime mover of a Literary Society' at Newcastle-Emlyn in the 1850s, recognising as he did the numerous class of people to whom English literature was 'neither accessible nor intelligible' and this society was open to all denominations with the object of 'advancing the interest of the rising generation'. There was a tradition of gentry patronage of educational establishments in the lower Teifi valley. The names of Dr. Philipps of Blaenpant, the Rev. Daniel Bowen of Waunifor and Archdeacon Beynon, in the mid-eighteenth and early nineteenth centuries, come to mind. The foundation of the National Society in 1811 and that of St. David's College at Lampeter were events much to the fore in the minds of enlightened gentry. One of the earliest National Schools in the area was that at Aberbanc: Thomas Davies Lloyd gave the land, and it was opened in August 1848. A *draft* conveyance drawn up by Thomas Davies Lloyd, earlier that year, stipulated the names of the rector of Llangunllo, the Rev. Thomas Howell Davies, John Howell Davies of Penybeili, Esq. five freehold farmers, a carpenter, Thomas Davies, Geulanfelen, Henllan, an auctioneer, and the Rev. Samuel Griffiths, the much respected minister of Horeb Congregational Chapel, and the Rev. John Jones vicar of Newcastle-Emlyn, as trustees and managers. The name of Samuel Griffiths is noteworthy – a clear statement of the donor's tolerance and regard for his nonconformist neighbours, and the latter's readiness to collaborate in the work of an educational establishment which was bound to subscribe to the doctrine of the Episcopal Anglican church.

The parcel of land was given 'freely, voluntarily and without valuable consideration (i.e. cash) for a school for the education of children and adults or children only of the labouring and manufacturing and other poorer classes in the several parishes of Llangunllo, Llanfair Orllwyn, Llandyfriog, Henllan and Bangor Teifi.' Later, it was decided to allow pupils from 'the lower districts' (along the banks of the Teifi) of the parishes of Llangeler and Penboyr, in Carmarthenshire, to be educated there. The trustees appointed eventually were the principal landowners on both banks of the river: Thomas Davies Lloyd, Rhys Jones Lloyd of Bronwydd, James Richard Lewes Lloyd of Dôl-Haidd, Esq. and Rees Goring Thomas of Llysnewydd Esq. In the event of a dispute arising relating to religious dogma, the matter was to be reported in writing to the Lord Bishop of St. David's who would be the final arbiter. Members of the management committee were expected to contribute sums ranging from one to five pounds every current year. Needless to say, the school was largely maintained by the Lloyd family of Bronwydd with gifts of books, repairs to the building, entertainment for the children and everything to do with its well being until the death of Lady Lloyd in 1937[21].

In August 1868, Sir Thomas Davies Lloyd laid the foundation stone of a new British school at St. Dogmaels. The '*Carmarthen Journal*' reported Sir Thomas Lloyd's speech in detail – a unique occasion in the seven hundred years since his ancestor Robert Fitzmartin had founded the abbey nearby! Sir Thomas commended the work of John Wycliffe and Queen Elizabeth, the latter in fostering the efforts of the Protestant translators of the Bible into Welsh. Praise of Wycliffe (and remarks on the need for a Bible based education and religious toleration) was a veiled thrust against the advance of Popery. The speech was an opportunity also to show his support for the Reform Bill which would extend power to the working classes, improve social conditions and, above all, bring about the 'co-operation of intelligence with the will of the people for the common good'. As has been observed already, the Lloyd family was noteworthy for their empathy with Methodism and Nonconformity. This continued after the passing of the Education Act of 1870, when important concessions were made to nonconformists in the famous 'Cowper Temple' clause prohibiting denominational teaching (of an Anglican or dissenting nature) in publicly controlled schools. There is no evidence to suggest that the Lloyds regarded the measure as a divisive force in local society. On the contrary, they accepted what had become the law of the land in the interest of the whole community and the Rev. Rhys Jones Lloyd as well as Sir Marteine Lloyd were active chairmen of the Newcastle-Emlyn School Boards in the 1880s and 90s. As Liberal Member of Parliament for the Cardigan Boroughs, Sir Thomas Davies Lloyd had the opportunity at the opening in 1871 of the University College of Wales Aberystwyth to enlarge on his educational and political philosophy. In a speech, which received loud acclaim, he spoke of the mine of intellectual wealth in Wales, and of those who had never been able to afford to enter the Universities of Oxford and Cambridge. Now, they were at the threshold of higher education. Moreover, he struck a political note by affirming his belief in nationality (like Kossuth in Hungary and Cavour in Italy). Education was the means of developing and improving the national and intellectual life of Wales. He compared the Welsh to the Greeks - their love of poetry, music and fine arts – and quoted the names of famous contemporaries –Brinley Richards and Thomas Brigstocke, the Carmarthen portrait painter, amongst others. He concluded his speech with the hope that the new university college would further assist in developing the genius for art, science, sculpture, poetry and music '. which I believe to be pre-eminent in the Welsh people.' In the narrower field of the conservation of archaeological and ancient artefacts, Sir Marteine and Lady Lloyd paid for the restoration of the 'beautiful wheel window' in the banqueting hall of the old bishop's palace at St. Davids in 1907, and in 1921, they were generous patrons of the new museum in Quay Street, Carmarthen to which they donated valuable historical items[22].

Apart from the benevolence and patronage of the Lloyd family towards their dependants' health, domestic welfare, their places of worship and education, they took part in sporting activities which were enjoyed by the commonalty of the countryside. For many centuries country folk had indulged in fishing, snaring, trapping birds and small animals, hunting the hare and running after horses and hounds, and in various rough ball games. But cock fighting was a

147

very popular sport which, along with bear baiting, had been prohibited by law in the early years of Queen Victoria's reign. The influence of Methodism and a stricter religious code led some of gentry in 'Tivyside', such as, the Lloyd family of Bronwydd to abandon the cruel and coarse sports of the past. But clownish and rustic pastimes, devoid of cruelty and marked rather, by rollicking good fund, still continued as before. 'Aquatic excursions' and 'rural diversions' provided entertainment for the gentry, as well as, for ordinary folk. In the summer of 1813, Thomas and James Lloyd of Bronwydd, had organised a function on Penbryn beach which was repeated on 'Cwmhayar Downs' Llandysul, a year later. The 'piece de resistance' amongst other acts of tomfoolery, was catching 'the sticky pig' – a pig whose tail had been previously close shaven and soaped. On Penbryn beach, they, also, indulged in horse and donkey races when the tide was out –and a good time was enjoyed by all.

Of the country diversions, which brought people together, none was looked forward to more than the hunt meet when the squire and a close community (those who had, perhaps, neither visited a large town nor left the border of their parish) congregated in social harmony. Thus, latent tensions were defused and all those present felt that they had their own rôle to play. On the north wall inside Llangunllo church there is a memorial to the late Sir Marteine Lloyd, and amongst the public distinctions he enjoyed, are engraved the letters M.F.H – Master of Fox Hounds. Like most of the gentry throughout the land (and the general populace who also participated) the Lloyd family had over the centuries indulged in field sports with passionate intensity. Keeping horses and hounds was part of the squire's upbringing, lifestyle and 'display'. The gentry hunted as children, while at the university, and at home were in the saddle up to six times a week. From its inception in the 1700's the 'Tivyside' Hunt had been supported by the local gentry and sporting farmers. After a temporary lapse from the 1790's (during the war against France) it was revived and was very active until the 1914-1918 and 1939-1945 wars. One of its prominent members was Colonel Thomas Lloyd.

When the Bronwydd pack was sold in 1845, it was replaced by a pack of beagles by Thomas Davies Lloyd in the following year and he remained master until his death in 1877.For several years Sir Thomas was successful in winning prizes at important national shows for the beagles he bred at Bronwydd. Later Sir Marteine took over as master until the outbreak of the Great War in 1914, when his horses were requisitioned and when food for the kennels had become unobtainable. The dispersal of the Bronwydd beagles was considered a great loss to the neighbourhood and apart from the Royal Rock Birkenhead, Pack (senior by some three months) was the oldest established in the kingdom. Sir Marteine also had otter hounds with which, and in conjunction with those of Colonel Pryse of Gogerddan, he used to hunt the rivers of mid and north Wales. But these he did not keep for many seasons because of the cost involved, not least, in feeding, labour and transport. Encouraged by John Pugh Vaughan

148

Pryse of Bwlchbychan, Sir Marteine tried 'foumart' (polecat) hunting with purebred otter hounds, but achieved no success. The hounds would not hold the line, and, they invariably got onto a fox or a hare. Another difficulty was that this hunting activity was carried on during the night, and because the dogs were liable to cause trouble the whole idea was abandoned. In any case, by the early 1900's this type of hunting was no longer fashionable. Incidental to his sporting activities, Sir Marteine Lloyd was recognised as one with the essential special knowledge of hounds to act as judge in the annual Royal Welsh show. He was regarded as one of the best known sporting squires of the day, in the company of Pryse of Gogerddan, Powell of Nanteos, Philipps of Mabws, Sir Watkin Williams Wynn, and nobility like Lord Cawdor, Lord Vane Tempest and the Marquess of Londonderry. Sir Marteine Lloyd's uncle, too, the Rev. Rhys Jones Lloyd, rector of Troedyraur was a well known sporting 'squarson' (who never missed a meet of the 'Tivyside Hunt') one of the most colourful characters of the time. Some analysts of the former social scene argue that it was an assertion of authority and prestige by the gentry against the monied mill and mine owners, and every Jorrocks of Mullygrubs Castle who invaded the countryside and bought land. But the interest and enthusiasm for the hunt was not only part of the 'display' of the gentry, it was the most public of pastimes – a spectacle enjoyed by the whole community which helped to preserve the peace and social harmony of the countryside. Unlike shooting, especially of game, there was no danger of any infringement of the law and the consequent social friction between landlord and poacher. Hunting involved every section of society who looked forward to the hunt meet at the 'Salutation' Newcastle-Emlyn, the 'Sergeants Inn' at Eglwyswrw and the 'Trewern Arms' Newport. To its supporters, it was an occasion to get rid of ravenous vermin, as the following homespun letter demonstrates: '. Dear Sir, I inform you that the owl Fox or Foxes took a 5s-0d of my Hens this morning. I am a poor man. Lost my hens bad job indeed. You please to come Dear Sir, to kill the Robbers as soon as you Cann.'

If farm crops, hedges fences and the like, were damaged, fair minded landowners, like the Lloyds of Bronwydd, were prepared to make recompense to the tenant, and where such an understanding did not exist, then the hunt, itself, could not survive. Farmers could after all, refuse to co-operate with the huntsmen, could destroy litters of foxes and even, and poison the hounds. By its very nature, hunting was an egalitarian activity linking various classes of society in what has been described a 'the democracy of the hunting field' and, one might add, a form of social and inter-dependent patronage, (long before the issue of cruelty to animals came to be seriously debated) –an activity, when squire, farmer, blacksmith, farrier, horseman, groom, labourer and cottager, as well as the country cleric, attorney, doctor, craftsman and artisan came together to participate in one common pastime, which, perhaps more than any other gave 'vitality, cohesion and stability to county society'[23].

Epilogue

There had always existed within the landowning system internal weaknesses, which were eventually to cripple and cause terminal damage to an estate and its owners. The strict settlement limited any personal interest and responsibility to that of the life tenant and was meant to secure the estate intact from one generation to the next. Other legal constraints, such as, - trusts to preserve rights of succession, long term mortgages to provide dowries, annuities, jointures to support the life tenant's widow and legitimate children, their up-bringing, education in a profession or trade – weighed heavily on the often flimsy economy of an estate. Apart from complicated legal arrangements, the character, temperament and behaviour, of a particular squire, could make or mar the well being of his patrimony.

The owner of a large estate was constantly and inevitably faced with a host of legal problems to safeguard his landed property: boundaries, manorial rights, minerals, road and rail developments and the like, not to mention the schemes of jealous and avaricious gentry neighbours.

As has been noticed already, the Lloyds of Bronwydd were afflicted with the same predilection to go to law as their Welsh gentry peers. The prolonged Cardigan Priory proceedings from the 1790's to about 1813 and the Bronwydd Peerage case from the early 1800's to the 1920's, were a drain on the estate. The election campaigns of Sir Thomas Davies Lloyd, an unrestrained lifestyle, in food and drink, horses and hounds, generous hospitality and entertaining, and all the ingredients of 'display' and to be 'in the mode', added further to the encumbrances[1].

The problems facing Sir Marteine Lloyd on his succession to the estate in 1877 – a mortgage of £94,000 and a bank overdraft, altogether, amounted to some £100,000. Stern measures were needed to remedy the serious situation he was faced with. The terms of the Settled Land Act of 1882 made it easier for landowners, hampered by entail and family settlements, to sell part of their estates in view of agricultural depression and the deterioration of land and buildings. So in order to repay the mortgagees Sir Marteine resorted to the sale of large portions of his estate and in 1890 about 1,436 acres of Bronwydd land were put on the market. But, most tenants were too poor to take advantage of such an offer.

The mass of correspondence between Sir Marteine Lloyd and his agents John Morgan Davies, Froodvale, John Evans, Cardigan, and his solicitors W. Evans George, illustrates the extremely serious financial straits he found himself in, and this lasted until his death in 1933. In addition, the agreements made with industrial magnates working mines and 'works' on the borders of Carmarthenshire and Glamorgan, led in 1909, to litigation (concerning the provision of accommodation works, culverts, watering ponds, approach roads and the like) and threats from the owners of the Llangennech colliery that they would terminate the lease, would be a blow in terms of loss of royalties and income coming into the Bronwydd coffers. The sale of part of the farm of Pentre Priscedwyn in the parish of Llandeilo-Talybont, for £1,174 was one ray of sunshine in an otherwise gloomy prospect. Although royalties from the coal mines of Brynlliw, Grovesend and Llangennech, from September, 1909, to March, 1914, brought in over £2,962 to the estate, there was a serious threat that 'some of the workings' would have to be closed because 'the coal was not workable' and the company claimed that they were losing £6,000, every half year, if they carried on.

Taking further advantage of the provisions of the Settled Land Act, 1882, Sir Marteine and Kemes Arundel Lloyd, his son and heir, arranged a re-settlement of the estate, and in 1911 put up for sale the home farm, the old mansion house of Cilrhiwe, and in all 2,290 acres in the parishes of Whitechurch (Eglwyswen), Cilgerran, Eglwyswrw and Llanfihangel-Penbedw. In addition, 350 acres in Llanfihangel Abercywyn and other scattered properties, making a total of over 4,500 acres were to be sold. Further sales were held between 1911 and 1914. It was estimated that all these would yield some £53,500. There were rumblings of trouble from Messrs. Pennington who wrote to Davies, Ffrwdfâl, concerning Sir Marteine's heavy bank overdraft of £12,000, and enquiring whether he was living 'in excess of his income'? The sum of money realised in the sale Cilrhiwe was to be divided between Sir Marteine and Capt. Kemes Lloyd. Payment of debts left £10,500 of which £8,000 was to be reinvested producing something like £348 per annum.

At the same time and partly on account of the sale of land, estate rents had diminished considerably, and (in further correspondence from Penningtons to Froodvale Davies) it appears that domestic problems were causing additional worry to Sir Marteine. There was the expense of the 'coming wedding' and the 'sums required to extricate Mr. Kemes Lloyd from the difficulties in which he found himself' as well as the 'large sums paid for Sir Marteine's own debts'[2]. The policy of selling off large acreages of the estate meant that the mortgage had been reduced to £73,000 and by May 1914, to £46,000. The continued debts through over-spending, reduction of his estate and diminished rents led Sir Marteine to write to Davies, Ffrwdfâl, expressing the hope '…that I shall not, in my old age be exiled from my home, let me die here whatever happens. I am so depressed and anxious re my affairs that it makes me feel quite ill, and I fear that I shall have a breakdown, to think that my family and myself may be reduced to absolute poverty … from many a sleepless night the doctor says that I have had a regular nervous breakdown …' Further sales were inevitable, and the proceeds of small holdings provided instant cash to keep things going – in September, 1916, Pantgwyn and Waun in the parish of Llanfair-Orllwyn were sold to Elias Rees, Nantypopty, Coedybryn, for £565. Furthermore in 1919,

250 acres were offered for sale in the parish of Llanstephan, Carmarthenshire, and a further 162 acres in Llanfair Orllwyn, almost within sight of Bronwydd. The Llandeilo-Talybont estate was valued at £7,450 for 514 acres (the minerals excepted) while Rhipin Du in the parish of Troedyraur with other small properties could realise a total of £8,865. Wealthy kinsfolk were, sometimes, ready to come to the rescue: Sir Owen Cosby Philipps, (later Lord Kylsant) bought in 1920 Pentrewin (Pentrewyn), a farm of 250 acres in Llansteffan parish for £8,712. According to figures provided by the new agent John Evans of Cardigan, the mortgage on the Bronwydd estate had been reduced to £30,000 in 1920, and by 1922, to £24,062.

What was most hurtful to Sir Marteine and Lady Lloyd was the claim, made by the Inland Revenue Department, that Kemes Lloyd had succeeded to the the estate (through the re-settlement) before his death on the Somme in 1916. This meant that they had to pay succession duty as well as death duty. Sir Marteine was reported to be 'little short of suicidal', and Lady Lloyd asked bitterly '…wasn't his life a great enough sacrifice to the state?'

In the next few years Sir Marteine and Lady Lloyd had to face the reality of their plight, and one incident illustrates the situation: a storm had caused much damage at Ffynnonwen, one of their farms near Bronwydd – 'What is to be done? Trades people are bothering me to pay the balance of their bills, which the £1,000 borrowed, did not. I am in dread of being served with writs…' wrote Sir Marteine to John Evans, Cardigan. To add to his problems, a deputation of farmers had arrived at Bronwydd to ask for a reduction of rent as a Mr Williams of Sandyhaven, had been given a reduction of £25; furthermore there was a poor output of coal in the industrial part of the estate.

The agent suggested a meeting with Sir Marteine and Lady Lloyd '…with reference to your finances, I have no doubt that if Lady Lloyd and yourself would arrange to keep within £150 a month, that things would right themselves in two or three years …' As a result, various ideas were considered – cutting down the number of servants at Bronwydd '…apart from Newman (the head gardener) and Bough the butler, two conscientious workers and thoroughly trustworthy, Whitbread too is very willing … the rest can go as far as I am concerned …' was Sir Marteine's reply[3].

Although not a very large house, even by Welsh standards, Bronwydd could no longer be run with the number of staff the Lloyds had been accustomed to – in house cleaning, preparing large quantities of food, serving meals, attending to the laundry, laying fires and tending them, to say nothing of grounds to be maintained, horses groomed, dogs fed and exercised – and much, much more. It is true that small sums of money came in from time to time, for example, the Welsh Church Commissioners awarded the trustees of the Bronwydd estate £463 in respect of Sir Marteine's loss of the right of presentation to the livings of Newport, Llanychllwydog, Llanllawer and Meline, when the Welsh church was disestablished in 1922.

A seasonal source of income was the letting of Newport Castle; it had been rented out many years before in the 1880s to 'Sir Henry Wrixom Becher of Ballygiblin in county Cork, Baronet' who spent his holidays there. But here again there were problems, for example, a Mrs. Kirkhouse, living near Llansamlet, (thinking that it would be in her favour to claim that she was a near relation of the widow of Mr. Jones, rector of Newport) had enquired whether the castle could be let for a very low rent '... as she and her husband wanted to make a living out of the Garden and a Poultry Farm ... fancy fowls in possession of the ancient ruins...!' Sir Marteine and Lady Lloyd were not amused. Even a titled lady like Lady Griffin had not come up to the expectations suggested by her rank: her domestics were so careless during the few weeks she was in residence that crockery, utensils and linen had been damaged and to claim compensation would be more costly than their value. Fortunately, Sir Stanley Read rented the castle in 1922-1923 at a rent of £62, an arrangement, which proved profitable, and there was no mention of broken pots and pans. But applicants 'of the right sort' were few indeed. In 1924, Sir Marteine (in sheer desperation) was compelled to let the castle to a family by the name of Pitchford. Reputedly, they were 'large [wealthy] farmers'. Even so, '..they had no servants, did everything for themselves, the lady bringing up everything from the town in a basket ... I hope to heaven that they are not going to turn my ancient ruins to cowhouses and pigsties ...' wrote Sir Marteine to his agent.

During the summer of 1923, Sir Marteine and Lady Lloyd spent most of their time staying with friends and relations in England and thus, a skeleton staff could look after Bronwydd. However, Lady Lloyd, during a short sojourn in Bath, insisted on staying in a hotel (expense notwithstanding). She proudly insisted that 'there were no suitable lodgings and the doctor had warned of the dangers from the drains and the rats ...' presumably, in the more ordinary and inferior establishments.

Sir Marteine, for his part, was most anxious to return home. He wrote of his 'hidreth adre' (sic. 'hiraeth am fynd adre' yearning for home) even for a few months, and then '...I think we must go and live abroad; the exchange is so good that one can live on half the money in Italy, and get 80/- for £1 note ..' But the thought of going to live in Switzerland depressed him greatly '... having to leave the old home is pain and grief to me...' Some years later, in September, 1929, Sir Marteine commented to his agent on a 'good sale' held at Glaneirw, near Gogerddan, '...it was a great pity that Col. (Harman) Brenchley did not have this sale during his lifetime which could have enabled him and his brother to have taken a smaller house and to have lived in comfort...' But he himself had not the heart to take his own medicine. On the contrary, he was at times oblivious of his own situation and also naively optimistic of the future. He gave instructions to his solicitor to recover the sum of £1,500, which he had invested in Russian Railway Bonds. Little did he understand of the Bolshevic mind! In 1927, he bought (against the advice of Lady Lloyd) the Llangunllo glebe farm for £1,850, because the occupant had the reputation of being a poacher, and another farm, Alltfawr, was bought merely because it was surrounded on three sides by the Bronwydd estate. The outlay in this transaction was offset (with some money to spare) two years later, with the sale of Tower Hill and Panteg, within easy reach of Bronwydd, along with the Court House at Eglwyswrw, for the total sum of £2,855[4].

Sir Marteine was often dazzled by smooth talk and bizarre schemes – Sambrook, the gamekeeper (the last person to advise on geology and mineralogy) had convinced him that gold could be mined from Foel Drigarn in the Precellies, and had started digging into an ancient site. But the excitement of a sudden fortune was short lived; the law had been broken and the Commissioners of Ancient Monuments could bring a court case against Sir Marteine. Indeed, the pot of gold had vanished somewhere at the end of the rainbow! Of a trusting nature and one who could not imagine any guile in those with whom he dealt, Sir Marteine was almost persuaded by one William Mate and? Leeson, his mining engineer, that the prospects of obtaining finance for working the mines at Llanfyrnach, were very good. Even John Evans, the agent, suggested that the property was worth £40,000, which seems disingenuous, to say the least, considering the state of the economy in the mid '20s. Again, Sir Marteine did not know that John Evans, shortly after his appointment as agent of the Bronwydd estate, had written to Messrs Pennington of Lincoln's Inn, a confidential letter suggesting a 50% increase in the Bronwydd rents, but -
'As Sir Marteine is rather sensitive on the point, would it be possible for you to write me a letter stating that the Trustees would wish me to revise the rents of the estate? The tenants have no idea who the Trustees are, and they would accept the inevitable.. in some cases an increase of 50% should be added without injustice to the tenant…'

Sentiment often clouded Sir Marteine's judgement: the Bronwydd Arms, a public house a few miles outside Carmarthen on the Cardigan road, had been built on Bronwydd land. It was leased to a tenant regarded as 'troublesome and feckless'; the rent was low and repairs were needed but Sir Marteine was not prepared to sell it, '…It's a landmark and I pass the house more than any house that I have got…' His estate agents and solicitors were constantly advising him to dispose of those properties which were uneconomic, but to which he clung tenaciously because of their position, richness in game or some family tradition such as that about a piece of land won on a game of Dominos! In 1921, the estate's London solicitors had estimated that the proceeds from sales of this kind even at a comparatively low price, would yield a larger income from investments than is now obtained from the land'

In spite of the strains and stresses on the estate and on the private life of Sir Marteine and Lady Lloyd, they were determined to celebrate their golden wedding in November 1928, with 'eclat' – 'it was a debt they owed to their tenants' – according to Lady Lloyd. How the occasion was celebrated has been described already. Both Sir Marteine and Lady Lloyd continued to encourage worthy causes, albeit, in an ever diminishing way and on a lesser scale. Sir Marteine, aware of the desperate need to find a stable market for Welsh farm produce, supported Lord Bledisloe and others who advocated Farmers'Co-operative Societies in county towns like Cardigan. He called a committee to develop means to improve the breeding of sheep. Lady Lloyd continued to hold functions to raise funds for the Nursing Association and other charities. Although there was no heir to succeed to the estate, and the succession of one of the daughters was very much in question, repairs and improvements were carried out at Bronwydd: tree planting has been mentioned; electric lighting was installed in 1928 generated by an oil engine, and Courts Leet were still held. Ignoring the fact those dues and other relics of mediaeval times were practically defunct, John Evans advised Sir Marteine '..not to tolerate interference with your rights..' and when the Carmarthenshire Motor Cycle and Light Car Club held their summer meeting at Pendine (which attracted large crowds) permission was given for them to do so on Bronwydd land on payment of a fee of 10s to Sir Marteine who was still the Lord of the Manor[5].

The story of Sir Marteine and Lady Lloyd's last years makes sad reading. The Prudential Assurance Co. had transferred the mortgage on the estate, which in 1920 was about £30,000, (and by 1925 had been further reduced to £21,102-10s) to three well-to-do Carmarthen ladies, but the prospect of clearing the mortgage in Sir Marteine's lifetime was grim. Sir Marteine Lloyd died in April, 1933, and advertisements appeared in 'Country Life' and estate journals '...to let on a short lease not exceeding three years – the attractive mansion house of Bronwydd, with rough shooting..' For a time it was occupied by gaunt and haggard young men – Basque refugees from the Spanish Civil War who wandered about disconsolately in what was to become a scene of decay and desolation. In the spring of 1937 Lady Lloyd died and a few months later, the mansion house of Bronwydd and 2,072 acres of land were offered for sale at the Cawdor Hotel, Newcastle-Emlyn. The Bronwydd demesne amounted to 90 acres and the home farm comprised over 189 acres in the parishes of Llangunllo and Llanfair Treflygen. The transaction was handled by John Evans, auctioneer and estate agent, Cardigan, Messrs John Francis, and Walters and Williams, solicitors, Carmarthen. The sale catalogue gave a detailed account of the house, the pleasure gardens and parkland, but included a very curious condition, namely, that a certain acreage of woodland (a unique feature of such an attractive property) was to be sold as a separate lot, with the complete right of entry by the purchaser with his waggons, lorries, horses, 'engines' of his trade and the like – which (in spite of covenants to make good any damage) would spoil the demesne and inevitably dissuade any potential buyer interested in acquiring a splendid country house– why this was done must remain a mystery unsolved[6].

Before long Bronwydd was denuded of its great trees; the gardens reverted to the wild. Nature had cynically reclaimed her own. One 'Ben Mowr' (Big Ben), notorious for his gross and shaggy bearing (albeit, perhaps a good fellow at heart) acted as a 'front man' for those whose aim was to exploit and plunder. The war years came and the house became the temporary home of a Jewish Boarding School evacuated from the cities to escape the Nazi Blitz. Thereafter, the pride and joy of Sir Thomas Davies Lloyd and Sir Marteine was dismantled: its panelling, fireplaces, gargoyles, timbers, roofing slates, lead and so on, were sought by those who desired to acquire a treasured memento of Bronwydd or (in the post-war shortage of building materials) to repair their more humble farm buildings and cottages. The post-war years brought the once impoverished farmers grants and government aid, new machinery and intensive farming methods. The home farm became a valuable and profitable holding. However, Bronwydd was one of the 'lost houses' of Wales – a sad relic of the glory of a bygone age. But, the memory remains[7].

"Floreat memoria Baroniae de Kemeys"

Notes and Sources

Ch.1.Introduction –

1. *NLW/Jn1*/iii.nos 1 and 2 Summer,1943,33-35;vii no.1 Summer 1951,33-45; no.2 Winter 1951,120-37; Bronwydd Mss/4251-4, 5822-81,6045-7,4971-8; J. Bateman: *The Great Landowners of Great Britain and Ireland.* 1876.

2. Personal recollections

Ch.2 Ancestry and Estate –

1. Rev.P.Warner: '*A Walk through Wales in August,1797…*'1798,95;Lady Katherine H.Lloyd: *The Lords Marcher of Kemes*,1930.
2. NLW/Bronwydd/679.
3. Lewis Dwnn:*Heraldic Visitations* i,19,21; NLW/Alcwyn Evans:A98,178,248,B18,125,F69,H79;T.Nicholas:*Annals…*1872,i; Francis Jones erroneously described Llan Ffynnonwen as a 'plas' in Llangunllo parish,see '*Cardiganshire Homes and their Families*',2001;*The Complete Peerage*,ii,1912,361-2;T.J.and Prys Morgan:Welsh Surnames,1985,201-2; Benjamin Williams(Gwynionydd): 'Cenarth yn Emlyn' in *Golud yr Oes*,i.rhif ii.1863,365; A.Wagner:*English Genealogy*,1983.77-81; for the romantic traditions about Urien see Ifor Williams:*Canu Llywarch Hen*,1935 xxx.
4. Bronwydd/2826,2310.
5. J.Davies:*Annals and Pedigrees of the Lloyds of Crynfryn…parish of Nantgwnlle,co.Cardigan*,1931,-7; WWHR.i,22;H Potter:*Historical Introduction to English Law*,1948.90; Bronwydd/2203-4,695; NLW/ Ms.12045E; J.Gwynfor Jones:*Early Modern Wales.c1545-1640*,1994.13; A Wagner:op.cit.195;Alcwyn Evans/12359D i.pt 2B28.
6. T.Barnes:Derry Ormond,Some New Evidence.*NLW/Jnl*.xii.2.1981,214;FG/ 25/16-7; Bronwydd/702.
7. NLW/SD/1634/40; J.R.S.Phillips:*The Justices of the Peace in Wales and Monmouthshire,1541-1689*,1975.189; Bronwydd/6018,2323- 5,2328,2868,2870-1,2312; E.A.Lewis: The Goods and Chattels of a Cardiganshire Esquire in 1663.*Cards.Antiq.Socy.Trans.xi*.1936,28-9; for Sir John Price of Newtown,'…originally a Royalist…but was keen enough to see which way the tide was turning…whose heart was always with the Parliament' J.R.Phillips: *The Civil War in Wales and the Marches*,1878.i.197,265,292;G.E.Mingay: *The Gentry, the Rise and Fall of a Ruling Class*,1976,68.
8. Bronwydd/ 4086,2868,2870-1,2206,1681,2332; PRO/HearthTax/ E179219/94; *WWHR*.ix.217-40.9. 9.
9. FG/8/98.15/35;Bronwydd/2332,2397;NLW/SD/1692/123;T Barnes:loc.cit;Lease and Release – a form of conveying real property which required two deeds,the 'Lease' executed on a certain date and the 'Release' usually on the following day.This procedure became obsolete after the Conveyance by Release Act,1841,and later statutes.

10. CRO/Golden Grove Book (s) ;T.Nicholas:op.cit.ii.884;J.R.Phillips op.cit.ii.163-4; DWB.for Phillips,Phillips,Tregibby,Cardigan,and Wogan; Francis Green:The Wogans of Pembrokeshire,*WWHR*,vi.1916,169-230,vii.1917-18,1-26; for Cambro-Norman Settlers in Ireland,see,M.T.Flanagan: *Irish Society,Anglo-Norman Settlers...*1989,ch.5. 'Adventurers from South Wales'137-63.

11. Bronwydd/1547,1775,2138,2315,1685-90,3085,2333;FG/22/187-8;SD/1743/175;D.Miles: *The Lords of Cemais*,1997,65.

12. Bronwydd/1560-1,2315,1951-2,1951-2.1960,2037-8,5021,5024,1946-7;FG/xiv/251: G.E.Mingay:op.cit.109-13.

13. Bronwydd/4000,4036,1572,1951-2,3997,1574,1575-6,2195,2900-1;F.Jones:Llanrheithan.*The Pembrokeshire Historian*,no.3.53-9.

14. Bronwydd/2001,4000,4036,1574,3418-27,1551-2,1711,7263,2847-8,2841,2347,3335,7264,2368-9,2872-3,2370-1,3469,2346,3473.

15. ibid:2301-3,2302-3,2347,2900-1,1951-2,2340-1,2317,1580,1692,3470,1778,2320,3473,3740-44.

16. FG/22/187;Bronwydd/2326,2346,2369,2873,3335,3445,3469,3448,28-3473;FG/22/187;DerryOrmond/51-2;T.Barnes:loc.cit.

17. Bronwydd/2008,2906,1933-4,1516,1575-6,3445,1793,1801,1992,1973,1994,3445,1767;D.Miles:op.cit.65-8; J.Hext Lewes:Llanllyr 1180-1980,*Ceredigion*,vi.4.1971,343;F.Jones:*Historic Cardiganshire Homes...*2000,174; J.Foster:*Alumni Oxonienses...1500-1714*,1888,92.

18. Bronwydd/1544,2811-2,1861,1692,2810,3468,1967,1999,1539,1629,1627,1887,1616.

19. ibid:1995,3628,3862,6804,5016;M.C.S.Evans: The Pioneers of Estate Mapping in Carmarthenshire. *The Carms. Antiquary*,xiii. 1977.53seq.

20. Bronwydd/1712-3,3116-7.2666-7,2668,3078-9,3090,3712,1613,2641-4,2011,1779;NLW/SD/1812/139;D.Miles:loc.cit; D.L.Baker-Jones: Notes on the Orielton Chancery proceedings. *NLW*/Jnl.xv.no.3.1968,344-61,no 4.1968,405-22; F.Jones:*Historic Houses of Pembrokeshire*. 1996.sub.Jordanstown Hall [Trewrdan]

21. D.Miles:op.cit.68-9;HRO/D/Pen/10/3,26/1.12; NLW/Court Henry/2,3; Bronwydd/2011,3264,3751,1778-9,2320,2733-4,2802-3; *Yr Haul*:Awst 1904,vi.369-71; H.M.Vaughan:*The South Wales Squires*,1926.123-5,148; Rhys Jones Lloyd's Journal (in private hands); CRO/EG/Box 61.

22. see section on 'The Lord Marcher'Bronwydd/1719-20,1715-6,4838-59,2088,2085,1495,2095,2068,2094,2551,2101,2111,2096,2099,2093,2082,2097-8,2090-1,2080,2092,2102,2081,2084,2086,1717-8,4602-17,4675-4702,3907,1785,1818,2113,5882-93.

23. ibid: 3907,2105,2107,2083,2110,2112-4,5882-93,4602-17.

24. ibid: 1785,3909-20,4602-17,4675-4702;D.Miles:loc.cit;DWB

25. ibid: 6781,7300,7305,4226-7,4979-97,5193-5221,6050,42233-4; *The Welshman*,27/7/1877;Cd.Ad.17/11/1871,27/7/1877; *Burke'sPeerage* ...1896; D.Miles, op.cit.69-73.

26. Burke, loc.cit; D Miles:op.cit 74-76;Cd.Ad.8/11/1878,29/9/1916,8/11/1916,7/4/1933,2/4/1938 Lady Katherine H.Lloyd op.cit; J Bateman: *The*

Great landowners of Great Britain and Ireland, 1876; Enumerators Returns 1871, but according to J.Foster's '*Alumnii...*' a Charles Robert Hutchings is mentioned, the son of the Rev. Robert Sparke Hutchings of Newton Abbot, Devon, Exhibitioner of Trinity College, Oxford, 1865-70, BA. 1870.

Chapter 3. Squire Lloyd – Farmer and Landowner.

1. D.W.Howell: *Patriarchs and Parasites*, 1986.11,14,16,32; G.E. Mingay:op.cit.109 .
2. Bronwydd/2325; E.A.Lewis:op.cit.109.
3. Cardiff Public Library/4.4669.
4. Bronwydd/Evans George/1587.
5. Bronwydd/3908.4229;*Cm.Jnl.*8/2/1828,26/9/1834,8/4/1842;H.M. Vaughan:*Welsh Outlook*,1926,25.
6. D.W.Howell:op.cit.52-3;-id- *Land and People*,1976,35; D.Jenkins: *The Agricultural Community in South West Wales*....1971,28;NLW/ Add.Mss/4572D;*The Cambrian*, 26/1/1805;Bronwydd/7234,5995- 9;G.E.Mingay:op.cit.82;information from the late John Jenkins,Llangeler.
7. D.W.Howell:op.cit.55-6;G.E.Mingay:op.cit.84;Bronwydd/ 5061,6804,2008,3468,3628,3862; CRO/Dynevor/154;Cawdor/2/ 141,145; *Research Notes-J.M.Eyles, Great Rissington, Glos.* NLW/ Falcondale/GP.vi.214.
8. Bronwydd/609;RCLWM/Evidence iii.Qu.44.751;information from the late H.W.T.Ll.Howell, Cardigan.
9. Bronwydd/1817-8,4223-4,5227,3522,5560-2,5222-7.
10. L.Baker-Jones:*Princelings,Privilege and Power*....1999,105-7;Cardiff Public Library/4.4669; R.Suggett: *John Nash, Architect*..1995,48-51; Bronwydd/2660-1,2019;Personal Knowledge.
11. D.W.Howell:op.cit.35; Bronwydd/5446-75,5476-84,3271,5505- 29;Cilgwyn/LB/Oct.1907-Mch.1909;see also ch.6 sources 17,18.
12. L.Baker-Jones:op.cit.99-100,102,300;D.W.Howell:op.cit.81;*Cm.Jnl.*1/ 11/1861,21/1/1870;NLW/Add Mss/5532E; D. Cannadine: *Aspects of Aristocracy – Grandeur and Decline in Modern Britain*, 1994,56-7.
13. Bronwydd/4389,5238-5304,3560,3563,3567,3786,3589.
14. L.Baker-Jones:op.cit. 88-9; J.Geraint Jenkins:The Maritime Heritage of Some Cardiganshire Villages. *Ceredigion*,ix,2,1982,111-27; NLW./ Ms.6431E.
15. D.W.Howell:op.cit 33; Bronwydd/3738,1958-9,1986; Llwyngwair/43; Owen Colby/7204; R.Fenton: *A Historical Tour Through Pembrokeshire*, 1811; G.W.Hall: *Metal Mines in Southern Wales*. 1971,3-7.
16. Bronwydd/2003,4340-75,5406-75,7304,6282;Cilgwyn/LB/35-11/1/ 1853; *Cm.Jnl.*22/11/1816,1/4/1825.
17. L.Baker-Jones:op.cit.93-5;Bronwydd/ 1309,1632-51,1615- 6,1627,6027,6954; Sir John Williams/119;Plas Llangoedmore/100;CRO/ JF/554;*Cm.Jnl.*6/3/1840.

18. Bronwydd/608,1652-3;Personal knowledge; note 18.the Plurarities Act, 1838,1885, Sales of Advowsons Act 1856.s 1-8,Ecclesiastical Benefices Act, 1898,s i.3; the Law Reports,London, 1898.ch.48.244-50; *Halsbury's Laws of England*, 4th.ed.vol.14.1975,paras-799,802,926,1359. The author is indebted to Mr B.L.V.Richards, Diocesan Registrar, Carmarthen, for drawing attention to these sources; Bishop Wm.Stubbs: *Constitutional History of England*, 1893,iii.353.

19. G.E.Mingay:op.cit.61;L.Baker-Jones:op.cit.300-03; Bronwydd/5006,4871-4902.4225,7237,4475-89.

20. B.G.Charles: *George Owen, a Welsh Elizabethan*, 1973,72-9; FG/9/418,6/421,14/351.

21. Bronwydd/6254-99,4065-8,4059,4070,3657,5402,5427-32,609,2921;Owen Colby/693,1940-5; L.Baker-Jones:loc.cit.

22. I.G.Jones: Cardiganshire Politics in the mid-Nineteenth century – *Ceredigion*,v.1.1964,2263,28,30,36; K.O.Morgan: Cardiganshire Politics, the Liberal Ascendancy, 1885-1923,ibid.v.4.1967,311,313,341 n.l; RCLWM/Qu.47,489;Bronwydd/3440,5016,6804.

23. G.E.Mingay:op.cit.20; Bronwydd/4071,2051,1865,1841,1885,1967,1959,2001,1997;H.M.Vaughan: *The South Wales Squires*,1926,180; information from Mr Gerallt D. Nash,St.Fagans.

24. Bronwydd/1812,2552,1901,2898,3282,1846,1710,1796,2875,1845.

25. –ibid-7026,2794-5; *Hansard*/188-27/5/1867;197-6/7/1869;RCLWM/Qu.44,303;personal knowledge.

26. H.M.Vaughan:op.cit.168-9; RCLWM/Qu.44271,44274,44337-8,44751,44837; J.Howard Davies: *The Social Structure and Economy of South West Wales in the Nineteenth Century (unpublished MA* thesis [Wales] 1967) 36-38,45, Bronwydd/5997,6149; *The Welshman*, 11/8/1893.

27. Bronwydd/601;L.Baker-Jones (ed): *The Glaspant Diary 1896,a Chronicle of Carmarthenshire Country Life*,2001,12-13; recollections of S.J. Havard Evans, Barrister-at-Law, Carmarthen; the late Mr. John Jenkins,Llangeler; Welshman, 31/10/1856, 3/1/1862.

Chapter 4. The Lord Marcher – the 'Governance' of Newport – the Peerage Case

1. *The Times*, 6/4/1933;Cm.Jnl.7/4/1933;T.Nicholas:op.cit.i.202-3;Burke:*Peerage, Baronetage and Knightage...*1896; J.H.Round: *The 'Lords of Kemes' in Family Origins*..(ed)W.W.Page,1921,705 seq; Sir Anthony Wagner op.cit.1983,51.

2. Bronwydd/1410-11,1182; B.E. and K.A.Howells:*The Extent of Kemes, 1594 (Pembs. Record Series)* 1977; B.G.Charles:o.p.cit.15-20; DWB.

3. B.G.Charles:op.cit.72-98,126,132,preface vii; *Baronia de Kemeys Arch.Camb.*1862.

4. Bronwydd/1022;D.Miles:*The Lords of Cemais*,1997,45seq.

5. Bronwydd/1788,2586,677-80; RCLWM/Appendix,457-8.

6. DWB;Bronwydd/6865,6462,3864-66,6570-6620,6411-20,6407-10,6846,597,6502-9,3654,6567-6619,3528,6433-66,6395-6400; public

notice re chief rents,-courtesy of Mr.Thomas Lloyd; *Report on the Barony of Kemes,1912-19*, in private hands; CRO/CAS/xiv,86-7.

7. Bronwydd/568,7318-24,6692,: Llwyngwair/2182.
8. Bronwydd/6784,3955,3596,6638,6041,6776,3825,6081-6109;*Cm.Jnl.*16/3/1838,23/3/1838.
9. Bronwydd/3822-61,566,559; *Cm.Jnl.*21/7/1810.
10. –bid- 505-6,5329-32,6804,5324-7,523.
11. –ibid-6805-19,7003-8; D.Miles: *The Ancient Borough of Newport in Pembrokeshire*,1995,59seq.
12. Bronwydd/5335-9,6948.
13. –ibid- 6949-13,539640.
14. –ibid-5315,6902-46,6696-6701;Pryse Williams/15638A.
15. Bronwydd/6635-6,3363;D.Miles:op.cit.33seq.
16. Bronwydd/3240,3346,7236,6948,6637.
17. Bronwydd/3410,9025,4418-9,3804-20,525,6863,563,3868-71,4710-4310,3962-5,4270-4310,3962-5.
18. Bronwydd/6466,6481-6,3863,4429,3410; *Royal Comm.Corporations in England and Wales*, 1835,353-4; I. Bowen: *the Statutes of Wales*, 1908,67-8,74; D.Miles:op.cit.25-7,33.
19. Bronwydd/3408-9,7044;D.Miles:op.cit.50-1;CRO/CAS/xxiv/1929.
20. Bronwydd/7271-2,7301,7294-5,7725.6523,6820,4391; *Baronia de Kemeys*,1862;*Burke:Landed gentry....*1906;R.J.H.Lloyd: Henry Leach,1770-1848,*THSC*,1956;information from the late Col.Stedman Lewis; D.Cannadine:op.cit.29-32;*Cd.Ad.*29/2/1867,29/5/1868, 15/12/1871;*Cm.Jnl.*14/7/1865,31/5/1867,3/2/1871; *The Welshman*,8/5/1868,30/1/1874;I. Gwynedd Jones:op.cit.14-21; I. Thomas:*Top Sawyer – A Biography of David Davies,Llandinam*,1938,116-29.
21. Bronwydd/6522,605,7328-9,6537-8;*The Gentlewoman*, 20/6/1908;Arthur Charles Fox Davies (1871-1928) of Coalbrookdale, Salop,author of books on genealogy, heraldry,etc. Tory candidate for Merthyr Tydfil in 1910, 1923-4, without success.
22. Bronwydd/3769,5027,3458,3750-63;J.B.Burke:*Dormant and Extinct Peerages*,1883,reprint 1969,359,612.

Chapter 5. Towers and Turrets – Perambulations

1. Bronwydd/679,2308;P.Smith: *Houses of the Welsh Countryside*, 1975,313; L.Baker-Jones:op.cit.11,141,144;P.Jenkins:*The Making of a Ruling Class*,the Glamorgan gentry,1640-1690,1983,21;E.A.Lewis;op.cit;PRO/E179/219/94/220/128/130;WWHR/ix.1920.217-240,x.1924,177-216.
2. Bronwydd/7301;E.A.Eastlake:*A History of the Gothic Revival in England*,1872,372-394; J.Stevens Curl:*Victorian Architecture*,1990 93-103; J. Sutherland:*The Life of Sir Walter Scott*.1995.48.153-7.
3. Bronwydd/4266,2997-3018.
4. J.S.Curl:loc.cit;DNB:DWB:*Arch.Camb.*1847.230;*Cd.Ad.*21/6/1872.

5. Bronwydd/4251-4.5822-82,4979-97; information from the late
Ll.Evans,J.Jenkins,Llangeler;E.Davies:*Hanes Plwyf Llangunllo*,1905,38
;Pierre Terrail, Seigneur de Bayard (c1476-1524) the archetypal knight
errant and soldier.
6. Bronwydd/6050,5829;CRO/JF/238;*Cm.Jnl*.17/11/1854.
7. T.Lloyd: *The Lost Houses of Wales*. 1986,53;old photographs by
J.Jenkins,Llangeler, R and G.Davies, Henllan;author's notes;
Enumerators Returns/1851,1871;RCHAM/notes by A.J.Parkinson/1975.
8. Recollections of the late Mr .B.Phillips, Drefach Velindre;D.S.Jones:
'Dyffryn Teifi', *Y Geninen*, Ionawr, 1901,97;
9. D.Miles:op.cit.19-25; *Inventory of Ancient Monuments/
Pembrokeshire.sub* Cilgerran,Newport;Canon G.Evans:The Story of
Newcastle Emlyn and Adpar to 1531...*Y Cymmrodor*,1922,150;
J.Sutherland:op.cit.154seq,NLW/D.Pryse Williams/15625B.
10. D.L.Baker-Jones: The Letters of the Reverend David Griffiths,
Nevern,1756-1834,
NLWJnl.x.2.1979,174;D.Miles:loc.cit;F.Jones:Bowen of Pentre Ifan and
Llwyngwair.*Pembs.Historian*,6,1979,76;Bronwydd/5832,3490-7,6278-
80,2997,3018;B.G.Charles:op.cit.29
11.   Inventory/Ancient Monuments/Pembs.-Felindre
Farchog;F.Jones:Jones:Historic Houses of Pembrokeshire,1996.
12. D.Miles:*The Lords of Cemais*,1997,65seq; F.M.Thompson:*Landed
Society in the Nineteenth Century*,1963.76seq;Bronwydd/614,6776
13. for Owen,Orielton,C.Hassall,Scourfield,see DWB;F.Jones:op.cit.Havod
Grove;Bronwydd/7363.6775,6778-9.
14. ibid 3953-4,594,3475-7;*Cm.Jnl*.15/5/1817;*British Press*10/8/1813
15. ibid 6452-66,3821,6733-68;*Cm.Jnl*.17/7/1846.
16. ibid:29/7/1860
17.   Cd.Ad.25/6/1875

Chapter 6. Family Celebrations – Benevolence and Patronage

1.   Cm.Jnl.23/2/1872l;Cd.Ad.9/2/1872.
2.   Cd.Ad.18/1/1875;Cm.Jnl.8/11/1878;The Welshman 15/11/1878;
Bronwydd/4965-70, 'Cwinten' - a local term for a large banner held by two
poles at each end and carried in processions.
3. loc.cit.
4. G.E.Mingay:op.cit.140seq;RCLWM/Evid.296.[Qu.37,826];Cd.Ad.12/8/
1921;J.Jenkins,Llangeler.
5. Lady Lloyd:op.cit.93;DWB;C.Cannon:*The Letters of Sir William
Jones*,I.1969,Letter 290,150;*Gent. Mag.*1774,262-5;M.Girouard:The
Return *to Camelot*.1981,96-110;*Cm.Jnl*.19/6/1810.
*6.   Cd.Ad.*6/1/1882;H.M.Vaughan:op.cit.45,108-10;M.Girouard:*A Country
House Companion*,1987,93;the late J.Williams,Blaenmorw,Capel
Newydd,Boncath.
7.   Cm.Jnl.and Welshman,9,16,30/11/1928;Bronwydd/5999.
8. L.Baker-Jones:op.cit.201,nn 13-16.

9. *Cd.Ad.*17/11/1871;*The Welshman*:17/1/1877,3/8/1877,6/7/1888;Mrs. Davies,Cilrhiwe,1960's.
10. *Cm.Jnl.*7/4/1933,14/4/1933;*The Times* 6/4/1933,2/4/1937.
11. Bronwydd/2318,2854,3663; L.Baker-Jones:op.cit.16,19;S.Meyrick:*History of Cardiganshire*,1810,174-5;Owen Chadwick:*The Victorian Church*,1971,i,167,301seq; M.Chandler:*The Life and Work of John Mason Neale,1818-1866*,1995.125-6;*WWHR*/1.291.ii.243,270,199-301.iii.224-5; Welsh periodicals like ' *Y Goleuad*' and *'Yr Haul'* in the nineteenth century are full of anti-Roman Catholic sentiments.
12. NLW/Add.Mss/2120D; J.Evans,Abermeurig: *Hanes Methodistiaeth De Aberteifi*,1904.235-43;D.Rees.Bronant:Teulu Bronwydd.*Cymru*.Chwefror,1902; *Western Mail* 20/5/1902.
13. Bronwydd/1778-9,2320,4376-88,5081,5565-71;D.Pryse Williams/ 1556OB:Charity Comm.Records.B17205,8 Dec.1915;CRO/Beckingsale/ 12/490;J.Jenkins,Llangeler;R.Evans,Penrhiwllan.
14. L.Baker-Jones:The *Glaspant Diary*...148,150;D.Pryse Williams/15664A; Cd.Ad.14/6/1872,29/9/1876,18/5/1883,1/11/1895;*The Welshman*,15/11/ 1851,10/3/1871; Bronwydd/3184-91;the Misses M. and D.Jones,Coedybryn; *RCLWM.loc.cit*; D.Jenkins:op.cit.29.
15. DWB,DNB; *Cd.Ad.*14/6/1872,26/7/1872,18/7/1873,27/9/1880,19/1/ 1883,1/6/1883; *Cm.Jnl.*8/6/1883.
16. I.Gwynedd Jones:The Rebuilding of Llanrhystud Church,Ceredigion.vii.2.1973,99-104; -id-: Church Restoration in Nineteenth Century Cardiganshire.NLW/Jnl.xx.4.1978,352-60;Bronwydd/ 3727;*Cm.Jnl.*20/1/1865,1/3/1867;*Cd.Ad.*7/12.1866,26/3/1869,1/11/1878.
17. For a description of Llangunllo Church,see – E.Davies:*Hanes Plwyf Llangunllo,*1905.72-84; *The Welshman,*29/4/1870; Recollections of the late Miss Lewis,Pwllgwair,Troedyraur; D.Jenkins:op.cit.27-8;Bronwydd/ 7304.
18. Bronwydd/531,4222;HRO/PQ/RC;*Cm.Jnl.*19/11/1815,1/12/1815,16/1/ 1852,17/11/1854;*Cd.Ad.*22/6/1860,2/9/1866,9/4/1869,14/12/1883,12/3/ 1885; *Yr Haul*,1863.28; D.L.Baker-Jones: 'To Supply the Sick Poor',*Carms.Historian* xv 1978,3-28; CRO/*Report:the Joint Counties Asylum,Carmarthen*,1887.
19. DWB;E.Pan Jones: *'Oes Gofion'*[nd];*Cm.Jnl.*7/6/1861,18/1/1864,19/1/ 1866,10/1/1879; *Cd.Ad.*5/1/1863,18/1/1864,26/12/1873,18/2/1876,16/3/ 1892; *The Welshman*,25/1/1867,1/2/1878; NLW/2152-9 [Cyfrinfa Tysul]; reminiscences of the late J.Rees Jones, Felindre;D.W.Howell: *The Rural Poor in Eighteenth CenturyWales.* 2000.76,94,111-2.169-70.
20. L.Baker-Jones: *Princelings*...222-34;*Cd.Ad.*5/2/1869;*Cm.Jnl.*11/8/1826,4/ 3/1836, 18/10/1850, 25/6/1875; *The Welshman*, 23/5/1851, 11/11/1835.
21. Bronwydd/4393-4401;*Cm.Jnl.* 14/8/1868; copies of *Chancery Court Records* from J.Jenkins, Llangeler; recollections of the late John Evans (John y Gwas), Felindre-one time assistant teacher at Aberbanc School and antiquary.
22. *Annual Report of the Association for the Preservation of Ancient Monuments, 1907; Trans. Carms. Antiquarian Society*, 1921-23, 23-28,

1923-25, 48.17-18; the memorial to Sir Marteine O.M.Lloyd, Bt. in Llangunllo Church was the work of Messrs.T.Mosford & Co. Ltd. Cardiff; CRO/CAS/xliii, 1934, 103;L Baker-Jones (ed): *The Glaspant Diary,* 1896...97. M. Cragoe: '*An Anglican aristocracy..... Carmarthenshire, 1862-1895'* 1996, 241

23. Cm.Jnl.15/7/1825, 3/3/1851, 13/12/1871; *British Press* 10/8/1813; *The Monthly Magazine,* Sept. 1814, 201; *Cd. Ad.* 18/1/1867; Capt.N.Wynne Apperly: *A Huntsman's Diary,* 1926, 165 seq; G.E.Mingay: op.cit.133, quoting F.M.L.Thompson: in the *English Landed Society in the Nineteenth Century.* 1963. 138-9, 144, 150; R.W.Malcomson: *Recreations in Rural England 1700-1850.* 1973. 52, 84.

Chapter 7. Epilogue

1. G.E.Mingay:op.cit.68,109-110,115-19;L.Baker-Jones:*Princelings*...129-37; H.Howard Davies;op.cit.169;
2. Bronwydd/7266-8,7282;J.Howard Davies:op.cit.134;CRO/JF/SC/642,342.
3. Bronwydd/4103,7304,7279,5476-84,5995,3411-7;CRO/Beckingsale/3000: Plas Llanstephan/1536-40.
4. Bronwydd/5484,6055,5557-8,3125,5433.
5. Bronwydd/34467,5455,5655,5481;J.Howard Davies:op.cit.163.
6. Bronwydd/5999; Bronwydd Estate Sale Catalogue,August,1937,(abstract of title) courtesy of J.Jenkins Llangeler.
7. Personal knowledge.

APPENDICES

Lloyd of Bronwydd Pedigree

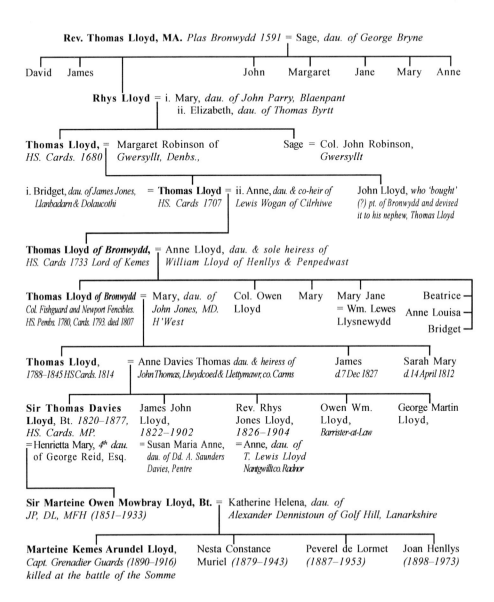

Rev. Thomas Lloyd, MA. *Plas Bronwydd 1591* = Sage, *dau. of George Bryne*

David   James   John   Margaret   Jane   Mary   Anne

Rhys Lloyd = i. Mary, *dau. of John Parry, Blaenpant*
ii. Elizabeth, *dau. of Thomas Byrtt*

Thomas Lloyd, = Margaret Robinson of   Sage = Col. John Robinson,
HS. Cards. 1680   Gwersyllt, Denbs.,   Gwersyllt

i. Bridget, *dau. of James Jones,* = **Thomas Lloyd** = ii. Anne, *dau. & co-heir of*   John Lloyd, *who 'bought'*
Llanbadarn & Dolaucothi   HS. Cards 1707   *Lewis Wogan of Cilrhiwe*   *(?) pt. of Bronwydd and devised*
                                                               it to his nephew, Thomas Lloyd

Thomas Lloyd *of Bronwydd,* = Anne Lloyd, *dau. & sole heiress of*
HS. Cards 1733 Lord of Kemes   William Lloyd of Henllys & Penpedwast

Thomas Lloyd *of Bronwydd* = Mary, *dau. of*   Col. Owen   Mary   Mary Jane   Beatrice ⌐
Col. Fishguard and Newport Fencibles.   John Jones, MD.   Lloyd   = Wm. Lewes   Anne Louisa ⌐
HS. Pembs. 1780, Cards. 1793. died 1807   H'West   Llysnewydd   Bridget ⌐

Thomas Lloyd, = Anne Davies Thomas *dau. & heiress of*   James   Sarah Mary
1788–1845 HS Cards. 1814   *John Thomas, Llwydcoed & Llettymawr, co. Carms*   *d. 7 Dec 1827*   *d. 14 April 1812*

Sir Thomas Davies   James John   Rev. Rhys   Owen Wm.   George Martin
Lloyd, Bt. *1820–1877,*   Lloyd,   Jones Lloyd,   Lloyd,   Lloyd,
HS. Cards. MP.   *1822–1902*   *1826–1904*   *Barrister-at-Law*
= Henrietta Mary, *4ᵗʰ dau.*   = Susan Maria Anne,   = Anne, *dau. of*
of George Reid, Esq.   *dau. of Dd. A. Saunders*   T. Lewis Lloyd
   Davies, Pentre   *Nantgwillt co. Radnor*

Sir Marteine Owen Mowbray Lloyd, Bt. = Katherine Helena, *dau. of*
JP, DL, MFH *(1851–1933)*   *Alexander Dennistoun of Golf Hill, Lanarkshire*

Marteine Kemes Arundel Lloyd,   Nesta Constance   Peverel de Lormet   Joan Henllys
Capt. Grenadier Guards (1890–1916)   Muriel *(1879–1943)*   *(1887–1953)*   *(1898–1973)*
killed at the battle of the Somme

NLW/Alcwyn Evans Mss; Burke's Peerage … 1898;
Dillwyn Miles, op. cit.

NOTICE.

We, the undersigned, being Cattle Dealers, Farmers, and Butchers, do agree to hold

AN ANNUAL

FAIR

IN THE

VILLAGE OF EGLWYSERW,

On the 18th of November,

For Horses & Cattle;

And on the 19th,

For Sheep and Pigs:

William Edwards, Swansea;
John Thomas, Swansea;
James Parry, Carmarthen;
Thomas Jones, Newcastle;
David Jones, Newcastle;
John Lewis, Newcastle;
John Jones, Carmarthen;
Walter Griffiths and Sons;
Charles Parry;
John Owens, Swansea;
John Abram, Swansea;
George Vaughan, Swansea;
James Evans, Swansea;

Henry Thomas, Llanddarog;
Thomas Watkins, Swansea;
John Daniel;
Thomas Morgans, Llandovery;
Daniel Davies, Penlanwen;
Rod. Evans & Son, Llanddewl;
John Griffiths, Forest;
Isaac Williams;
Evan Evans, Llandre;
John Evans, Llandre;
David Davies, Shop;
Thomas Davies, Tanlan;
George Partington;

J. Williams, Black Lane, Llandovery;
John Myers;
Richard Lewis, Butcher, Carmarthen;
John Lewis, Butcher, Carmarthen;
Phillip Lewis, Butcher, Carmarthen;
Thos. Morgan, Butcher, Carmarthen;
Evan Evans, Cwmbychan;
John Jones, Newcastle;
John Jones, Pwllmelin;
James Davies, Kilgerran;
Evan Felix, Cardigan;
Jonah Morris, Kilgerran;
Stephen Jones.

ISAAC THOMAS, PRINTER, ST. MARY-STREET, CARDIGAN.

166

EGLWYSERW FAIR.

TAKE NOTICE,

that Thomas Davies Lloyd, of Bronwydd, in the County of Cardigan, Esquire, is entitled to certain Tolls, Pickages, Stallages, and Profits arising from and out of the Fair held in a certain Field situate at the Farm of Penycoed, in the Parish of Eglwyserw, in the County of Pembroke, on the first Monday after the 22nd of November;

AND WE DO HEREBY CAUTION YOU

not to hold a Fair in the Village of Eglwyserw, on the 18th November, for Horses and Cattle, and on the 19th, for Sheep and Pigs, as advertized by you in certain hand Bills, bearing your Name, with others, the same being a Nuisance.

AND WE GIVE YOU FURTHER NOTICE,

that the said Fair, held on the first Monday after the 22nd day of November, will be held on Monday the 24th instant; And that if the said Thomas Davies Lloyd shall lose, or be in any way deprived of any Toll, Pickage, Stallage, or other Profit, or receive any prejudice in the Profits and Emoluments arising from the said last mentioned Fair, in consequence of your having advertized the Fair on the 18th and 19th November instant, one or more Action or Actions at Law, will be brought against you; or such other Proceedings taken, as the said Thomas Davies Lloyd may be advised.

Dated the 6th Day of November, 1851.

Cardigan

Attorneys for the said Thomas Davies Lloyd, Esquire.

ISAAC THOMAS, PRINTER, ST. MARY-STREET, CARDIGAN.

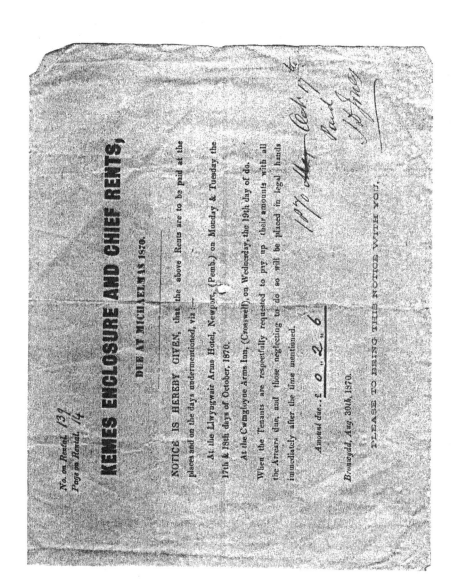

KEMES ENCLOSURE AND CHIEF RENTS,

DUE AT MICHAELMAS 1870.

No. on Rental 13/
Page on Rental, 1/4

NOTICE IS HEREBY GIVEN, that the above Rents are to be paid at the places and on the days undermentioned, viz:—

At the Llwyngwair Arms Hotel, Newport, (Pemb.) on Monday & Tuesday, the 17th & 18th days of October, 1870.

At the Cwmgloyne Arms Inn, (Croeswell), on Wednesday, the 19th day of do.

When the Tenants are respectfully requested to pay up their amounts with all the Arrears due, and those neglecting to do so will be placed in legal hands immediately after the time mentioned.

Amount due..£ 0 ,, 2 ,, 6

Bronwydd, Aug. 30th, 1870.

PLEASE TO BRING THIS NOTICE WITH YOU.

Extracts from a lengthy lament (21 vv.anon) for Sir Marteine and Lady Lloyd and the splendour of Bronwydd

Hen balas y Bronwydd a'i dyrau a'i do
    Trwy'r oesau fu'n ymffrost a balchder y fro,
Ei fonedd dihafal, ei gyfoeth a'i fri
    Sy'n bennod ddiddorol anfarwol inni.

Bu enw Syr Marteine a'i deidiau o'i flan
    Yn noddi traddodiad a'i gadw yn lan,
Efe oedd ein harglwydd, ein ceidwad a'n tad
    Efe oedd y brenin i ddeiliad y stad.

Ymdyrrai penaethiaid y gwledydd i'r plas
    Uchelwyr o urddas, doethineb a thras,
Ei deulu a'i hanes ei gysgod a'i rad,
    Fu'n gefndir a nodded i werin y wlad.

Ei goedydd mawreddog llydanfrig eu tw'
    Na welwyd yn Liban(us) rai cyfled a nhw,
Ei erddi cyfoethog, cyforiog eu rhin
    Ei ddyfnion seleri, ei gafnau a'i win.

Pendefig pob helfa a'i farch yn dyheu
    Am swn y bytheiaid a dilyn y crei,
Addurnodd ei furiau a phennau ei brae
    A swyn ei orchestion oedd enaid ei swae.

One wele! daeth chwalfa a'r pomp ddaeth i lawr
    Fe syrthiodd y castell a'i gwymp a fu mawr,
Y Bronwydd mawr breiniol arswydol ei sedd
    Sydd heddiw yn garnedd a'r Syr yn ei fedd.

Y coedydd brenhinol yn dderi ac ynn
    A loriwyd o'r Drindod i fanc Coedybryn,
D'oes un ffenest Gothig i'w gweld yn y lle
    A'i seiliau yn gandryll a noethion i'r ne'.

Ni cherdd y cardotyn i'r cefen yn awr
    Yn llwyd a phenisel a'i gallon ar lawr,
Ni ddaw Ladi Lloyd a'i thynerwch a'i gwen
    I estyn ei frechdan a'i gildwrn i'r hen

Mae'r bleiddiaid fel cynt ar bileri y glwyd
    Yn arwydd symbolig o statws a nwyd,
Y 'Baedd' ar y dorau – er cadw mewn co'
    Y rhamant a'r mawredd a'r holl 'Dali Ho'.

Gogoniant y Plas oedd ei goedydd bythwyrdd
    A'r blodau fu'n gwisgo ymylon y ffyrdd.
Fe wylodd y Marchog pan syrthiodd y pin
    Fe wylodd y wlad pan syrthiodd ei hun.

'Yr Hen Ardner' (???)

(courtesy of the late John Jenkins)

170

Englynion – Stanzas in the strict metre by the antiquary, poet and cleric, the Rev. Benjamin Williams (Gwynionydd) 1821 – 1891, composed in honour of Sir Thomas Davies Lloyd, Bart. who received the title in 1863 (Yr Haul-Mawrth, 1863, tt81 – 2)

ENGLYNION

I Syr Thomas Davies Lloyd, Bronwydd, ar ei ddyrchafiad yn Farwnig.

Barwnig hyglod Bronwydd – yn ei wlad,
    Anwyl yw a chlodrydd;
Lleda, ymdaena bob dydd,
Ei glod ar g'oedd y gwledydd.

Hen lys olynol oesau – yn y sir,
    Yn sedd i rinweddau;
O bell, gogoniant y bau,
Yw Bronwydd rhwng ei bryniau.

Hen deulu yn y dalaeth – gyrhaedda,
    Gwreiddiau'r Dywysogaeth;
Yn lled hir o bell y daeth,
Dylif o hen waedoliaeth.

Cyrhaedd drwy fonedd Caron – rhyglyddawl
    Arglwyddi glyn Aeron: [darddiad,
O Rys Chwith mae'r rhes wech hon – o
Goreu eu dygaid drwy Geredigion.

Hen Gemmaes enwog yma – yr henwaed
    Barwnaidd feddianna:
Drwy fonedd yn dorf hana,
Yn ol i'r Martiniaid wna.

Daw eilwaith mewn modd dilys – o achau
    Mwy uchel, mae'n hysbys;
Breninoedd brie in hynys,
Aurdorchog drwy'r enwog Rys.*

Ein hanwyl, hoff Freuines – o wybod,
    Gydnabu ei achres;
Ei alw i radd uchel res,
Haeddawl ddyrchafiad roddes.

---

*Rhys ab Tewdwr Mawr, Prince of South Wales.

Rhyw hyawdl fawr Orhoian! – ei genedl
    Yn gynnes wna ddadgan;
    E ddaeth gorfoledd weithian,
    Mae'r wlad, gan deimlad, yn dân!

Drwy'r awyr, ceir swn arwyrain – bryniau
    A bronydd wnânt adsain;
    Hwylus o hyd daw ail sain,
    Nis paid y diaspedain!

Gorlanw mae gwir lawenydd – a mawr drwst,
    Fel môr dros ei lenydd:
    Yn y swn pa beth y sydd? – O, mawrhau,
    Hyd y wybrenau, Syr Thomas Lloyd, Bronwydd.

Ei ryglyddawl Arglwyddes, - lon orchwyl,
    Anerchir yn gynnes;
    Taenu, dywedyd hanes,
    Yn un llaw dymuno'i lles.

Ei etifedd fo'n tyfu – yn addurn
    I foneddion Cymru;
    Dal anrhydedd ei deulu – dewrgalon,
    Yn enwog wron, a'i wlad fo'n garu.

Hir einioes llawn o rinwedd – oll iddynt,
    Llwyddo b'ont yr unwed;
    Eu nod fo gwladgar nodwedd – yn wastad,
    Ym mlaen eu rhediad yn nheml anrhydedd.

GWYNIONYDD.

The Bronwydd Demesne 1847

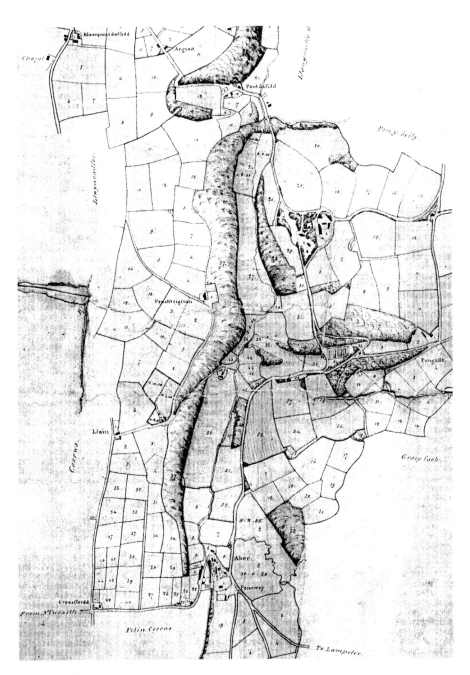

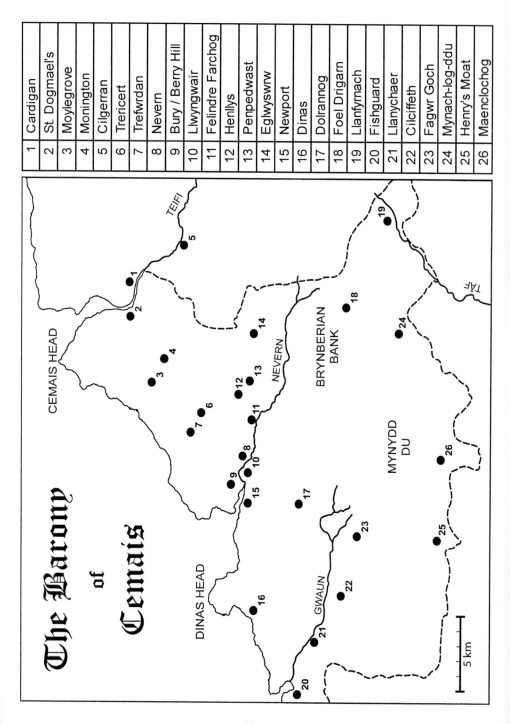

The Barony of Cemais

1	Cardigan
2	St. Dogmael's
3	Moylegrove
4	Monington
5	Cilgerran
6	Trericert
7	Trefwrdan
8	Nevern
9	Bury / Berry Hill
10	Llwyngwair
11	Felindre Farchog
12	Henllys
13	Penpedwast
14	Eglwyswrw
15	Newport
16	Dinas
17	Dolrannog
18	Foel Drigarn
19	Llanfyrnach
20	Fishguard
21	Llanychaer
22	Cilciffeth
23	Fagwr Goch
24	Mynach-log-ddu
25	Henry's Moat
26	Maenclochog

Index